THE WAY OF ZEN

禅道

ALAN W. WATTS

THE WAY OF ZEN

VINTAGE BOOKS

A DIVISION OF RANDOM HOUSE, INC., NEW YORK

Vintage Books Edition, August 1989

Library of Congress Cataloging-in-Publication Data
Watts, Alan, 1915–1973.
    The way of Zen = [Zendō] / Alan W. Watts—1st Vintage Books ed.
        p.   cm.
    Parallel title in Japanese characters.
    Reprint. Originally published: New York: Pantheon, 1957.
    Bibliography: p.
    Includes index.
    ISBN 0-679-72301-3
    1. Zen Buddhism.   I. Title.   II. Title: Zendō.
[BQ9265.4.W38   1989]
294.3'927—dc19   88-40502
                                                      CIP

Manufactured in the United States of America
13579B8642

To
TIA, MARK, AND RICHARD
who will understand it all the better
for not being able to read it.

CONTENTS

LIST OF ILLUSTRATIONS

PREFACE

During the past twenty years there has been an extraordinary growth of interest in Zen Buddhism. Since the Second World War this interest has increased so much that it seems to be becoming a considerable force in the intellectual and artistic world of the West. It is connected, no doubt, with the prevalent enthusiasm for Japanese culture which is one of the constructive results of the late war, but which may amount to no more than a passing fashion. The deeper reason for this interest is that the viewpoint of Zen lies so close to the "growing edge" of Western thought.

The more alarming and destructive aspects of Western civilization should not blind us to the fact that at this very time it is also in one of its most creative periods. Ideas and insights of the greatest fascination are appearing in some of the newer fields of Western science–in psychology and psychotherapy, in logic and the philosophy of science, in semantics and communications theory. Some of these developments might be due to suggestive influences from Asian philosophy, but on the whole I am inclined to feel that there is more of a parallelism than a direct influence. We are, however, becoming aware of the parallelism, and it promises an exchange of views which should be extremely stimulating.

Western thought has changed so rapidly in this century that we are in a state of considerable confusion. Not only are there serious difficulties of communication between the intellectual and the general public, but the course of our thinking and of our very history has seriously undermined the common-sense assumptions which lie at the roots of our social conventions and institutions. Familiar concepts of space, time, and motion, of nature and natural law, of history and social change, and of human personality itself have dissolved, and we find ourselves adrift without landmarks in a universe which more and more resembles the Buddhist principle of the "Great Void." The various wisdoms of the West, religious, philosophical, and scientific, do not offer much guidance to the art of living in such a universe, and we find the prospects of making our way in so trackless an ocean of relativity rather frightening. For we are used to absolutes, to firm principles and laws to which we can cling for spiritual and psychological security.

This is why, I think, there is so much interest in a culturally productive way of life which, for some fifteen hundred years, has felt thoroughly at home in "the Void," and which not only feels no terror for it but rather a positive delight. To use its own words, the situation of Zen has always been–

> *Above, not a tile to cover the head;*
> *Below, not an inch of ground for the foot.*

Such language should not actually be so unfamiliar to us, were we truly prepared to accept the meaning of "the foxes have holes, and the birds of the air have nests; but the Son of Man hath not where to lay his head."

I am not in favor of "importing" Zen from the Far East, for it has become deeply involved with cultural institutions which are quite foreign to us. But there is no doubt that there are things which we can learn, or unlearn, from it and apply in our own way. It has the special merit of a mode of expressing itself which is as intelligible–or perhaps as baffling–to the intellectual as to the illiterate, offering possibilities of communication which we have not explored. It has a directness, verve, and humor, and a sense of both beauty and nonsense at once exasperating and delightful. But above all it has a way of being able to turn one's mind inside out, and dissolving what seemed to be the most oppressive human problems into questions like "Why is a mouse when it spins?" At its heart there is a strong but completely unsentimental compassion for human beings suffering and perishing from their very attempts to save themselves.

There are many excellent books about Zen, though some of the best are out of print or otherwise difficult to obtain. But as yet no one—not even Professor Suzuki—has given us a comprehensive account of the subject which includes its historical background and its relation to Chinese and Indian ways of thought. The three volumes of Suzuki's *Essays in Zen Buddhism* are an unsystematic collection of scholarly papers on various aspects of the subject, enormously useful for the advanced student but quite baffling to the general reader without an understanding of the general principles. His delightful *Introduction to Zen Buddhism* is rather narrow and specialized. It omits the essential information about the relation of Zen to Chinese Taoism and Indian Buddhism, and is in some respects rather more mystifying than it need be. His other works are studies of special aspects of Zen, all of which require general background and historical perspective.

R. H. Blyth's *Zen in English Literature and Oriental Classics* is one of the best introductions available, but it is published only in Japan and, again, lacks the background information. As a series of rambling and marvelously perceptive observations, it makes no attempt to give an orderly presentation of the subject. My own *Spirit of Zen* is a popularization of Suzuki's earlier works, and besides being very unscholarly it is in many respects out of date and misleading, whatever merits it may have in the way of lucidity and simplicity. Christmas Humphreys' *Zen Buddhism*, published only in England, is likewise a popularization of Suzuki and, once more, does not really begin to put Zen in its cultural context. It is written in a clear and sprightly fashion, but the author finds identities between Buddhism and Theosophy which I feel to be highly questionable. Other studies of Zen by both Western and Asian authors are of a more specialized character, or are discussions of Zen *à propos* of something else—psychology, art, or cultural history.

In default, then, of a fundamental, orderly, and comprehensive account of the subject, it is no wonder that Western impressions of Zen are somewhat confused, despite all the enthusiasm and interest which it has aroused. The problem, then, is to write such a book—and this I have tried to do since no one who understands the subject better than I seems willing or able to do so. Ideally, I suppose, such a work should be written by an accomplished and recognized Zen master. But at present no such person has sufficient command of English. Furthermore, when one speaks from within a tradition, and especially from within its institutional hierarchy, there is always apt to be a certain lack of perspective and grasp of the outsider's viewpoint. Again, one of the biggest obstacles to communication between Japanese Zen masters and Westerners is the absence of clarity as to difference of basic cultural premises. Both sides are so "set in their ways" that they are unaware of the limitations of their means of communication.

Perhaps, then, the most appropriate author of such a work would be a Westerner who had spent some years under a Japanese master, going through the whole course of Zen training. Now from the standpoint of Western "scientific scholarship" this would not do at all, for such a person would have become an "enthusiast" and "partisan" incapable of an objective and disinterested view. But, fortunately or unfortunately, Zen is above all an experience, nonverbal in character, which is simply inaccessible to the purely literary and scholarly approach. To know what Zen is, and especially what it is not, there is no alternative but to practice it, to experiment with it in the concrete so as to discover the meaning which underlies the words. Yet such Westerners as have undergone some of the special type of training followed in Rinzai Zen tend to become "cagey" and uncommunicative on the principle that

Those who know do not speak;
Those who speak do not know.

Although, however, they do not "put up," they do not completely "shut up." On the one hand, they would love to share their understanding with others. But on the other hand, they are convinced that words are ultimately futile, and are, furthermore, under an agreement not to discuss certain aspects of their training. They begin, therefore, to take the characteristically Asian attitude of "Come and find out for yourself." But the scientifically trained Westerner is, not without reason, a cautious and skeptical fellow who likes to know what he is "getting into." He is acutely conscious of the capacity of the mind for self-deception, for going into places where entrance is impossible without leaving one's critical perspective at the door. Asians tend so much to despise this attitude, and their Western devotees even more so, that they neglect to tell the scientific inquirer many things that are still well within the possibilities of human speech and intellectual understanding.

To write about Zen is, therefore, as problematic for the outside, "objective" observer as for the inside, "subjective" disciple. In varying situations I have found myself on both sides of the dilemma. I have associated and studied with the "objective observers" and am convinced that, for all their virtues, they invariably miss the point and eat the menu instead of the dinner. I have also been on the inside of a traditional hierarchy—not Zen—and am equally convinced that from this position one does not know what dinner is being eaten. In such a position one becomes technically "idiotic," which is to say, out of communication with those who do not belong to the same fold.

It is both dangerous and absurd for our world to be a group of communions mutually excommunicate. This is especially true of the great cultures of the East and the West, where the potentialities of communication are the richest, and the dangers of failure to communicate the worst. As one who has spent somewhat more than twenty years trying to interpret the East to the West, I have become increasingly certain that to interpret such a phenomenon as Zen there is a clear principle to be followed.

On the one hand, it is necessary to be sympathetic and to experiment personally with the way of life to the limit of one's possibilities. On the other hand, one must resist every temptation to "join the organization," to become involved with its institutional commitments. In this friendly neutral position one is apt to be disowned by both sides. But, at the worst, one's misrepresentations provoke them to express themselves more clearly. For the relationship between two positions becomes far more clear when there is a third with which to compare them. Thus even if this study of Zen does no more than express a standpoint which is neither Zen nor anything Western, it will at least provide that third point of reference.

However, there can be no doubt that the essential standpoint of Zen refuses to be organized, or to be made the exclusive possession of any institution. If there is anything in this world which transcends the relativities of cultural conditioning, it is Zen–by whatever name it may be called. This is an excellent reason for Zen's not being institutionalized, and for the fact that many of its ancient exponents were "universal individualists" who were never members of any Zen organization, and never sought the acknowledgment of any formal authority.

This, then, is my position with respect to Zen–and I feel I should be frank with the reader in a day when there is so much anxiety about people's credentials or "quantifications." I cannot represent myself as a Zenist, or even as a Buddhist, for this seems to me to be like trying to wrap up and label the sky. I cannot represent myself as a scientifically objective academician, for– with respect to Zen–this seems to me to be like studying birdsong in a collection of stuffed nightingales. I claim no rights to speak of Zen. I claim only the pleasure of having studied its literature and observed its art forms since I was hardly more than a boy, and of having had the delight of informal association with a number of Japanese and Chinese travelers of the same trackless way.

This book is intended both for the general reader and for the more serious student, and I trust that the former will be tolerant of the use of some technical terminology, a Chinese character appendix, and other critical apparatus most useful for those who wish to explore the subject more deeply. The book is divided into two parts, the first dealing with the background and history of Zen, and the second with its principles and practice. The sources of information are of three types. I have, firstly, used almost all the studies of Zen in European languages. Naturally, I have made considerable use of the works of Professor D. T. Suzuki, but at the same time I have tried not to rely upon them too heavily—not because of any defect in them, but because I think readers are entitled to something more, by way of a fresh viewpoint, than a mere summarization of his views.

Secondly, I have based the essential view of Zen here presented upon a careful study of the more important of its early Chinese records, with special reference to the *Hsin-hsin Ming*, the *T'an Ching* or *Sutra of the Sixth Patriarch*, the *Lin-chi Lu*, and the *Ku-tsun-hsü Yü-lu*. My own knowledge of T'ang dynasty Chinese is certainly not enough to deal with some of the finer points of this literature, but sufficient, I think, to get what I wanted, which was a clear view of the essential doctrine. In all this, my efforts have been greatly aided by colleagues and research associates at the American Academy of Asian Studies, and I wish in particular to express my thanks to Professors Sabro Hasegawa and Gi-ming Shien, to Dr. Paul and Dr. George Fung, Dr. Frederick Hong, Mr. Charles Yick, and to Mr. Kazumitsu Kato, priest of the Soto-Zen School.

Thirdly, my information is derived from a large number of personal encounters with teachers and students of Zen, spread over more than twenty years.

In the following pages the translations from the original texts are my own, unless otherwise indicated. For the convenience of those who read Chinese, I have supplied, following the Bibliography, an appendix of the original Chinese forms of the more important quotations and technical terms. I have found these almost essential for the more serious student, for even among the most highly qualified scholars there is still much uncertainty as to the proper translation of T'ang dynasty Zen texts. References to this appendix are by superscribed index letters in alphabetical order.

References to other works are by surname of the author and number, directing the reader to the Bibliography for full details. Scholarly readers will have to excuse me for not using the absurd diacritical marks in romanized Sanskrit words, since these are merely confusing to the general reader and unnecessary to the Sanskritist who will at once call to mind the Devanagiri script. As to the proper names of Zen masters and titles of Zen texts, these are given in the romanized forms of Mandarin or Japanese according to the country of origin, and technical terms are given in Mandarin unless used in the discussion of specifically Japanese Zen. For Mandarin one is almost compelled by general usage to adopt the Wade-Giles romanization, for which I have appended a table of pronunciation following this Preface, since it has so little relation to the actual sounds.

I am most grateful to Mr. R. H. Blyth for his kind permission to quote a number of his translations of *haiku* poems from his magnificent four-volume anthology, *Haiku*, published by the Hokuseido Press in Tokyo; to Professor Sabro Hasegawa for his generous help in preparing the jacket and providing illustrations; and to my daughter Joan for the photographs of Ryoanji.

In conclusion, I am most happy to express my thanks to the Bollingen Foundation for a three-year fellowship, during which much of the preliminary study was done for the writing of this book.

ALAN W. WATTS

Mill Valley, California
July 1956

Consonants   Aspirated: Read *p'*, *t'*, *k'*, *ch'*, and *ts'* as in p*in*, t*ip*, *k*ilt, *ch*in, and bi*ts*.

Unaspirated: Read *p*, *t*, *k*, *ch*, and *ts* (or *tz*) as in *b*in, *d*ip, *g*ilt, *g*in, and bi*ds*.

hs or *sh,* as in *sh*oe.

j is nearly like an "unrolled" *r*, so that *jen* is nearly the English *wren*.

Vowels   Usually Italian values,

a as in f*a*ther

e as in *ei*ght

eh as in broth*er*

i as in mach*i*ne and p*i*n

ih as in sh*ir*t

o as in s*o*ap

u as in g*oo*se

ü as in German *ü*ber

Diphthongs   *ai* as in l*igh*t

ao as in l*ou*d

ei as in w*eigh*t

ia as in Willi*a*m

ieh as in Kor*ea*

ou as in gr*ou*p

ua as in sw*a*n

ueh as in d*oer*

ui as in sw*ay*

uo as in *whoah!*

Combinations   *an* and *ang* as in b*un* and b*ung*

en and *eng* as in wood*en* and am*ong*

in and *ing* as in s*in* and s*ing*

un and *ung* with the *u* as in l*oo*k.

PART ONE

BACKGROUND AND HISTORY

One

THE PHILOSOPHY OF THE TAO

Zen Buddhism is a way and a view of life which does not belong to any of the formal categories of modern Western thought. It is not religion or philosophy; it is not a psychology or a type of science. It is an example of what is known in India and China as a "way of liberation," and is similar in this respect to Taoism, Vedanta, and Yoga. As will soon be obvious, a way of liberation can have no positive definition. It has to be suggested by saying what it is not, somewhat as a sculptor reveals an image by the act of removing pieces of stone from a block.

Historically, Zen may be regarded as the fulfillment of long traditions of Indian and Chinese culture, though it is actually much more Chinese than Indian, and, since the twelfth century, it has rooted itself deeply and most creatively in the culture of Japan. As the fruition of these great cultures, and as a unique and peculiarly instructive example of a way of liberation, Zen is one of the most precious gifts of Asia to the world.

The origins of Zen are as much Taoist as Buddhist, and, because its flavor is so peculiarly Chinese, it may be best to begin by inquiring into its Chinese ancestry—illustrating, at the same time, what is meant by a way of liberation by the example of Taoism.

Much of the difficulty and mystification which Zen presents to the Western student is the result of his unfamiliarity with Chinese ways of thinking—ways which differ startlingly from our own and which are, for that very reason, of special value to us in attaining a critical perspective upon our own ideas. The problem here is not simply one of mastering different ideas, differing from our own as, say, the theories of Kant differ from those of Descartes, or those of Calvinists from those of Catholics. The

3

problem is to appreciate differences in the basic premises of thought and in the very methods of thinking, and these are so often overlooked that our interpretations of Chinese philosophy are apt to be a projection of characteristically Western ideas into Chinese terminology. This is the inevitable disadvantage of studying Asian philosophy by the purely literary methods of Western scholarship, for words can be communicative only between those who share similar experiences.

This is not to go so far as to say that so rich and subtle a language as English is simply incapable of expressing Chinese ideas. On the contrary, it can say much more than has been believed possible by some Chinese and Japanese students of Zen and Taoism whose familiarity with English leaves something to be desired. The difficulty is not so much in the language as in the thought-patterns which have hitherto seemed inseparable from the academic and scientific way of approaching a subject. The unsuitability of these patterns for such subjects as Taoism and Zen is largely responsible for the impression that the "Oriental mind" is mysterious, irrational, and inscrutable. Furthermore, it need not be supposed that these matters are so peculiarly Chinese or Japanese that they have no point of contact with anything in our own culture. While it is true that none of the *formal* divisions of Western science and thought corresponds to a way of liberation, R. H. Blyth's marvelous study of *Zen in English Literature* has shown most clearly that the essential insights of Zen are universal.

The reason why Taoism and Zen present, at first sight, such a puzzle to the Western mind is that we have taken a restricted view of human knowledge. For us, almost all knowledge is what a Taoist would call *conventional* knowledge, because we do not feel that we really know anything unless we can represent it to ourselves in words, or in some other system of conventional signs such as the notations of mathematics or music. Such knowledge is called conventional because it is a matter of social agreement as to the codes of communication. Just as people speaking the same language have tacit agreements as to what words shall stand for what things, so the members of every society and every culture are united by bonds of communication resting upon all kinds of agreement as to the classification and valuation of actions and things.

Thus the task of education is to make children fit to live in a society by persuading them to learn and accept its codes–the rules and conventions of communication whereby the society holds itself together. There is first the spoken language. The child is taught to accept "tree" and not "boojum" as the agreed sign for *that* (pointing to the object). We have no difficulty in understanding that the word "tree" is a matter of convention. What is much less obvious is that convention also governs the delineation of the thing to which the word is assigned. For the child has to be taught not only what words are to stand for what things, but also the way in which his culture has tacitly agreed to divide things from each other, to mark out the boundaries within our daily experience. Thus scientific convention decides whether an eel shall be a fish or a snake, and grammatical convention determines what experiences shall be called objects and what shall be called events or actions. How arbitrary such conventions may be can be seen from the question, "What happens to my fist [noun-object] when I open my hand?" The object miraculously vanishes because an action was disguised by a part of speech usually assigned to a thing! In English the differences between things and actions are clearly, if not always logically, distinguished, but a great number of Chinese words do duty for both nouns and verbs–so that one who thinks in Chinese has little difficulty in seeing that objects are also events, that our world is a collection of processes rather than entities.

Besides language, the child has to accept many other forms of code. For the necessities of living together require agreement as to codes of law and ethics, of etiquette and art, of weights, measures, and numbers, and, above all, of role. We have difficulty in communicating with each other unless we can identify ourselves in terms of roles–father, teacher, worker, artist, "regular guy," gentleman, sportsman, and so forth. To the extent that we identify ourselves with these stereotypes and the rules of behavior associated with them, we ourselves feel that we *are* someone because our fellows have less difficulty in accepting us–that is, in identifying us and feeling that we are "under control." A meeting of two strangers at a party is always somewhat embarrassing when the host has not identified their roles in introducing them, for neither knows what rules of conversation and action should be observed.

Once again, it is easy to see the conventional character of roles. For a man who is a father may also be a doctor and an artist, as well as an employee and a brother. And it is obvious that even the sum total of these role labels will be far from supplying an adequate description of the man himself, even though it may place him in certain general classifications. But the conventions which govern human identity are more subtle and much less obvious than these. We learn, very thoroughly though far less explicitly, to identify ourselves with an equally conventional view of "myself." For the conventional "self" or "person" is composed mainly of a history consisting of selected memories, and beginning from the moment of parturition. According to convention, I am not simply what I am doing now. I am also what I have done, and my conventionally edited version of my past is made to seem almost more the real "me" than what I am at this moment. For what I *am* seems so fleeting and intangible, but what I *was* is fixed and final. It is the firm basis for predictions of what I will be in the future, and so it comes about that I am more closely identified with what no longer exists than with what actually is!

It is important to recognize that the memories and past events which make up a man's historical identity are no more than a selection. From the actual infinitude of events and experiences some have been picked out–abstracted–as significant, and this significance has of course been determined by conventional standards. For the very nature of conventional knowledge is that it is a system of abstractions. It consists of signs and symbols in which things and events are reduced to their general outlines, as the Chinese character *jen* [a] stands for "man" by being the utmost simplification and generalization of the human form.

The same is true of words other than ideographs. The English words "man," "fish," "star," "flower," "run," "grow," all denote classes of objects or events which may be recognized as members of their class by very simple attributes, abstracted from the total complexity of the things themselves.

Abstraction is thus almost a necessity for communication, since it enables us to represent our experiences with simple and rapidly made "grasps" of the mind. When we say that we can think only of one thing at a time, this is like saying that the Pacific Ocean cannot be swallowed at a gulp. It has to be taken in a cup, and downed bit by bit. Abstractions and conventional signs are like the cup; they reduce experience to units simple enough to be comprehended one at a time. In a similar way, curves are measured by reducing them to a sequence of tiny straight lines, or by thinking of them in terms of the squares which they cross when plotted on graph paper.

Other examples of the same process are the newspaper photograph and the transmission of television. In the former, a natural scene is reproduced in terms of light and heavy dots arranged in a screen or gridlike pattern so as to give the general impression of a black-and-white photograph when seen without a magnifying glass. Much as it may look like the original scene, it is only a reconstruction of the scene in terms of dots, somewhat as our conventional words and thoughts are reconstructions of experience in terms of abstract signs. Even more like the thought process, the television camera transmits a natural scene in terms of a linear series of impulses which may be passed along a wire.

Thus communication by conventional signs of this type gives

us an abstract, one-at-a-time translation of a universe in which things are happening altogether-at-once–a universe whose concrete reality always escapes perfect description in these abstract terms. The perfect description of a small particle of dust by these means would take everlasting time, since one would have to account for every point in its volume.

The linear, one-at-a-time character of speech and thought is particularly noticeable in all languages using alphabets, representing experience in long strings of letters. It is not easy to say why we must communicate with others (speak) and with ourselves (think) by this one-at-a-time method. Life itself does not proceed in this cumbersome, linear fashion, and our own organisms could hardly live for a moment if they had to control themselves by taking thought of every breath, every beat of the heart, and every neural impulse. But if we are to find some explanation for this characteristic of thought, the sense of sight offers a suggestive analogy. For we have two types of vision–central and peripheral, not unlike the spotlight and the floodlight. Central vision is used for accurate work like reading, in which our eyes are focused on one small area after another like spotlights. Peripheral vision is less conscious, less bright than the intense ray of the spotlight. We use it for seeing at night, and for taking "subconscious" notice of objects and movements not in the direct line of central vision. Unlike the spotlight, it can take in very many things at a time.

There is, then, an analogy–and perhaps more than mere analogy–between central vision and conscious, one-at-a-time thinking, and between peripheral vision and the rather mysterious process which enables us to regulate the incredible complexity of our bodies without thinking at all. It should be noted, further, that we *call* our bodies complex as a result of trying to understand them in terms of linear thought, of words and concepts. But the complexity is not so much in our bodies as in the task of trying to understand them by this means of thinking. It is like trying to make out the features of a large room with no other light than a single bright ray. It is as complicated as trying to drink water with a fork instead of a cup.

In this respect, the Chinese written language has a slight advantage over our own, and is perhaps symptomatic of a different way of thinking. It is still linear, still a series of abstractions taken in one at a time. But its written signs are a little closer to life than spelled words because they are essentially pictures, and, as a Chinese proverb puts it, "One showing is worth a hundred sayings." Compare, for example, the ease of showing someone how to tie a complex knot with the difficulty of telling him how to do it in words alone.

Now the general tendency of the Western mind is to feel that we do not really understand what we cannot represent, what we cannot communicate, by linear signs—by thinking. We are like the "wallflower" who cannot learn a dance unless someone draws him a diagram of the steps, who cannot "get it by the feel." For some reason we do not trust and do not fully use the "peripheral vision" of our minds. We learn music, for example, by restricting the whole range of tone and rhythm to a notation of fixed tonal and rhythmic intervals—a notation which is incapable of representing Oriental music. But the Oriental musician has a rough notation which he uses only as a reminder of a melody. He learns music, not by reading notes, but by listening to the performance of a teacher, getting the "feel" of it, and copying him, and this enables him to acquire rhythmic and tonal sophistications matched only by those Western jazz artists who use the same approach.

We are not suggesting that Westerners simply do not use the "peripheral mind." Being human, we use it all the time, and every artist, every workman, every athlete calls into play some special development of its powers. But it is not academically and philosophically respectable. We have hardly begun to realize its possibilities, and it seldom, if ever, occurs to us that one of its most important uses is for that "knowledge of reality" which we try to attain by the cumbersome calculations of theology, metaphysics, and logical inference.

When we turn to ancient Chinese society, we find two "philosophical" traditions playing complementary parts–Confucianism and Taoism. Generally speaking, the former concerns itself with the linguistic, ethical, legal, and ritual conventions which provide the society with its system of communication. Confucianism, in other words, preoccupies itself with conventional knowledge, and under its auspices children are brought up so that their originally wayward and whimsical natures are made to fit the Procrustean bed of the social order. The individual defines himself and his place in society in terms of the Confucian formulae.

Taoism, on the other hand, is generally a pursuit of older men, and especially of men who are retiring from active life in the community. Their retirement from society is a kind of outward symbol of an inward liberation from the bounds of conventional patterns of thought and conduct. For Taoism concerns itself with unconventional knowledge, with the understanding of life directly, instead of in the abstract, linear terms of representational thinking.

Confucianism presides, then, over the socially necessary task of forcing the original spontaneity of life into the rigid rules of convention–a task which involves not only conflict and pain, but also the loss of that peculiar naturalness and un-self-consciousness for which little children are so much loved, and which is sometimes regained by saints and sages. The function of Taoism is to undo the inevitable damage of this discipline, and not only to restore but also to develop the original spontaneity, which is termed *tzu-jan* [b] or "self-so-ness." For the spontaneity of a child is still childish, like everything else about him. His education fosters his rigidity but not his spontaneity. In certain natures, the conflict between social convention and repressed spontaneity is so violent that it manifests itself in crime, insanity, and neurosis,

which are the prices we pay for the otherwise undoubted benefits
of order.

But Taoism must on no account be understood as a revolution
against convention, although it has sometimes been used as a
pretext for revolution. Taoism is a way of liberation, which never
comes by means of revolution, since it is notorious that most
revolutions establish worse tyrannies than they destroy. To be
free from convention is not to spurn it but not to be deceived by
it. It is to be able to use it as an instrument instead of being
used by it.

The West has no recognized institution corresponding to
Taoism because our Hebrew-Christian spiritual tradition identifies the Absolute—God—with the moral and logical order of
convention. This might almost be called a major cultural catas-
trophe, because it weights the social order with excessive authority, inviting just those revolutions against religion and tradition which have been so characteristic of Western history.
It is one thing to feel oneself in conflict with socially sanctioned
conventions, but quite another to feel at odds with the very root
and ground of life, with the Absolute itself. The latter feeling
nurtures a sense of guilt so preposterous that it must issue either
in denying one's own nature or in rejecting God. Because the
first of these alternatives is ultimately impossible—like chewing
off one's own teeth—the second becomes inevitable, where such
palliatives as the confessional are no longer effective. As is the
nature of revolutions, the revolution against God gives place to
the worse tyranny of the absolutist state—worse because it cannot even forgive, and because it recognizes nothing outside the
powers of its jurisdiction. For while the latter was theoretically
true of God, his earthly representative the Church was always
prepared to admit that though the laws of God were immutable,
no one could presume to name the limits of his mercy. When
the throne of the Absolute is left vacant, the relative usurps it
and commits the real idolatry, the real indignity against God—

the absolutizing of a concept, a conventional abstraction. But it is unlikely that the throne would have become vacant if, in a sense, it had not been so already–if the Western tradition had had some way of apprehending the Absolute directly, outside the terms of the conventional order.

Of course the very word "Absolute" suggests to us something abstract and conceptual, such as "Pure Being." Our very idea of "spirit" as opposed to "matter" seems to have more kinship with the abstract than the concrete. But with Taoism, as with other ways of liberation, the Absolute must never be confused with the abstract. On the other hand, if we say that the *Tao*,° as the ultimate Reality is called, is the concrete rather than the abstract, this may lead to still other confusions. For we are accustomed to associate the concrete with the material, the physiological, the biological, and the natural, as distinct from the supernatural. But from the Taoist and Buddhist standpoints these are still terms for conventional and abstract spheres of knowledge.

Biology and physiology, for example, are types of knowledge which represent the real world in terms of their own special abstract categories. They measure and classify that world in ways appropriate to the particular uses they want to make of it, somewhat as a surveyor deals with earth in terms of acres, a contractor in truckloads or tons, and a soil analyst in types of chemical structures. To say that the concrete reality of the human organism *is* physiological is like saying that the earth *is* so many tons or acres. And to say that this reality is natural is accurate enough if we mean spontaneous (*tzu-jan*) or *natura naturans* ("nature naturing"). But it is quite inaccurate if we mean *natura naturata* ("nature natured"), that is to say, nature classified, sorted into "natures" as when we ask, "What is the *nature* of this thing?" It is in this sense of the word that we must think of "scientific naturalism," a doctrine which has nothing in common with the naturalism of Taoism.

Thus to begin to understand what Taoism is about, we must at least be prepared to admit the possibility of some view of the world other than the conventional, some knowledge other than the contents of our surface consciousness, which can apprehend reality only in the form of one abstraction (or thought, the Chinese *nien* [d]) at a time. There is no real difficulty in this, for we will already admit that we "know" how to move our hands, how to make a decision, or how to breathe, even though we can hardly begin to explain how we do it in words. We know how to do it because we just do it! Taoism is an extension of this kind of knowledge, an extension which gives us a very different view of ourselves from that to which we are conventionally accustomed, and a view which liberates the human mind from its constricting identification with the abstract ego.

According to tradition, the originator of Taoism, Lao-tzu, was an older contemporary of Kung Fu-tzu, or Confucius, who died in 479 B.C.[1] Lao-tzu is said to have been the author of the *Tao Te Ching*, a short book of aphorisms, setting forth the principles of the Tao and its power or virtue (*Te* [e]). But traditional Chinese philosophy ascribes both Taoism and Confucianism to a still earlier source, to a work which lies at the very foundation of Chinese thought and culture, dating anywhere from 3000 to 1200 B.C. This is the *I Ching*, or *Book of Changes*.

The *I Ching* is ostensibly a book of divination. It consists of oracles based on sixty-four abstract figures, each of which is composed of six lines. The lines are of two kinds—divided (negative) and undivided (positive)—and the six-line figures, or hexagrams, are believed to have been based on the various ways in which a tortoise shell will crack when heated.[2] This refers to an ancient method of divination in which the soothsayer bored a hole in

---

[1] Modern scholarship has questioned both the date and the historicity of Lao-tzu, but it is hard to say whether this is really more than a manifestation of fashion, since there are periodic tendencies to cast doubts on the existence of great sages or to question the hoariness of their antiquity. One recalls similar doubts in connection with Jesus and the Buddha. There are some serious arguments for a later date, but it seems best to keep the traditional date until evidence to the contrary becomes more conclusive. See Fung Yu-lan (1), vol. 1, pp. 170–76.

[2] Fung Yu-lan (1), vol. 1, pp. 379–80.

the back of a tortoise shell, heated it, and then foretold the future from the cracks in the shell so formed, much as palmists use the lines on the hand. Naturally, these cracks were most complicated, and the sixty-four hexagrams are supposed to be a simplified classification of the various patterns of cracks. For many centuries now the tortoise shell has fallen into disuse, and instead the hexagram appropriate to the moment in which a question is asked of the oracle is determined by the random division of a set of fifty yarrow stalks.

But an expert in the *I Ching* need not necessarily use tortoise shells or yarrow stalks. He can "see" a hexagram in anything— in the chance arrangement of a bowl of flowers, in objects scattered upon a table, in the natural markings on a pebble. A modern psychologist will recognize in this something not unlike a Rorschach test, in which the psychological condition of a patient is diagnosed from the spontaneous images which he "sees" in a complex ink-blot. Could the patient interpret his own projections upon the ink-blot, he would have some useful information about himself for the guidance of his future conduct. In view of this, we cannot dismiss the divinatory art of the *I Ching* as mere superstition.

Indeed, an exponent of the *I Ching* might give us quite a tough argument about the relative merits of our ways for making important decisions. We feel that we decide rationally because we base our decisions on collecting relevant data about the matter in hand. We do not depend upon such irrelevant trifles as the chance tossing of a coin, or the patterns of tea leaves or cracks in a shell. Yet he might ask whether we really know what information is relevant, since our plans are constantly upset by utterly unforeseen incidents. He might ask how we know when we have collected enough information upon which to decide. If we were rigorously "scientific" in collecting information for our decisions, it would take us so long to collect the data that the time for action would have passed long before the work had been completed. So how do we know when we have enough? Does the information itself tell us that it is enough? On the contrary, we go through the motions of gathering the necessary information in a rational way, and then, just because of a hunch, or because we are tired of thinking, or because the time has come to decide, we act. He would ask whether this is not depending just as much upon "irrelevant trifles" as if we had been casting the yarrow stalks.

In other words, the "rigorously scientific" method of predicting the future can be applied only in special cases—where prompt action is not urgent, where the factors involved are largely mechanical, or in circumstances so restricted as to be trivial. By far the greater part of our important decisions depend upon "hunch"—in other words, upon the "peripheral vision" of the mind. Thus the reliability of our decisions rests ultimately upon our ability to "feel" the situation, upon the degree to which this "peripheral vision" has been developed.

Every exponent of the *I Ching* knows this. He knows that the book itself does not contain an exact science, but rather a useful tool which will work for him if he has a good "intuition," or if, as he would say, he is "in the Tao." Thus one does not consult the oracle without proper preparation, without going quietly and meticulously through the prescribed rituals in order to bring the mind into that calm state where the "intuition" is felt to act more effectively. It would seem, then, that if the origins of Taoism are to be found in the *I Ching,* they are not so much in the text of the book itself as in the way in which it was used and in the assumptions underlying it. For experience in making decisions by intuition might well show that this "peripheral" aspect of the mind works best when we do not try to interfere with it, when we trust it to work by itself—*tzu-jan,* spontaneously, "self-so."

Thus the basic principles of Taoism begin to unfold themselves. There is, first of all, the Tao—the indefinable, concrete "process" of the world, the Way of life. The Chinese word means originally a way or road, and sometimes "to speak," so that the first line of the *Tao Te Ching* contains a pun on the two meanings:

The Tao which can be spoken is not eternal Tao.[3] *

But in trying at least to suggest what he means, Lao-tzu says:

> There was something vague before heaven and earth arose. How calm! How void! It stands alone, unchanging; it acts everywhere, untiring. It may be considered the mother of everything under heaven. I do not know its name, but call it by the word *Tao*. (25)

And again:

> *The Tao is something blurred and indistinct.*
> *How indistinct! How blurred!*
> *Yet within it are images.*
> *How blurred! How indistinct!*
> *Yet within it are things.*
> *How dim! How confused!*
> *Yet within it is mental power.*
> *Because this power is most true,*
> *Within it there is confidence.* (21)

"Mental power" is *ching*,[g] a word which combines the ideas of essential, subtle, psychic or spiritual, and skillful. For the point seems to be that as one's own head looks like nothing to the eyes yet is the source of intelligence, so the vague, void-seeming, and indefinable Tao is the intelligence which shapes the world with a skill beyond our understanding.

The important difference between the Tao and the usual idea of God is that whereas God produces the world by making (*wei*[h]), the Tao produces it by "not-making" (*wu-wei*[i])—which is approximately what we mean by "growing." For things made are separate parts put together, like machines, or things fashioned from without inwards, like sculptures. Whereas things grown divide themselves into parts, from within outwards. Because the nat-

---

[3] Duyvendak (1) suggests that *tao* did not have the meaning of "to speak" at this date, and so translates the passage, "The Way that may truly be regarded as the Way is other than a permanent way." It really comes to the same thing, for what Duyvendak means by a "permanent way" is a fixed concept of the Tao—i.e., a definition. Almost every other translator, and most of the Chinese commentators, take the second *tao* to mean "spoken."

ural universe works mainly according to the principles of growth, it would seem quite odd to the Chinese mind to ask how it was made. If the universe were made, there would of course be someone who knows *how* it is made–who could explain how it was put together bit by bit as a technician can explain in one-at-a-time words how to assemble a machine. But a universe which grows utterly excludes the possibility of knowing how it grows in the clumsy terms of thought and language, so that no Taoist would dream of asking whether the Tao knows how it produces the universe. For it operates according to spontaneity, not according to plan. Lao-tzu says:

The Tao's principle is spontaneity. (25) [f]

But spontaneity is not by any means a blind, disorderly urge, a mere power of caprice. A philosophy restricted to the alternatives of conventional language has no way of conceiving an intelligence which does not work according to plan, according to a (one-at-a-time) order of thought. Yet the concrete evidence of such an intelligence is right to hand in our own thoughtlessly organized bodies.[3a] For the Tao does not "know" how it produces the universe just as we do not "know" how we construct our brains. In the words of Lao-tzu's great successor, Chuang-tzu:

Things are produced around us, but no one knows the whence. They issue forth, but no one sees the portal. Men one and all value that part of knowledge which is known. They do not know how to avail themselves of the Unknown in order to reach knowledge. Is not this misguided? [4]

[3a] The above was written before I had seen the second volume of Joseph Needham's masterly *Science and Civilization in China*, where he discusses the organismic nature of the Chinese, and especially the Taoist, conception of the universe. See especially Section 13*f*, pp. 279 ff. Needham also draws attention to the essential differences between Hebrew-Christian and Chinese views of natural law, the former deriving from the "word" of a lawgiver, God, and the latter from a relationship of spontaneous processes working in an organismic pattern. See Section 18, *f* and *h*, esp. pp. 557–64 and 572–83.

[4] H. A. Giles (1), p. 345.

The conventional relationship of the knower to the known is often that of the controller to the controlled, and thus of lord to servant. Thus whereas God is the master of the universe, since "he knows about it all! He knows! He knows!," the relationship of the Tao to what it produces is quite otherwise.

> *The great Tao flows everywhere,*
> *to the left and to the right.*
> *All things depend upon it to exist,*
> *and it does not abandon them.*
> *To its accomplishments it lays no claim.*
> *It loves and nourishes all things,*
> *but does not lord it over them.* (34)

In the usual Western conception God is also self-knowing– transparent through and through to his own understanding, the image of what man would like to be: the conscious ruler and controller, the absolute dictator of his own mind and body. But in contrast with this, the Tao is through and through mysterious and dark (*hsüan* [k]). As a Zen Buddhist said of it in later times:

There is one thing: above, it supports Heaven; below, it upholds Earth. It is black like lacquer, always actively functioning.[5] [l]

Hsüan is, of course, a metaphorical darkness–not the darkness of night, of black as opposed to white, but the sheer inconceivability which confronts the mind when it tries to remember the time before birth, or to penetrate its own depths.

Western critics often poke fun at such nebulous views of the Absolute, deriding them as "misty and mystical" in contrast with their own robustly definite opinions. But as Lao-tzu said:

> *When the superior man hears of the Tao,*
> *he does his best to practice it.*
> *When the middling man hears of the Tao,*
> *he sometimes keeps it, and sometimes loses it.*

[5] T'ung-shan Liang-chieh. Dumoulin and Sasaki (1), p. 74.

When the inferior man hears of the Tao,
he will laugh aloud at it.
If he did not laugh, it would not be the Tao. (41)

For it is really impossible to appreciate what is meant by the Tao without becoming, in a rather special sense, stupid. So long as the conscious intellect is frantically trying to clutch the world in its net of abstractions, and to insist that life be bound and fitted to its rigid categories, the mood of Taoism will remain incomprehensible; and the intellect will wear itself out. The Tao is accessible only to the mind which can practice the simple and subtle art of *wu-wei*, which, after the Tao, is the second important principle of Taoism.

We saw that the *I Ching* had given the Chinese mind some experience in arriving at decisions spontaneously, decisions which are effective to the degree that one knows how to let one's mind alone, trusting it to work by itself. This is *wu-wei*, since *wu* means "not" or "non-" and *wei* means "action," "making," "doing," "striving," "straining," or "busyness." To return to the illustration of eyesight, the peripheral vision works most effectively—as in the dark—when we see out of the corners of the eyes, and do not look at things directly. Similarly, when we need to see the details of a distant object, such as a clock, the eyes must be relaxed, not staring, not *trying* to see. So, too, no amount of working with the muscles of the mouth and tongue will enable us to taste our food more acutely. The eyes and the tongue must be trusted to do the work by themselves.

But when we have learned to put excessive reliance upon central vision, upon the sharp spotlight of the eyes and mind, we cannot regain the powers of peripheral vision unless the sharp and staring kind of sight is first relaxed. The mental or psychological equivalent of this is the special kind of stupidity to which Lao-tzu and Chuang-tzu so often refer. It is not simply calmness of mind, but "non-graspingness" of mind. In Chuang-tzu's words, "The perfect man employs his mind as a mirror. It grasps nothing; it refuses nothing. It receives, but does not keep." One might almost say that it "fuzzes" itself a little to compensate for too harsh a clarity. Thus Lao-tzu says of himself:

> Cut out cleverness and there are no anxieties! . . .
> People in general are so happy, as if enjoying a feast,
> Or as going up a tower in spring.
> I alone am tranquil, and have made no signs,
> Like a baby who is yet unable to smile;
> Forlorn as if I had no home to go to.
> Others all have more than enough,
> And I alone seem to be in want.
> Possibly mine is the mind of a fool,
> Which is so ignorant!
> The vulgar are bright,
> And I alone seem to be dull.
> The vulgar are discriminative,
> And I alone seem to be blunt.
> I am negligent as if being obscure;
> Drifting, as if being attached to nothing.
> The people in general all have something to do,
> And I alone seem to be impractical and awkward.
> I alone am different from others,
> But I value seeking sustenance from the Mother (Tao). (20) [6]

In most Taoist writings there is a slight degree of exaggeration or overstatement of the point which is actually a kind of humor, a self-caricature. Thus Chuang-tzu writes on the same theme:

> The man of character (te) lives at home without exercising his mind and performs actions without worry. The notions of right and wrong and the praise and blame of others do not disturb him. When within the four seas all people can enjoy themselves, that is happiness for him. . . . Sorrowful in countenance, he looks like a baby who has lost his mother; appearing stupid, he goes about

[6] Save for the first line, I have followed Ch'u Ta-kao (1), p. 30.

like one who has lost his way. He has plenty of money to spend, but does not know where it comes from. He drinks and eats just enough and does not know where the food comes from. (3:13) [7]

Lao-tzu is still more forceful in his apparent condemnation of conventional cleverness:

> Cut out sagacity; discard knowingness,
> and the people will benefit an hundredfold.
> Cut out "humanity"; discard righteousness,
> and the people will regain love of their fellows.
> Cut out cleverness; discard the utilitarian,
> and there will be no thieves and robbers. . . .
> Become unaffected; [8]
> Cherish sincerity;
> Belittle the personal;
> Reduce desires. (19)

The idea is not to reduce the human mind to a moronic vacuity, but to bring into play its innate and spontaneous intelligence by using it without forcing it. It is fundamental to both Taoist and Confucian thought that the natural man is to be trusted, and from their standpoint it appears that the Western mistrust of human nature—whether theological or technological—is a kind of schizophrenia. It would be impossible, in their view, to believe oneself innately evil without discrediting the very belief, since all the notions of a perverted mind would be perverted notions. However religiously "emancipated," the technological mind shows that it has inherited the same division against itself when it tries to subject the whole human order to the control of conscious reason. It forgets that reason cannot be trusted if the brain cannot be trusted, since the power of reason

[7] Lin Yutang (1), p. 129.
[8] "Unaffected" is an attempt to render su,[m] a character which refers originally to unbleached silk, or to the unpainted silk background of a picture. "Humanity" refers to the central Confucian principle of jen,[n] which would ordinarily mean "human-heartedness," though it is obvious that Lao-tzu refers to its self-conscious and affected form.

depends upon organs that were grown by "unconscious intelligence."

The art of letting the mind alone is vividly described by another Taoist writer, Lieh-tzu (*c.* 398 B.C.), celebrated for his mysterious power of being able to ride upon the wind. This, no doubt, refers to the peculiar sensation of "walking on air" which arises when the mind is first liberated. It is said that when Professor D. T. Suzuki was once asked how it feels to have attained *satori*,[o] the Zen experience of "awakening," he answered, "Just like ordinary everyday experience, except about two inches off the ground!" Thus when asked to explain the art of riding on the wind, Lieh-tzu gave the following account of his training under his master Lao Shang:

> After I had served him . . . for the space of three years, my mind did not venture to reflect on right and wrong, my lips did not venture to speak of profit and loss. Then, for the first time, my master bestowed one glance upon me—and that was all.
>
> At the end of five years a change had taken place; my mind was reflecting on right and wrong, and my lips were speaking of profit and loss. Then, for the first time, my master relaxed his countenance and smiled.
>
> At the end of seven years, there was another change. I let my mind reflect on what it would, but it no longer occupied itself with right and wrong. I let my lips utter whatsoever they pleased, but they no longer spoke of profit and loss. Then, at last, my master led me in to sit on the mat beside him.
>
> At the end of nine years, my mind gave free rein to its reflections,[p] my mouth free passage to its speech. Of right and wrong, profit and loss, I had no knowledge, either as touching myself or others. . . . Internal and external were blended into unity. After that, there was no distinction between eye and ear, ear and nose, nose and mouth: all were the same. My mind was frozen, my body in dissolution, my flesh and bones all melted together. I was wholly unconscious of what my body was resting on, or what was under my feet. I was borne this way and that on the wind, like dry chaff or leaves falling from a tree. In fact, I knew not whether the wind was riding on me or I on the wind.[9]

[9] L. Giles (1), pp. 40–42. From *Lieh-tzu*, ii.

The state of consciousness described sounds not unlike being pleasantly drunk–though without the "morning after" effects of alcohol! Chuang-tzu noticed the similarity, for he wrote:

> A drunken man who falls out of a cart, though he may suffer, does not die. His bones are the same as other people's; but he meets the accident in a different way. His spirit is in a condition of security. He is not conscious of riding in the cart; neither is he conscious of falling out of it. Ideas of life, death, fear, etc., cannot penetrate his breast; and so he does not suffer from contact with objective existences. And if such security is to be got from wine, how much more is it to be got from Spontaneity. (19) [10]

Since Lao-tzu, Chuang-tzu, and Lieh-tzu were all conscious enough to write very intelligible books, it may be assumed that some of this language is, again, exaggerated or metaphorical. Their "unconsciousness" is not coma, but what the exponents of Zen later signified by *wu-hsin*,[q] literally "no-mind," which is to say un-self-consciousness. It is a state of wholeness in which the mind functions freely and easily, without the sensation of a second mind or ego standing over it with a club. If the ordinary man is one who has to walk by lifting his legs with his hands, the Taoist is one who has learned to let the legs walk by themselves.

Various passages in the Taoist writings suggest that "no-mindedness" is employing the whole mind as we use the eyes when we rest them upon various objects but make no special effort to take anything in. According to Chuang-tzu:

> The baby looks at things all day without winking; that is because his eyes are not focussed on any particular object. He goes without knowing where he is going, and stops without knowing what he is doing. He merges himself with the surroundings and moves along with it. These are the principles of mental hygiene. (23) [11]

And again:

[10] H. A. Giles (1), p. 232.
[11] Lin Yutang (1), p. 86.

If you regulate your body and unify your attention, the harmony of heaven will come upon you. If you integrate your awareness, and unify your thoughts, spirit will make its abode with you. *Te* (virtue) will clothe you, and the Tao will shelter you. Your eyes will be like those of a new-born calf, which seeks not the wherefore. (22)

Each of the other senses might similarly be used to illustrate the "non-active" functioning of the mind–listening without straining to hear, smelling without strong inhalation, tasting without screwing up the tongue, and touching without pressing the object. Each is a special instance of the mental function which works through all, and which Chinese designates with the peculiar word *hsin*.[r]

This term is so important for the understanding of Zen that some attempt must be made to say what Taoism and Chinese thought in general take it to mean.[12] We usually translate it as "mind" or "heart," but neither of these words is satisfactory. The original form of the ideograph [s] seems to be a picture of the heart, or perhaps of the lungs or the liver, and when a Chinese speaks of the *hsin* he will often point to the center of his chest, slightly lower than the heart.

The difficulty with our translations is that "mind" is too intellectual, too cortical, and that "heart" in its current English usage is too emotional–even sentimental. Furthermore, *hsin* is not always used with quite the same sense. Sometimes it is used for an obstruction to be removed, as in *wu-hsin*, "no-mind." But sometimes it is used in a way that is almost synonymous

[12] The central Zen principle of "no-mind" or *wu-hsin* is already found in Chuang-tzu. Cf. *Chuang-tzu* (22):

> Body like dry bone,
> Mind like dead ashes;
> This is true knowledge,
> Not to strive after knowing the whence.
> In darkness, in obscurity,
> The mindless (wu-hsin) cannot plan;–
> What manner of man is that?

H. A. Giles (1), p. 28L

with the Tao. This is especially found in Zen literature, which abounds with such phrases as "original mind" (*pen hsin*ᵗ), "Buddha mind" (*fu hsin*ᵘ), or "faith in mind" (*hsin hsin*ᵛ). This apparent contradiction is resolved in the principle that "the true mind is no mind," which is to say that the *hsin* is true, is working properly, when it works as if it were not present. In the same way, the eyes are seeing properly when they do not see themselves, in terms of spots or blotches in the air.

All in all, it would seem that *hsin* means the totality of our psychic functioning, and, more specifically, the center of that functioning, which is associated with the central point of the upper body. The Japanese form of the word, *kokoro*, is used with even more subtleties of meaning, but for the present it is enough to realize that in translating it "mind" (a sufficiently vague word) we do not mean exclusively the intellectual or thinking mind, nor even the surface consciousness. The important point is that, according to both Taoism and Zen, the center of the mind's activity is not in the conscious thinking process, not in the ego.

When a man has learned to let his mind alone so that it functions in the integrated and spontaneous way that is natural to it, he begins to show the special kind of "virtue" or "power" called *te*. This is not virtue in the current sense of moral rectitude but in the older sense of effectiveness, as when one speaks of the healing virtues of a plant. *Te* is, furthermore, unaffected or spontaneous virtue which cannot be cultivated or imitated by any deliberate method. Lao-tzu says:

> *Superior* te *is not* te,
> *and thus has* te.
> *Inferior* te *does not let go of* te,
> *and thus is not* te.
> *Superior* te *is non-active* [wu-wei] *and aimless.*
> *Inferior* te *is active and has an aim.* (38)

The literal translation has a strength and depth which is lost in such paraphrases as "Superior virtue is not conscious of itself as virtue, and thus really is virtue. Inferior virtue cannot dispense with virtuosity, and thus is not virtue."

When the Confucians prescribed a virtue which depended upon the artificial observance of rules and precepts, the Taoists pointed out that such virtue was conventional and not genuine. Chuang-tzu made up the following imaginary dialogue between Confucius and Lao-tzu:

> "Tell me," said Lao-tzu, "in what consist charity and duty to one's neighbour?"
>
> "They consist," answered Confucius, "in a capacity for rejoicing in all things; in universal love, without the element of self. These are the characteristics of charity and duty to one's neighbour."
>
> "What stuff!" cried Lao-tzu. "Does not universal love contradict itself? Is not your elimination of self a positive manifestation of self? Sir, if you would cause the empire not to lose its source of nourishment,—there is the universe, its regularity is unceasing; there are the sun and moon, their brightness is unceasing; there are the stars, their groupings never change; there are the birds and beasts, they flock together without varying; there are trees and shrubs, they grow upwards without exception. Be like these: follow Tao, and you will be perfect. Why then these vain struggles after charity and duty to one's neighbour, as though beating a drum in search of a fugitive. Alas! Sir, you have brought much confusion into the mind of man." (13) [13]

The Taoist critique of conventional virtue applied not only in the moral sphere but also in the arts, crafts, and trades. According to Chuang-tzu:

> Ch'ui the artisan could draw circles with his hand better than with compasses. His fingers seemed to accommodate themselves so naturally to the thing he was working at, that it was unnecessary to fix his attention. His mental faculties thus remained One (i.e., integrated), and suffered no hindrance. To be unconscious of one's feet implies that the shoes are easy. To be unconscious of a waist implies that the girdle is easy. The intelligence being unconscious of positive and negative implies that the heart (*hsin*) is at ease. . . . And he who, beginning with ease, is never not at ease, is unconscious of the ease of ease. (19) [14]

[13] H. A. Giles (1), p. 167.
[14] H. A. Giles (1), p. 242.

Just as the artisan who had mastered *te* could do without the artificiality of the compass, so the painter, the musician, and the cook would have no need for the conventional classifications of their respective arts. Thus Lao-tzu said:

> The five colours will blind a man's sight.
> The five sounds will deaden a man's hearing.
> The five tastes will spoil a man's palate.
> Chasing and hunting will drive a man wild.
> Things hard to get will do harm to a man's conduct.
> Therefore the sage makes provision for the stomach
>   and not for the eye. (12) [15]

This must by no means be taken as an ascetic's hatred of sense experience, for the point is precisely that the eye's sensitivity to color is impaired by the fixed idea that there are just five true colors. There is an infinite continuity of shading, and breaking it down into divisions with names distracts the attention from its subtlety. This is why "the sage makes provision for the stomach and not for the eye," which is to say that he judges by the concrete content of the experience, and not by its conformity with purely theoretical standards.

In sum, then, *te* is the unthinkable ingenuity and creative power of man's spontaneous and natural functioning—a power which is blocked when one tries to master it in terms of formal methods and techniques. It is like the centipede's skill in using a hundred legs at once.

> The centipede was happy, quite,
> Until a toad in fun
> Said, "Pray, which leg goes after which?"
> This worked his mind to such a pitch,
> He lay distracted in a ditch,
> Considering how to run.

A profound regard for *te* underlies the entire higher culture of the Far East, so much so that it has been made the basic principle of every kind of art and craft. While it is true that these arts em-

[15] Ch'u Ta-kao (1), p. 22.

ploy what are, to us, highly difficult technical disciplines, it is always recognized that they are instrumental and secondary, and that superior work has the quality of an accident. This is not merely a masterful mimicry of the accidental, an assumed spontaneity in which the careful planning does not show. It lies at a much deeper and more genuine level, for what the culture of Taoism and Zen proposes is that one might become the kind of person who, without intending it, is a source of marvelous accidents.

Taoism is, then, the original Chinese way of liberation which combined with Indian Mahayana Buddhism to produce Zen. It is a liberation *from* convention and *of* the creative power of *te*. Every attempt to describe and formulate it in words and one-at-a-time thought symbols must, of necessity, distort it. The foregoing chapter has perforce made it seem one of the "vitalist" or "naturalistic" philosophical alternatives. For Western philosophers are constantly bedeviled by the discovery that they *cannot* think outside certain well-worn ruts—that, however hard they may try, their "new" philosophies turn out to be restatements of ancient positions, monist or pluralist, realist or nominalist, vitalist or mechanist. This is because these are the only alternatives which the conventions of thought can present, and they cannot discuss anything else without presenting it in their own terms. When we try to represent a third dimension upon a two-dimensional surface, it will of necessity seem to belong more or less to the two alternatives of length and breadth. In the words of Chuang-tzu:

> Were language adequate, it would take but a day fully to set forth Tao. Not being adequate, it takes that time to explain material existences. Tao is something beyond material existences. It cannot be conveyed either by words or by silence. (25) [16]

[16] H. A. Giles (1), p. 351.

Two

THE ORIGINS OF BUDDHISM

Chinese civilization was at least two thousand years old when it first encountered Buddhism. Thus the new philosophy entered into a solidly established culture in which it could hardly become acceptable without major adaptations to the Chinese mentality, even though there were some resemblances between Taoism and Buddhism so strong that they have aroused speculation as to whether contacts between the two were much earlier than has been supposed. China absorbed Buddhism as it has absorbed so many other external influences—not only philosophies and ideas, but also alien populations and invaders. Undoubtedly this is due in some measure to the extraordinary stability and maturity which the Chinese have derived from Confucianism. Reasonable, unfanatical, humanistic, Confucianism is one of the most workable patterns of social convention that the world has known. Coupled with the "let well enough alone" attitude of Taoism, it nurtured a mellow and rather easygoing type of mentality which, when it absorbed Buddhism, did much to make it more "practical." That is to say, it made Buddhism a possible way of life for *human* beings, for people with families, with everyday work to do, and with normal instincts and passions.

It was a basic Confucian principle that "it is man who makes truth great, not truth which makes man great." For this reason, "humanness" or "human-heartedness" (*jen* [a]) was always felt to be superior to "righteousness" (*i* [b]), since man himself is greater than any idea which he may invent. There are times when men's passions are much more trustworthy than their principles. Since opposed principles, or ideologies, are irreconcilable, wars fought over principle will be wars of mutual annihilation. But wars fought for simple greed will be far less destructive, because the aggressor will be careful not to destroy what he is fighting to capture. Reasonable—that is, human—men will always be capable of compromise, but men who have dehumanized themselves by becoming the blind worshipers of an idea or an ideal are fanatics whose devotion to abstractions makes them the enemies of life.

Modified by such attitudes, Far Eastern Buddhism is much more palatable and "according to nature" than its Indian and Tibetan counterparts, with ideals of life which seem at times to be superhuman, more suited to angels than to men. Even so, all forms of Buddhism subscribe to the Middle Way between the extremes of angel (*deva*) and demon (*preta*), ascetic and sensualist, and claim that supreme "awakening" or Buddhahood can be attained only from the human state.

There are some serious difficulties in the way of giving an historically accurate account of Indian Buddhism, as of the whole philosophical tradition from which it arose. No student of Asian thought should be unaware of these difficulties, because they make it necessary to take almost every important pronouncement about ancient Indian thought with caution. Thus before attempting to describe Indian Buddhism, some of these difficulties should be mentioned.

The first, and most serious, is the problem of interpreting the Sanskrit and Pali texts in which ancient Indian literature is preserved. This is especially true of Sanskrit, the sacred language of India, and more particularly the form of Sanskrit used in the Vedic period. Both Western and Indian scholars are uncertain as to its exact interpretation, and all modern dictionaries rely heavily on a single source—the lexicon compiled by Böthlingk and Roth in the latter part of the last century, and now admitted to contain a great deal of guesswork. This seriously affects our understanding of the primary sources of Hinduism—the *Vedas* and *Upanishads*. The discovery of proper European equivalents for philosophical terms has been hindered by the fact that early lexicographers were all too ready to find correspondences with Western theological terms, since one of the primary objects of their studies was to assist the missionaries.[1]

The second is that it is extremely hard to know what was the original form of Buddhism. There are two sets of Buddhist scriptures: the Pali Canon of the Theravada or Southern School of Buddhism, which flourishes in Ceylon, Burma, and Thailand, and the Sanskrit-Tibetan-Chinese Canon of the Mahayana, or Northern School. There is a general consensus of scholars that the Pali Canon is, on the whole, the earlier of the two, and that the principal *sutras* (as the sacred texts are called) of the Mahayana Canon were all compiled after 100 B.C. However, the literary form of the Pali Canon does not suggest that it represents the actual words of Gautama the Buddha. If the *Upanishads* are characteristic of the style of discourse of an Indian teacher between 800 and 300 B.C., they bear little resemblance to the tediously repetitious and scholastic style of most Buddhist scriptures. There can be little doubt that the greater part of both Buddhist Canons is the work of the pandits of the Sangha, the Buddhist monastic order, for it shows every sign of being the reverential elaboration of an original doctrine. As with Russian icons, the original painting has been almost lost to sight in the overlay of jewels and gold.

The third is that the Hindu-Buddhist tradition has never had the historical sense of the Hebrew-Christian tradition, so that there are few, if any, marks to indicate the date of a given text. Scriptures were handed down by oral tradition for an indeterminable period of time before being committed to writing, and it is quite possible that historical references could have been changed to suit the times as the oral form was handed down. Furthermore, a Buddhist monk writing in A.D. 200 would have no compunction in attributing his own words to the Buddha if he felt sincerely that they were an expression, not of personal

[1] See Monier-Williams, *Sanskrit-English Dictionary*, p. ix. (Oxford, 1951.)

opinion, but of the supra-personal state of awakening to which he had attained. He would attribute the words to the Buddha as speaking in a spiritual rather than material body.

The danger of scholarship is always that, in extreme specialization, it may be unable to see the forest for the trees. But the problem of gaining some idea of the thought of India at the time of the Buddha, six centuries before Christ, is not to be solved by careful piece-work alone–necessary as this may be. There is, however, enough reliable information to suggest the grand and beautifully ordered form of Upanishadic Hinduism if we do not read it with our noses against the page.

Fundamental to the life and thought of India from the very earliest times is the great mythological theme of *atma-yajna*–the act of "self-sacrifice" whereby God gives birth to the world, and whereby men, following the divine pattern, reintegrate themselves with God. The act by which the world is created is the same act by which it is consummated–the giving up of one's life– as if the whole process of the universe were the type of game in which it is necessary to pass on the ball as soon as it is received. Thus the basic myth of Hinduism is that the world is God playing hide-and-seek with himself. As Prajapati, Vishnu, or Brahma, the Lord under many names creates the world by an act of self-dismemberment or self-forgetting, whereby the One becomes Many, and the single Actor plays innumerable parts. In the end, he comes again to himself only to begin the play once more–the One dying into the Many, and the Many dying into the One.

A thousand heads hath Purusha, a thousand eyes, a thousand feet.
On every side pervading earth he fills a space ten fingers wide.

This Purusha is all that yet hath been and all that is to be;
The lord of immortality that waxes greater still by food.

So mighty is his greatness; yea, greater than this is Purusha.
All creatures are one fourth of him, three-fourths eternal life in heaven. . . .

When the gods prepared the sacrifice with Purusha as their offering,
Its oil was spring, the holy gift was autumn; summer was the wood.

From that great general sacrifice the dripping fat was gathered up.
He formed the creatures of the air, and animals both wild and tame. . . .

When they divided Purusha, how many portions did they make?
What do they call his mouth, his arms? What do they call his thighs and feet?

The Brahman (caste) was his mouth, of both his arms was the Rajanya (Kshatriya caste) made.
His thighs became Vaishya, from his feet the Shudra was produced.

The moon was gendered from his mind, and from his eye the sun had birth;
Indra and Agni from his mouth were born, and Vayu from his breath.

Forth from his navel came mid-air; the sky was fashioned from his head;
Earth from his feet, and from his ear the regions. Thus they formed the worlds.[2]

The thousand heads, eyes, and feet of the Purusha are the members of men and other beings, for the point is that That which knows in and through every individual is God himself, the *atman* or Self of the world. Every life is a part or role in which the mind of God is absorbed, somewhat as an actor absorbs himself in being Hamlet and forgets that in real life he is Mr. Smith. By the act of self-abandonment God becomes all beings, yet at the same time does not cease to be God. "All creatures are one fourth of him, three-fourths eternal life in heaven." For God is divided in play, in make-believe, but remains undivided in reality. So that when the play comes to an end, the individualized consciousness awakes to find itself divine.

In the beginning this world was *Atman* (the Self), alone in the form of Purusha. Looking about he saw nothing other than himself.

[2] *Rigveda* x. 90. The translation is from R. T. H. Griffith. Purusha is "the Person," i.e., the original consciousness behind the world.

He said first, "I am." Thence came the word "I." Thus even now, when one is spoken to, he first answers simply, "It is I," and then tells whatever name he has.[3]

> On all sides That has hands and feet;
> On all sides eyes, heads, and faces;
> On all sides in the world it hears;
> All things it embraces.[4]

It is important to remember that this picture of the world as the play (*lila*) of God is mythological in form. If, at this stage, we were to translate it directly into philosophical statement it would be a crude type of pantheism, with which Hindu philosophy is generally and erroneously confused. Thus the idea of each man, each thing, as a part which the Purusha plays in the state of self-forgetting must not be confused with a logical or scientific statement of fact. The form of statement is poetic, not logical. In the words of the *Mundaka Upanishad*,

> Truly this *atman* (Self)—the poets say—travels on this earth from body to body. (ii. 7)

Hindu philosophy has not made the mistake of imagining that one can make an informative, factual, and positive statement about the ultimate reality. As the same *Upanishad* says,

> Where knowledge is without duality, without action, cause, or effect, unspeakable, incomparable, beyond description, what is that? It is impossible to say! (vi. 7)

Every positive statement about ultimate things must be made in the suggestive form of myth, of poetry. For in this realm the direct and indicative form of speech can say only *"Neti, neti"* ("No, no"), since what can be described and categorized must always belong to the conventional realm.

Hindu mythology elaborates the theme of the divine play on a fabulous scale, embracing not only colossal concepts of time and

[3] *Brihadaranyaka Upanishad* i. 4. 5.
[4] *Bhagavad-Gita* xiii. 13.

space, but also the widest extremes of pleasure and pain, virtue and depravity. The inmost Self of saint and sage is no less the veiled Godhead than the inmost Self of the debauchee, the coward, the lunatic, and the very demons. The opposites (*dvandva*) of light and darkness, good and evil, pleasure and pain, are the essential elements of the game, for although the Godhead is identified with Truth (*sat*), Consciousness (*chit*), and Bliss (*ananda*), the dark side of life has its integral part in the game just as every drama must have its villain, to disrupt the *status quo,* and as the cards must be shuffled, thrown into chaos, in order that there may be a significant development of the play. For Hindu thought there is no Problem of Evil. The conventional, relative world is necessarily a world of opposites. Light is inconceivable apart from darkness; order is meaningless without disorder; and, likewise, up without down, sound without silence, pleasure without pain. In the words of Ananda Coomaraswamy:

> For anyone who holds that "God made the world," the question, Why did He permit the existence in it of any evil, or of that Evil One in whom all evil is personified, is altogether meaningless; one might as well enquire why He did not make a world without dimensions or one without temporal succession.[5]

According to the myth, the divine play goes on through endless cycles of time, through periods of manifestation and withdrawal of the worlds measured in units of *kalpas,* the *kalpa* being a span of 4,320,000,000 years. From the human standpoint such a conception presents a terrifying monotony, since it goes on aimlessly for ever and ever. But from the divine standpoint it has all the fascination of the repetitious games of children, which go on and on because time has been forgotten and has reduced itself to a single wondrous instant.

The foregoing myth is not the expression of a formal philoso-

[5] Coomaraswamy (1), p. 77.

phy, but of an experience or state of consciousness which is called *moksha* or "liberation." On the whole it is safer to say that Indian philosophy is primarily this experience; it is only quite secondarily a system of ideas which attempt to translate the experience into conventional language. At root, then, the philosophy becomes intelligible only by sharing the experience which consists of the same type of nonconventional knowledge found in Taoism. It is also termed *atma-jnana* (Self-knowledge) or *atma-bodha* (Self-awakening), since it may be considered as the discovery of who or what I am, when I am no longer identified with any role or conventional definition of the person. Indian philosophy does not describe the content of this discovery except in mythological terms, using the phrase "I am Brahman" (*aham brahman*) or "That art thou" (*tat tvam asi*) to suggest that Self-knowledge is a realization of one's original identity with God.

But this does not imply what "claiming to be God" means in a Hebrew-Christian context, where mythical language is ordinarily confused with factual language so that there is no clear distinction between God as described in the terms of conventional thought and God as he is in reality. A Hindu does not say "I am Brahman" with the implication that he is personally in charge of the whole universe and informed as to every detail of its operation. On the one hand, he is not speaking of identity with God at the level of his superficial personality. On the other, his "God"–Brahman–is not in charge of the universe in a "personal" way; he does not know and act in the manner of a person since he does not know the universe in terms of conventional facts nor act upon it by means of deliberation, effort, and will. It may be of significance that the word "Brahman" is from the root *brih-*, "to grow," since his creative activity, like that of the Tao, is with the spontaneity proper to growth as distinct from the deliberation proper to making. Furthermore, though Brahman is said to "know" himself, this knowing is not a matter of information, a knowledge such as one has of objects distinct from a subject. In the words of Shankara,

For He is the Knower, and the Knower can know other things, but cannot make Himself the object of His own knowledge, in the same way that fire can burn other things, but cannot burn itself.[6]

To the Western mind the puzzle of Indian philosophy is that it has so much to say about what the *moksha* experience is not, and little, or nothing, to say about what it is. This is naturally bewildering, for if the experience is really without content, or if it is so lacking in relation to the things which we consider important, how is one to explain the immense esteem which it holds in the Indian scheme of life?

Even at the conventional level it is surely easy to see that knowing what is not so is often quite as important as knowing what is. Even when medicine can suggest no effective remedy for the common cold, there is some advantage in knowing the uselessness of certain popular nostrums. Furthermore, the function of negative knowledge is not unlike the uses of space—the empty page upon which words can be written, the empty jar into which liquid can be poured, the empty window through which light can be admitted, and the empty pipe through which water can flow. Obviously the value of emptiness lies in the movements it permits or in the substance which it mediates and contains. But the emptiness must come first. This is why Indian philosophy concentrates on negation, on liberating the mind from concepts of Truth. It proposes no *idea*, no description, of what is to fill the mind's void because the idea would exclude the fact—somewhat as a picture of the sun on the windowpane would shut out the true sun's light. Whereas the Hebrews would not permit an image of God in wood or stone, the Hindus will not permit an image of thought—unless it be so obviously mythological as not to be mistaken for the reality.

Therefore the practical discipline (*sadhana*) of the way of

[6] *Bashya* on *Kena Upanishad*, 9–11. "Cannot" may give the wrong implication since the word is ordinarily privative. The point is that, as light has no need to shine upon itself since it is luminous already, so there is no advantage to be gained and, indeed, no meaning in the notion of Brahman's being the object of his own knowledge.

liberation is a progressive disentanglement of one's Self (*atman*) from every identification. It is to realize that I am not this body, these sensations, these feelings, these thoughts, this consciousness. The basic reality of my life is not any conceivable object. Ultimately it is not even to be identified with any idea, as of God or *atman*. In the words of the *Mandukya Upanishad:*

> (It is) That which is conscious neither of the subjective nor of the objective, nor of both; which is neither simple consciousness, nor undifferentiated sentience, nor mere darkness. It is unseen, without relations, incomprehensible, uninferable, and indescribable—the essence of Self-consciousness, the ending of *maya*. (vii)

The *atman* is to our total consciousness what the head is to the sense of sight—neither light nor darkness, neither full nor empty, only an inconceivable beyond. In the moment when every last identification of the Self with some object or concept has ceased, in the state called *nirvikalpa* or "without conception," there flashes forth from its unknown depths the state of consciousness which is called divine, the knowledge of Brahman.

Translated into conventional and—let it be repeated—mythopoetic language, the knowledge of Brahman is represented as the discovery that this world which seemed to be Many is in truth One, that "all is Brahman" and that "all duality is falsely imagined." Taken as statements of fact, such utterances are logically meaningless and convey no information. Yet they seem to be the best possible expression in words of the experience itself, though it is as if in the moment of saying the "last word" the tongue were paralyzed by its own revelation, and compelled to babble nonsense or be silent.

Moksha is also understood as liberation from *maya*—one of the most important words in Indian philosophy, both Hindu and Buddhist. For the manifold world of facts and events is said to be *maya*, ordinarily understood as an illusion which veils the one underlying reality of Brahman. This gives the impression that *moksha* is a state of consciousness in which the whole varied world of nature vanishes from sight, merged in a boundless ocean of vaguely luminous space. Such an impression should be dismissed at once, for it implies a duality, an incompatibility, between Brahman and *maya* which is against the whole principle of Upanishadic philosophy. For Brahman is not One *as opposed* to Many, not simple *as opposed* to complex. Brahman is without duality (*advaita*), which is to say without any opposite since Brahman is not in any class or, for that matter, outside any class.

Now classification is precisely *maya*. The word is derived from the Sanskrit root *matr-*, "to measure, form, build, or lay out a plan," the root from which we obtain such Greco-Latin words as meter, matrix, material, and matter. The fundamental process of measurement is division, whether by drawing a line with the finger, by marking off or by enclosing circles with the span of the hand or dividers, or by sorting grain or liquids into measures (cups). Thus the Sanskrit root *dva-* from which we get the word "divide" is also the root of the Latin *duo* (two) and the English "dual."

To say, then, that the world of facts and events is *maya* is to say that facts and events are terms of measurement rather than realities of nature. We must, however, expand the concept of measurement to include setting bounds of all kinds, whether by descriptive classification or selective screening. It will thus be easy to see that facts and events are as abstract as lines of latitude or as feet and inches. Consider for a moment that it is impossible to isolate a single fact, all by itself. Facts come in pairs at the very least, for a single body is inconceivable apart from a space in which it hangs. Definition, setting bounds, delineation—these are always acts of *division* and thus of duality, for as soon as a boundary is defined it has two sides.

This point of view is somewhat startling, and even quite hard to understand, for those long accustomed to think that things, facts, and events are the very building-blocks of the world, the most solid of solid realities. Yet a proper understanding of the *maya* doctrine is one of the most essential prerequisites for the study of Hinduism and Buddhism, and in trying to grasp its meaning one must try to put aside the various "idealist" philosophies of the West with which it is so often confused—even by modern Indian Vedantists. For the world is not an illusion of the mind in the sense that—to the eyes of the liberated man (*jivan-mukta*)—there is nothing to be seen but a trackless void. He sees the world that we see; but he does not mark it off, measure it, divide it in the same way. He does not look upon it as really or concretely broken down into separate things and events. He sees that the skin may just as well be regarded as what joins us to our environment as what separates us from it. He sees, furthermore, that the skin will be considered as joining only if it has first been considered as separating, or vice versa.

Thus his point of view is not monistic. He does not think that all things are in reality One because, concretely speaking, there never were any "things" to be considered One. To join is as much *maya* as to separate. For this reason both Hindus and Buddhists prefer to speak of reality as "nondual" rather than "one," since the concept of one must always be in relation to that of many. The doctrine of *maya* is therefore a doctrine of relativity. It is saying that things, facts, and events are delineated, not by nature, but by human description, and that the way in which we describe (or divide) them is relative to our varying points of view.

It is easy to see, for example, that an event called the First World War can only rather arbitrarily be said to have begun on August 4, 1914, and to have ended on November 11, 1918. Historians can discover "actual" beginnings of the war long before and "resumptions" of the same strife long after these formal boundaries of the event. For events can divide and merge like blobs of mercury according to the changing fashions of historical description. The boundaries of events are conventional rather than natural, in the sense that a man's life is said to have begun at the moment of parturition, rather than at conception on the one hand or weaning on the other.

Similarly, it is easy to see the conventional character of things.

Ordinarily a human organism is counted as one thing, though from the physiological standpoint it is as many things as it has parts or organs, and from the sociological standpoint it is merely part of a larger thing called a group.

Certainly the world of nature abounds with surfaces and lines, with areas of density and vacuity, which we employ in marking out the boundaries of events and things. But here again, the *maya* doctrine asserts that these forms (*rupa*) have no "own-being" or "self-nature" (*svabhava*): they do not exist in their own right, but only in relation to one another, as a solid cannot be distinguished save in relation to a space. In this sense, the solid and the space, the sound and the silence, the existent and the nonexistent, the figure and the ground are inseparable, interdependent, or "mutually arising," and it is only by *maya* or conventional division that they may be considered apart from one another.

Indian philosophy also thinks of *rupa* or form as *maya* because it is impermanent. Indeed, when Hindu and Buddhist texts speak of the "empty" or "illusory" character of the visible world of nature–as distinct from the conventional world of things–they refer precisely to the impermanence of its forms. Form is flux, and thus *maya* in the slightly extended sense that it cannot be firmly marked down or grasped. Form is *maya* when the mind attempts to comprehend and control it in the fixed categories of thought, that is, by means of names (*nama*) and words. For these are precisely the nouns and verbs by means of which the abstract and conceptual categories of things and events are designated.

To serve their purpose, names and terms must of necessity be fixed and definite like all other units of measurement. But their use is–up to a point–so satisfactory that man is always in danger of confusing his measures with the world so measured, of identifying money with wealth, fixed convention with fluid reality. But to the degree that he identifies himself and his life with these rigid and hollow frames of definition, he condemns himself to the perpetual frustration of one trying to catch water in a sieve. Thus Indian philosophy speaks constantly of the un-wisdom of pursuing things, of striving for the permanence of particular entities and events, because it sees in all this nothing more than an infatuation with ghosts, with the abstract meas-ures of the mind (*manas*).[7]

Maya is, then, usually equated with *nama-rupa* or "name-and-form," with the mind's attempt to grasp the fluid forms of nature in its mesh of fixed classes. But when it is understood that form is ultimately void—in the special sense of ungraspable and im-measurable—the world of form is immediately seen as Brahman rather than *maya*. The formal world becomes the real world in the moment when it is no longer clutched, in the moment when its changeful fluidity is no longer resisted. Hence it is the very transitoriness of the world which is the sign of its divinity, of its actual identity with the indivisible and immeasurable infinity of Brahman.

This is why the Hindu-Buddhist insistence on the imper-manence of the world is not the pessimistic and nihilistic doc-trine which Western critics normally suppose it to be. Transitori-ness is depressing only to the mind which insists upon trying to grasp. But to the mind which lets go and moves with the flow of change, which becomes, in Zen Buddhist imagery, like a ball in a mountain stream, the sense of transience or emptiness becomes a kind of ecstasy. This is perhaps why, in both East and West, impermanence is so often the theme of the most profound and moving poetry—so much so that the splendor of change shines through even when the poet seems to resent it the most.

> *Tomorrow, and tomorrow, and tomorrow,*
> *Creeps in this petty pace from day to day*
> *To the last syllable of recorded time,*
> *And all our yesterdays have lighted fools*

[7] From the same root as *maya*, and from which also come our words "mensu-ration" (Lat., *mensura*), "mental" (Lat., *mens*), "dimension," and "man" himself, "the measure of all things." Cf. also the Latin *mensis* (month).

The way to dusty death. Out, out, brief candle!
Life's but a walking shadow, a poor player
That struts and frets his hour upon the stage
And then is heard no more: it is a tale
Told by an idiot, full of sound and fury,
Signifying nothing.

Stated thus—as R. H. Blyth observes—it seems not so bad after all.

In sum, then, the *maya* doctrine points out, firstly, the impossibility of grasping the actual world in the mind's net of words and concepts, and, secondly, the fluid character of those very forms which thought attempts to define. The world of facts and events is altogether *nama,* abstract names, and *rupa,* fluid form. It escapes both the comprehension of the philosopher and the grasp of the pleasure-seeker like water from a clutching fist. There is even something deceptive in the idea of Brahman as the eternal reality underlying the flux, and of the *atman* as the divine ground of human consciousness, for in so far as these are concepts they are as incapable of grasping the real as any other.

It is precisely this realization of the *total* elusiveness of the world which lies at the root of Buddhism. This is the special shift of emphasis which, more than anything else, distinguishes the doctrine of the Buddha from the teaching of the *Upanishads,* which is the *raison d'être* for the growth of Buddhism as a distinct movement in Indian life and thought.

For Gautama the "Awakened One" or Buddha (died *c.* 545 B.C.) lived at a time when the major *Upanishads* were already in existence, and their philosophy must be seen as the point of departure for his own teaching. It would be a serious mistake, however, to look upon the Buddha as the "founder" or "reformer" of a religion which came into being as some kind of organized revolt against Hinduism. For we are speaking of a time when there was no consciousness of "religions," when such terms as "Hindu-ism" or "Brahman-ism" would have meant nothing. There was simply a tradition, embodied in the orally transmitted doctrine of the *Vedas* and *Upanishads,* a tradition that was not specifically "religious" in that it involved a whole way of life and concerned everything from the methods of agriculture to the knowledge of the ultimate reality. The Buddha was acting in full accord with this tradition when he became a *rishi* or "forest sage," who had abandoned the life of the householder and divested himself of caste in order to follow a way of liberation. As with every other *rishi*, the method of his way of liberation had certain characteristic features, and his doctrine contained criticisms of men's failure to practice the tradition which they professed.

Furthermore, he was being entirely traditional in his abandonment of caste and in accepting a following of casteless and homeless students. For the Indian tradition, even more than the Chinese, specifically encourages the abandonment of the conventional life at a certain age, after the duties of family and citizenship have been fulfilled. Relinquishment of caste is the outward and visible sign of the realization that one's true state is "unclassified," that one's role or person is simply conventional, and that one's true nature is "no-thing" and "no-body."

This realization was the crux of the Buddha's experience of awakening (*bodhi*) which dawned upon him one night, as he sat under the celebrated Bo Tree at Gaya, after seven years of meditation in the forests. From the standpoint of Zen, this experience is the essential content of Buddhism, and the verbal doctrine is quite secondary to the wordless transmission of the experience itself from generation to generation. For seven years Gautama had struggled by the traditional means of *yoga* and *tapas,* contemplation and ascesis, to penetrate the cause of man's enslavement to *maya,* to find release from the vicious circle of clinging-to-life (*trishna*) which is like trying to make the hand grasp itself. All his efforts had been in vain. The eternal *atman,* the real Self, was not to be found. However much he concentrated upon his own mind to find its root and ground, he found only his own effort to concentrate. The evening before his awakening he simply "gave up," relaxed his ascetic diet, and ate some nourishing food.

Thereupon he felt at once that a profound change was coming over him. He sat beneath the tree, vowing never to rise until he had attained the supreme awakening, and—according to a tradition—sat all through the night until the first glimpse of the morning star suddenly provoked a state of perfect clarity and understanding. This was *anuttara samyak sambodhi*, "unexcelled, complete awakening," liberation from *maya* and from the everlasting Round of birth-and-death (*samsara*), which goes on and on for as long as a man tries in any way whatsoever to grasp at his own life.

Yet the actual content of this experience was never and could never be put into words. For words are the frames of *maya*, the meshes of its net, and the experience is of the water which slips through. Thus so far as words are concerned the most that may be said of this experience are the words attributed to the Buddha in the *Vajracchedika*:

> Just so, Subhuti, I obtained not the least thing from unexcelled, complete awakening, and for this very reason it is called "unexcelled, complete awakening." (22)

Thus from the standpoint of Zen the Buddha "never said a word," despite the volumes of scriptures attributed to him. For his real message remained always unspoken, and was such that, when words attempted to express it, they made it seem as if it were nothing at all. Yet it is the essential tradition of Zen that what cannot be conveyed by speech can nevertheless be passed on by "direct pointing," by some nonverbal means of communication without which the Buddhist experience could never have been handed down to future generations.

In its own (probably rather late) tradition, Zen maintains that the Buddha transmitted awakening to his chief disciple, Mahakasyapa, by holding up a flower and remaining silent. The Pali Canon, however, relates that immediately after his awakening the

Buddha went to the Deer Park at Benares, and set forth his doctrine to those who had formerly been his companions in the ascetic life, expressing it in the form of those Four Noble Truths which provide so convenient a summary of Buddhism.

These Four Truths are patterned on the traditional Vedic form of a physician's diagnosis and prescription: the identification of the disease, and of its cause, the pronouncement as to whether it may be cured, and the prescription for the remedy.

The First Truth is concerned with the problematic word *duhkha*, loosely translatable as "suffering," and which designates the great disease of the world for which the Buddha's method (*dharma*) is the cure.

> Birth is *duhkha*, decay is *duhkha*, sickness is *duhkha*, death is *duhkha*, so also are sorrow and grief. . . . To be bound with things which we dislike, and to be parted from things which we like, these also are *duhkha*. Not to get what one desires, this also is *duhkha*. In a word, this body, this fivefold aggregation based on clutching (*trishna*), this is *duhkha*.[8]

This, however, cannot quite be compressed into the sweeping assertion that "life is suffering." The point is rather that life as we usually live it is suffering—or, more exactly, is bedeviled by the peculiar frustration which comes from attempting the impossible. Perhaps, then, "frustration" is the best equivalent for *duhkha*, even though the word is the simple antonym of *sukha*, which means "pleasant" or "sweet." [9]

In another formulation of the Buddha's teaching *duhkha* is one of the three characteristics of being, or becoming (*bhava*), whereof the other two are *anitya*, impermanence, and *anatman*, absence of any Self. These two terms are of basic importance. The *anitya* doctrine is, again, not quite the simple assertion that the world is impermanent, but rather that the more one grasps at

[8] *Samyutta Nikaya*, 421.
[9] Or, if we were to translate *duhkha* as "sour," we might say that the Buddha's doctrine is that life is soured by man's grasping attitude towards it—as milk turns sour when kept too long.

the world, the more it changes. Reality in itself is neither permanent nor impermanent; it cannot be categorized. But when one tries to hold on to it, change is everywhere apparent, since, like one's own shadow, the faster one pursues it, the faster it flees.

In the same way, the *anatman* doctrine is not quite the bald assertion that there is no real Self (*atman*) at the basis of our consciousness. The point is rather that there is no Self, or basic reality, which may be grasped, either by direct experience or by concepts. Apparently the Buddha felt that the doctrine of the *atman* in the *Upanishads* lent itself too easily to a fatal misinterpretation. It became an object of belief, a desideratum, a goal to be reached, something to which the mind could cling as its one final abode of safety in the flux of life. The Buddha's view was that a Self so grasped was no longer the true Self, but only one more of the innumerable forms of *maya*. Thus *anatman* might be expressed in the form, "The true Self is non-Self," since any attempt to conceive the Self, believe in the Self, or seek for the Self immediately thrusts it away.

The *Upanishads* distinguish between *atman*, the true, supraindividual Self, and the *jivatman* or individual soul, and the Buddha's *anatman* doctrine agrees with them in denying the reality of the latter. It is fundamental to every school of Buddhism that there is no ego, no enduring entity which is the constant subject of our changing experiences. For the ego exists in an abstract sense alone, being an abstraction from memory, somewhat like the illusory circle of fire made by a whirling torch. We can, for example, imagine the path of a bird through the sky as a distinct line which it has taken. But this line is as abstract as a line of latitude. In concrete reality, the bird left no line, and, similarly, the past from which our ego is abstracted has entirely disappeared. Thus any attempt to cling to the ego or to make it an effective source of action is doomed to frustration.

The Second Noble Truth relates to the cause of frustration, which is said to be *trishna*, clinging or grasping, based on *avidya*, which is ignorance or unconsciousness. Now *avidya* is the formal opposite of awakening. It is the state of the mind when hypnotized or spellbound by *maya*, so that it mistakes the abstract world of things and events for the concrete world of reality. At a still deeper level it is lack of self-knowledge, lack of the realization that all grasping turns out to be the futile effort to grasp oneself, or rather, to make life catch hold of itself. For to one who has self-knowledge, there is no duality between himself and the external world. *Avidya* is "ignoring" the fact that subject and object are relational, like the two sides of a coin, so that when one pursues, the other retreats. This is why the egocentric attempt to dominate the world, to bring as much of the world as possible under the control of the ego, has only to proceed for a little while before it raises the difficulty of the ego's controlling itself.

This is really a simple problem of what we now call cybernetics, the science of control. Mechanically and logically it is easy to see that any system approaching perfect self-control is also approaching perfect self-frustration. Such a system is a vicious circle, and has the same logical structure as a statement which states something about itself, as for example, "I am lying," when it is implied that the statement is itself a lie. The statement circulates fatuously forever, since it is always true to the extent that it is false, and false to the extent that it is true. Expressed more concretely, I cannot throw a ball so long as I am holding on to it—so as to maintain perfect control of its movement.

Thus the desire for perfect control, of the environment and of oneself, is based on a profound mistrust of the controller. *Avidya* is the failure to see the basic self-contradiction of this position. From it therefore arises a futile grasping or controlling of life which is pure self-frustration, and the pattern of life which follows is the vicious circle which in Hinduism and Buddhism is called *samsara*, the Round of birth-and-death.[10]

[10] The dynamic structure of the Round is called *pratitya-samutpada*, the twelvefold chain of "dependent origination," in which the twelve causal links give rise to one another mutually, constituting a closed circle without

The active principle of the Round is known as *karma* or "conditioned action," action, that is, arising from a motive and seeking a result—the type of action which always requires the necessity for further action. Man is involved in *karma* when he interferes with the world in such a way that he is compelled to go on interfering, when the solution of a problem creates still more problems to be solved, when the control of one thing creates the need to control several others. *Karma* is thus the fate of everyone who "tries to be God." He lays a trap for the world in which he himself gets caught.

Many Buddhists understand the Round of birth-and-death quite literally as a process of reincarnation, wherein the *karma* which shapes the individual does so again and again in life after life until, through insight and awakening, it is laid to rest. But in Zen, and in other schools of the Mahayana, it is often taken in a more figurative way, as that the process of rebirth is from moment to moment, so that one is being reborn so long as one identifies himself with a continuing ego which reincarnates itself afresh at each moment of time. Thus the validity and interest of the doctrine does not require acceptance of a special theory of survival. Its importance is rather that it exemplifies the whole problem of action in vicious circles and its resolution, and in this respect Buddhist philosophy should have a special interest for students of communication theory, cybernetics, logical philosophy, and similar matters.

The Third Noble Truth is concerned with the ending of self-frustration, of grasping, and of the whole viciously circular pattern of *karma* which generates the Round. The ending is called

beginning or end. Thus ignorance (*avidya*) gives rise to motivation (*samskara*), and this in series to consciousness (*vijnana*), name-and-form (*namarupa*), the six senses (*shadayatana*), sense stimulation (*sparsa*), sense experience (*vedana*), grasping (*trishna*), possessiveness (*upadana*), coming-to-be (*bhava*), birth (*jati*), and old-age-and-death (*jaramarana*), which again gives rise to *avidya*. The Buddha explained that *avidya* was put first on the list, not because it was the temporal beginning of the series, but for simple convenience of exposition. The whole series arises together, and its terms exist only in relation to one another.

nirvana, a word of such dubious etymology that a simple trans-lation is exceedingly difficult. It has been variously connected with Sanskrit roots which would make it mean the blowing out of a flame, or simply blowing out (ex- or de-spiration), or with the cessation of waves, turnings, or circlings (*vritti*) of the mind.

The two latter interpretations seem, on the whole, to make most sense. If *nirvana* is "de-spiration" it is the act of one who has seen the futility of trying to hold his breath or life (*prana*) indefinitely, since to hold the breath is to lose it. Thus *nirvana* is the equivalent of *moksha,* release or liberation. Seen from one side, it appears to be despair–the recognition that life utterly defeats our efforts to control it, that all human striving is no more than a vanishing hand clutching at clouds. Seen from the other side, this despair bursts into joy and creative power, on the principle that to lose one's life is to find it–to find freedom of action unimpeded by self-frustration and the anxiety inherent in trying to save and control the Self.

If *nirvana* is related to the cessation (*nir-*) of turnings (*vritti*), the term is synonymous with the aim of *yoga,* defined in the *Yogasutra* as *citta vritti nirodha*–the cessation of turnings of the mind. These "turnings" are the thoughts whereby the mind endeavors to grasp the world and itself. *Yoga* is the practice of trying to stop these thoughts by thinking about them, until the utter futility of the process is *felt* so vividly that it simply drops away, and the mind discovers its natural and unconfused state.

It is obvious, however, that both etymologies give us the same essential meaning. *Nirvana* is the way of life which ensues when clutching at life has come to an end. In so far as all definition is clutching, *nirvana* is necessarily indefinable. It is the natural, "un-self-grasped" state of the mind; and here, of course, the mind has no specific meaning, for what is not grasped is not known in the conventional sense of knowledge. More popularly and literally understood, *nirvana* is the disappearance of the

being from the Round of incarnations, not into a state of annihilation, but simply into a state escaping definition, and thus
immeasurable and infinite.

To attain *nirvana* is also to attain Buddhahood, awakening.
But this is not attainment in any ordinary sense, because no
acquisition and no motivation are involved. It is impossible to
desire *nirvana,* or to intend to reach it, for anything desirable
or conceivable as an object of action is, by definition, not *nirvana.*
Nirvana can only arise unintentionally, spontaneously, when the
impossibility of self-grasping has been thoroughly perceived. A
Buddha, therefore, is a man of no rank. He is not above, like
an angel; he is not below, like a demon. He does not appear anywhere in the six divisions of the Round, and it would be mistaken
to think of him as superior to the angels, for the law of the
Round is that what goes up must come down, and vice versa.
He has transcended all dualities whatsoever, and thus it would
mean nothing to him to think of himself as a superior person or a
spiritual success.

The Fourth Noble Truth describes the Eightfold Path of the
Buddha's *Dharma,* that is, the method or doctrine whereby self-
frustration is brought to an end. Each section of the path has a
name preceded by the word *samyak* (Pali, *samma*), which has
the meaning of "perfect" or "complete." The first two sections
have to do with thought; the following four have to do with action; and the final two have to do with contemplation or awareness. We therefore have:

1 *Samyag-drishti,* or complete view.
2 *Samyak-samkalpa,* or complete understanding.

3 *Samyag-vak,* or complete (i.e., truthful) speech.
4 *Samyak-karmanta,* or complete action.
5 *Samyagajiva,* or complete vocation.
6 *Samyag-vyayama,* or complete application.

7 *Samyak-smriti,* or complete recollectedness.
8 *Samyak-samadhi,* or complete contemplation.

Without discussing these sections in detail, it may simply be said that the first two are concerned with a proper understanding of the doctrine and of the human situation. In some ways the first section, "complete view," contains all the others, since the method of Buddhism is above all the practice of clear awareness, of seeing the world *yathabhutam*–just as it is. Such awareness is a lively attention to one's direct experience, to the world as immediately sensed, so as not to be misled by names and labels. *Samyak-samadhi*, the last section of the path, is the perfection of the first, signifying pure experience, pure awareness, wherein there is no longer the dualism of the knower and the known.

The sections dealing with action are often misunderstood because they have a deceptive similarity to a "system of morals." Buddhism does not share the Western view that there is a moral law, enjoined by God or by nature, which it is man's duty to obey. The Buddha's precepts of conduct–abstinence from taking life, taking what is not given, exploitation of the passions, lying, and intoxication–are voluntarily assumed rules of expediency, the intent of which is to remove the hindrances to clarity of awareness. Failure to observe the precepts produces "bad *karma*," not because *karma* is a law or moral retribution, but because all motivated and purposeful actions, whether conventionally good or bad, are *karma* in so far as they are directed to the grasping of life. Generally speaking, the conventionally "bad" actions are rather more grasping than the "good." But the higher stages of Buddhist practice are as much concerned with disentanglement from "good *karma*" as from "bad." Thus complete action is ultimately free, uncontrived, or spontaneous action, in exactly the same sense as the Taoist *wu-wei*.[11]

Smriti, recollectedness, and *samadhi*, contemplation, constitute the section dealing with the life of meditation, the inner, mental practice of the Buddha's way. Complete recollectedness is a constant awareness or watching of one's sensations, feelings, and

[11] Technically such action would be called *akarma*, unconditioned action, or *asamskrita*, uncontrived action.

thoughts–without purpose or comment. It is a total clarity and presence of mind, actively passive, wherein events come and go like reflections in a mirror: nothing is reflected except what *is*.

> In walking, standing, sitting, or lying down he understands that he is so doing, so that, however his body is engaged, he understands it just as it is. . . . In setting out or returning, in looking before or around, in bending or stretching his arm, . . . he acts with clear awareness.[12]

Through such awareness it is seen that the separation of the thinker from the thought, the knower from the known, the subject from the object, is purely abstract. There is not the mind on the one hand and its experiences on the other: there is just a process of experiencing in which there is nothing to be grasped, as an object, and no one, as a subject, to grasp it. Seen thus, the process of experiencing ceases to clutch at itself. Thought follows thought without interruption, that is, without any need to divide itself from itself, so as to become its own object.

> "Where there is an object, there thought arises." Is then the thought one thing, and the object another? No, what is the object, just that is the thought. If the object were one thing, and the thought another, then there would be a double state of thought. So the object itself is just thought. Can then thought review thought? No, thought cannot review thought. As the blade of a sword cannot cut itself, as a finger-tip cannot touch itself, so a thought cannot see itself.[13]

This nonduality of the mind, in which it is no longer divided against itself, is *samadhi*, and because of the disappearance of that fruitless threshing around of the mind to grasp itself, *samadhi* is a state of profound peace. This is not the stillness of total inactivity, for, once the mind returns to its natural state, *samadhi* persists at all times, in "walking, standing, sitting, and lying." But, from the earliest times, Buddhism has especially emphasized the practice of recollectedness and contemplation while sitting.

[12] *Majjhima Nikaya*, I. 56.
[13] *Sikshasamuccaya*, 234. In Conze (2), p. 163.

Most images of the Buddha show him in the posture of sitting meditation, in the particular attitude known as *padmasana,* the posture of the lotus, with the legs crossed and the feet resting, soles upward, upon the thighs.

Sitting meditation is not, as is often supposed, a spiritual "exercise," a practice followed for some ulterior object. From a Buddhist standpoint, it is simply the proper way to sit, and it seems perfectly natural to remain sitting so long as there is nothing else to be done, and so long as one is not consumed with nervous agitation. To the restless temperament of the West, sitting meditation may seem to be an unpleasant discipline, because we do not seem to be able to sit "just to sit" without qualms of conscience, without feeling that we ought to be doing something more important to justify our existence. To propitiate this restless conscience, sitting meditation must therefore be regarded as an exercise, a discipline with an ulterior motive. Yet at that very point it ceases to be meditation (*dhyana*) in the Buddhist sense, for where there is purpose, where there is seeking and grasping for results, there is no *dhyana.*

This word *dhyana* (Pali, *jhana*) is the original Sanskrit form of the Chinese *ch'an* ᵉ and the Japanese *zen,* and thus its meaning is of central importance for an understanding of Zen Buddhism. "Meditation" in the common sense of "thinking things over" or "musing" is a most misleading translation. But such alternatives as "trance" or "absorption" are even worse, since they suggest states of hypnotic fascination. The best solution seems to be to leave *dhyana* untranslated and add it to the English language as we have added Nirvana and Tao.[14]

[14] The Pali Canon (*Vinaya Pitaka,* III. 3–6, and *Majjhima Nikaya,* I. 349–52) lists eight types of *jhana*–the four *rupa-jhana* and the four *arupa-jhana* –the states of *jhana* with form and without form. The first four involve the progressive settling of conception (*vitakka*) and discursive thought (*vicara*) into a state of equanimity (*upekkha*) through the practice of *samadhi.* In other words, as the mind returns to its natural state of integrity and nonduality, it ceases to clutch at experience with the symbols of discursive thought. It simply perceives without words or concepts. Beyond this lie the four *arupa-jhana,* described as the spheres of Boundless Space, Boundless

As used in Buddhism, the term *dhyana* comprises both recollectedness (*smriti*) and *samadhi*, and can best be described as
the state of unified or one-pointed awareness. On the one hand,
it is one-pointed in the sense of being focused on the present,
since to clear awareness there is neither past nor future, but just
this one moment (*ekaksana*) which Western mystics have called
the Eternal Now. On the other hand, it is one-pointed in the
sense of being a state of consciousness without differentiation
of the knower, the knowing, and the known.

> A Tathagata (i.e., a Buddha) is a seer of what is to be seen, but
> he is not mindful (*na mannati*, or does not conceive) of the seen,
> the unseen, the seeable, or the seer. So too with the heard, the
> sensed, and the known: he does not think of them in these cate-
> gories.[15]

The difficulty of appreciating what *dhyana* means is that the
structure of our language does not permit us to use a transitive
verb without a subject and a predicate. When there is "knowing,"
grammatical convention requires that there must be someone
who knows and something which is known. We are so accustomed to this convention in speaking and thinking that we fail
to recognize that it is simply a convention, and that it does not
necessarily correspond to the actual experience of knowing. Thus
when we say, "A light flashed," it is somewhat easier to see
through the grammatical convention and to realize that the flash-
ing is the light. But *dhyana* as the mental state of the liberated
or awakened man is naturally free from the confusion of conventional entities with reality. Our intellectual discomfort in trying
to conceive knowing without a distinct "someone" who knows
and a distinct "something" which is known, is like the discomfort of arriving at a formal dinner in pajamas. The error is conventional, not existential.

Consciousness, Nothingness, and Neither-Perception-nor-Nonperception,
which are stages of the mind's realization of its own nature. At the time of
his death, the Buddha is said to have entered into *parinirvana* (i.e., final
nirvana) from the fourth *rupa-jhana*.

[15] *Anguttara Nikaya*, II. 25.

Once again, therefore, we see how convention, how the *maya* of measurement and description, populates the world with those ghosts which we call entities and things. So hypnotic, so persuasive is the power of convention that we begin to feel these ghosts as realities, and make of them our loves, our ideals, our prized possessions. But the anxiety-laden problem of what will happen to me when I die is, after all, like asking what happens to my fist when I open my hand, or where my lap goes when I stand up. Perhaps, then, we are now able to understand the celebrated summary of the Buddha's doctrine given in the *Visuddhimagga*:

> *Suffering alone exists, none who suffer;*
> *The deed there is, but no doer thereof;*
> *Nirvana is, but no one seeking it;*
> *The Path there is, but none who travel it.* (16)

Three

MAHAYANA BUDDHISM

Because the teaching of the Buddha was a way of liberation, it had no other object than the experience of *nirvana*. The Buddha did not attempt to set forth a consistent philosophical system, trying to satisfy that intellectual curiosity about ultimate things which expects answers in words. When pressed for such answers, when questioned about the nature of *nirvana*, the origin of the world, and the reality of the Self, the Buddha maintained a "noble silence," and went on to say that such questions were irrelevant and did not lead to the actual experience of liberation.

It has often been said that the later development of Buddhism was due to the inability of the Indian mind to rest content with that silence, so that at last it had to indulge its overwhelming urge for "abstract metaphysical speculations" about the nature of reality. Such a view of the genesis of Mahayana Buddhism is, however, rather misleading. The vast body of Mahayana doctrine arose not so much to satisfy intellectual curiosity as to deal with the practical psychological problems encountered in following the Buddha's way. Certainly the treatment of these problems is highly scholastic, and the intellectual level of the Mahayana texts is very lofty. But the consistent aim is to bring about the experience of liberation, not to construct a philosophical system. In the words of Sir Arthur Berriedale Keith:

> The metaphysics of the Mahayana in the incoherence of its systems shows clearly enough the secondary interest attaching to it in the eyes of the monks, whose main interest was concentrated on the attainment of release; the Mahayana no less than the Hinayana is concerned vitally with this practical end, and its philosophy is of value merely in so far as it helps men to attain their aim.[1]

[1] Keith (1), p. 273.

57

There are, no doubt, respects in which Mahayana Buddhism is a concession both to intellectual curiosity and to a popular desire for short cuts to the goal. But at root it is the work of highly sensitive and perceptive minds studying their own inner workings. To anyone who is highly self-aware, the Buddhism of the Pali Canon leaves many practical problems unanswered. Its psychological insight goes little further than the construction of analytical catalogues of mental functions, and though its precepts are clear it is not always helpful in explaining their practical difficulties. Perhaps it is too sweeping a generalization, but one receives the impression that whereas the Pali Canon would unlock the door to *nirvana* by sheer effort, the Mahayana would jiggle the key until it turns smoothly. Thus the great concern of the Mahayana is the provision of "skillful means" (*upaya*) for making *nirvana* accessible to every type of mentality.

How and when the Mahayana doctrines arose is a matter of historical guesswork. The great Mahayana *sutras* are ostensibly the teachings of the Buddha and his immediate disciples, but their style is so different and their doctrine so much more subtle than that of the Pali Canon that scholars almost unanimously assign them to later dates. There is no evidence of their existence in the time of the great Buddhist emperor Asoka, grandson of Chandragupta Maurya, who was converted to Buddhism in 262 B.C. Asoka's rock inscriptions reflect no more than the social teachings of the Pali Canon, its insistence on *ahimsa* or nonviolence to both men and animals and its general precepts for the life of the laity. The principal Mahayana texts were being translated into Chinese by Kumarajiva shortly after A.D. 400, but our knowledge of Indian history during the intervening six hundred years from Asoka's death is so fragmentary, and the internal evidences of the *sutras* themselves so vague, that we can do little more than assign them to the four hundred years between 100 B.C. and A.D. 300. Even specific individuals associated with their development–Asvaghosha, Nagarjuna, Asanga, and Vasubandhu–can be dated only very approximately.

The traditional Mahayanist account of its own origin is that its teachings were delivered by the Buddha to his intimate disciples but their public revelation withheld until the world was ready for them. The principle of "delayed revelation" is a well-known expedient for permitting the growth of a tradition, for exploring the implications contained in the original seed. Apparent contradictions between earlier and later doctrines are explained by assigning them to different levels of truth, ranging from the most relative to the absolute, and of which the (probably quite late) Avatamsaka School distinguishes no less than five. However, the problem of the historical origins of the Mahayana is of no very direct importance for an understanding of Zen, which, as a Chinese rather than Indian form of Buddhism, came into being when Indian Mahayana was fully grown. We can pass on, therefore, to the central Mahayana doctrines from which Zen arose.

The Mahayana distinguishes itself from the Buddhism of the Pali Canon by terming the latter the Little (*hina*) Vehicle (*yana*) of liberation and itself the Great (*maha*) Vehicle–great because it comprises such a wealth of *upaya,* or methods for the realization of *nirvana.* These methods range from the sophisticated dialectic of Nagarjuna, whose object is to free the mind of all fixed conceptions, to the Sukhavati or Pure Land doctrine of liberation through faith in the power of Amitabha, the Buddha of Boundless Light, who is said to have attained his awakening many aeons before the time of Gautama. They include even the Tantric Buddhism of medieval India, wherein liberation may be realized through the repetition of sacred words and formulae called *dharani,* and through special types of *yoga* involving sexual intercourse with a *shakti* or "spiritual wife." [2]

[2] The alleged "obscenity" of *maithuna,* as this practice is called, is entirely in the minds of Christian missionaries. In fact, the relationship with the *shakti* was anything but promiscuous, and involved the mature and all-too-infrequent notion of a man and a woman undertaking their spiritual development in common. This included a sanctification of the sexual relationship which should logically have been part of the Catholic view of marriage as a sacrament. For a full treatment see S. B. Dasgupta, *An Introduction to Tantric Buddhism* (Calcutta, 1952), and Sir John Woodroffe, *Shakti and Shakta* (Madras and London, 1929).

A preliminary study of the Pali Canon will certainly give the impression that *nirvana* is to be realized only through rigorous effort and self-control, and that the aspirant should lay aside all other concerns for the pursuit of this ideal. Mahayanists may be perfectly correct in assuming that the Buddha intended this emphasis as an *upaya,* a skillful means of enabling one to realize, concretely and vividly, the absurd vicious circle of desiring not to desire, or of trying to get rid of selfishness by oneself. For this is certainly the conclusion to which the practice of the Buddha's doctrine led. It may be attributed to laziness and loss of nerve, but it seems more plausible to suggest that those who remained in the path of self-deliverance were merely unconscious of the paradox involved. For wherever the Mahayana continues to teach the way of liberation by one's own effort, it does so as an expedient for bringing the individual to a vivid awareness of his own futility.

Various indications suggest that one of the earliest notions of the Mahayana was the conception of the Bodhisattva, not simply as a potential Buddha, but as one who by renouncing *nirvana* was at a higher spiritual level than one who attained it and so withdrew from the world of birth-and-death. In the Pali Canon the disciples of the Buddha who attain *nirvana* are termed Arhans or "worthy ones," but in the Mahayana texts the ideal of the Arhan is accounted almost selfish. It is fit only for the *sravaka,* the "hearer" of the doctrine who has progressed only so far as to get a theoretical understanding. The Bodhisattva, however, is one who realizes that there is a profound contradiction in a *nirvana* attained by himself and for himself. From the popular standpoint, the Bodhisattva became a focus of devotion (*bhakti*), a savior of the world who had vowed not to enter the final *nirvana* until all other sentient beings had likewise attained it. For their sakes he consented to be born again and again into the Round of *samsara,* until, in the course of innumerable ages, even the grass and the dust had attained Buddhahood.

But from a deeper standpoint it became obvious that the idea of the Bodhisattva is implicit in the logic of Buddhism, that it flows naturally from the principle of not-grasping and from the doctrine of the unreality of the ego. For if *nirvana* is the state in which the attempt to grasp reality has wholly ceased, through the realization of its impossibility, it will obviously be absurd to think of *nirvana* itself as something to be grasped or attained. If, furthermore, the ego is merely a convention, it is nonsense to think of *nirvana* as a state to be attained by some being. As is said in the *Vajracchedika:*

All Bodhisattva-heroes should cultivate their minds to think: all sentient beings of whatever class . . . are caused by me to attain the boundless liberation of *nirvana.* Yet when vast, innumerable, and immeasurable numbers of beings have thus been liberated, in truth no being has been liberated! Why is this, Subhuti? It is because no Bodhisattva who is truly a Bodhisattva holds to the idea of an ego, a personality, a being, or a separate individual. (3)

The corollary of this position is that if there is no *nirvana* which can be attained, and if, in reality, there are no individual entities, it will follow that our bondage in the Round is merely apparent, and that in fact we are already in *nirvana*—so that to seek *nirvana* is the folly of looking for what one has never lost. Naturally, then, the Bodhisattva makes no motion to depart from the Round of *samsara,* as if *nirvana* were somewhere else, for to do so would imply that *nirvana* is something that needs to be attained and that *samsara* is an actual reality. In the words of the *Lankavatara Sutra:*

Those who, afraid of the sufferings arising from the discrimination of birth-and-death (*samsara*), seek for Nirvana, do not know that birth-and-death and Nirvana are not to be separated from one another; and, seeing that all things subject to discrimination have no reality, (they) imagine that Nirvana consists in the future annihilation of the senses and their fields. (II. 18) [3]

To strive, then, to blot out the conventional world of things and events is to admit that it exists in reality. Hence the Mahayanist

[3] In Suzuki (3), p. 55. The "fields" of the senses are the areas or aspects of the external world to which the particular sense organs are related.

principle that "what has never arisen does not have to be annihilated." [a]

These are not the idle speculations and sophistries of a system
of subjective idealism or nihilism. They are answers to a practical problem which may be expressed thus: "If my grasping of
life involves me in a vicious circle, how am I to learn not to
grasp? How can I try to let go when trying is precisely not letting
go?" Stated in another way, to try not to grasp is the same thing
as to grasp, since its motivation is the same—my urgent desire to
save myself from a difficulty. I cannot get rid of this desire, since
it is one and the same desire as the desire to get rid of it! This is
the familiar, everyday problem of the psychological "double-
bind," of creating the problem by trying to solve it, of worrying
because one worries, and of being afraid of fear.

Mahayana philosophy proposes a drastic but effective answer
which is the theme of a class of literature called *Prajna-paramita,*
or "wisdom for crossing to the other shore," a literature closely
associated with the work of Nagarjuna (*c.* A.D. 200), who ranks
with Shankara as one of the greatest minds of India. Stated
baldly, the answer is that all grasping, even for *nirvana,* is futile—
for there is nothing to be grasped. This is Nagarjuna's celebrated
Sunyavada, his "Doctrine of the Void," otherwise known as the
Madhyamika, the "middle way," because it refutes all metaphysical propositions by demonstrating their relativity. From the
standpoint of academic philosophy, the *Prajna-paramita* and the
doctrine of Nagarjuna are no doubt some form of nihilism or
"absolute relativism." But this is not Nagarjuna's standpoint. The
dialectic with which he demolishes every conception of reality
is merely a device for breaking the vicious circle of grasping, and
the terminus of his philosophy is not the abject despair of
nihilism but the natural and uncontrived bliss (*ananda*) of
liberation.

The Sunyavada takes its name from the term *sunya,* void, or
sunyata, voidness, with which Nagarjuna described the nature of
reality, or rather, of the *conceptions* of reality which the human

mind :an form. Conceptions here include not only metaphysical views but also ideals, religious beliefs, ultimate hopes and ambitions of every kind–everything which the mind of man seeks and grasps for his physical or spiritual security. Not only does the Sunyavada demolish the beliefs which one consciously adopts; it also seeks out the hidden and unconscious premises of thought and action, and submits them to the same treatment until the very depths of the mind are reduced to a total silence. Even the idea of *sunya* is itself to be voided.

> *It cannot be called void or not void,*
> *Or both or neither;*
> *But in order to point it out,*
> *It is called "the Void."* [4]

Stcherbatsky (1) is certainly right in thinking that the Sunyavada is best called a doctrine of relativity. For Nagarjuna's method is simply to show that all things are without "self-nature" (*svabhava*) or independent reality since they exist only in relation to other things. Nothing in the universe can stand by itself–no thing, no fact, no being, no event–and for this reason it is absurd to single anything out as the ideal to be grasped. For what is singled out exists only in relation to its own opposite, since what is is defined by what is not, pleasure is defined by pain, life is defined by death, and motion is defined by stillness. Obviously, the mind can form no idea of what "to be" means without the contrast of "not to be," since the ideas of being and non-being are abstractions from such simple experiences as that there is a penny in the right hand and no penny in the left.

From one point of view, the same relativity exists between *nirvana* and *samsara, bodhi* (awakening) and *klesa* (defilement). That is to say, the search for *nirvana* implies the existence and the problem of *samsara,* and the quest for awakening implies that one is in the state of defilement with delusion. To put it in another way: as soon as *nirvana* is made an object of desire, it be-

[4] *Madhyamika Shastra,* XV. 3.

comes an element of *samsara*. The real *nirvana* cannot be desired
because it cannot be conceived. Thus the *Lankavatara Sutra* says:

> Again, Mahamati, what is meant by non-duality? It means that
> light and shade, long and short, black and white, are relative terms,
> Mahamati, and not independent of each other; as Nirvana and
> Samsara are, all things are not-two. There is no Nirvana except
> where is Samsara; there is no Samsara except where is Nirvana; for
> the condition of existence is not of a mutually exclusive character.
> Therefore it is said that all things are non-dual as are Nirvana and
> Samsara. (II. 28) [5]

But the equation "*Nirvana* is *samsara*" is true in another sense
as well–namely, that what appears to us to be *samsara* is really
nirvana, and that what appears to be the world of form (*rupa*)
is really the void (*sunya*). Hence the famous saying:

> Form is not different from emptiness; emptiness is not different
> from form. Form is precisely emptiness; emptiness is precisely
> form.[6]

Once again, this is not to say that awakening will cause the
world of form to vanish without trace, for *nirvana* is not to be
sought as "the future annihilation of the senses and their fields."
The *sutra* is saying that form is void just as it is, in all its prickly
uniqueness.

The point of this equation is not to assert a metaphysical
proposition but to assist the process of awakening. For awakening will not come to pass when one is trying to escape or change
the everyday world of form, or to get away from the particular
experience in which one finds oneself at this moment. Every
such attempt is a manifestation of grasping. Even the grasping
itself is not to be changed by force, for

> *bodhi* [awakening] is the five offenses, and the five offenses are
> *bodhi*. . . . If anyone regards *bodhi* as something to be attained,
> to be cultivated by discipline, he is guilty of the pride of self.[7]

[5] In Suzuki (3), p. 67.
[6] *Prajna-paramita-hridaya Sutra* (Chinese version).
[7] *Saptasatika-prajna-paramita Sutra*, 232, 234.

Some of these passages may suggest that the Bodhisattva may just as well be an easygoing, worldly fellow, who–because *samsara* is *nirvana* anyhow–can go on living just as he pleases. He may be thoroughly deluded, but since even delusion is *bodhi* there would be no point in trying to change it. There is often a deceptive resemblance between opposite extremes. Lunatics frequently resemble saints, and the unaffected modesty of the sage often lets him seem to be a very ordinary person. Yet there is no easy way of pointing out the difference, of saying what it is that the ordinary, worldly fellow does or does not do which makes him different from a Bodhisattva, or vice versa. The entire mystery of Zen lies in this problem, and we shall return to it at the proper time. It is enough to say here that the so-called "ordinary person" is only apparently natural, or perhaps that his real naturalness feels unnatural to him. In practice it is simply impossible to decide, intentionally, to stop seeking for *nirvana* and to lead an ordinary life, for as soon as one's "ordinary" life is intentional it is not natural.

It is for this reason that the insistence of the Mahayana texts on the unattainability of *nirvana* and *bodhi* is not something to be accepted theoretically, as a mere philosophical opinion. One has to know "in one's bones" that there is nothing to be grasped.

> Thereupon the thought came to some of the Gods in that assembly: What the fairies talk and murmur, that we understand though mumbled. What Subhuti has just told us, that we do not understand!
>
> Subhuti read their thoughts and said: There is nothing to understand, there is nothing to understand. For nothing in particular has been indicated, nothing in particular has been explained. . . . No one will grasp this perfection of wisdom as here explained. For no Dharma (doctrine) at all has been indicated, lit up, or communicated. So there will be no one who can grasp it.[8]

The point arrives, then, when it is clearly understood that all one's intentional acts–desires, ideals, stratagems–are in vain. In the whole universe, within and without, there is nothing whereon

8 *Ashtasahasrika*, II. 38, 40. In Conze (2), pp. 177–78.

to lay any hold, and no one to lay any hold on anything. This has been discovered through clear awareness of everything that seemed to offer a solution or to constitute a reliable reality, through the intuitive wisdom called *prajna*, which sees into the relational character of everything. With the "eye of *prajna*" the human situation is seen for what it is–a quenching of thirst with salt water, a pursuit of goals which simply require the pursuit of other goals, a clutching of objects which the swift course of time renders as insubstantial as mist. The very one who pursues, who sees and knows and desires, the inner subject, has his existence only in relation to the ephemeral objects of his pursuit. He sees that his grasp upon the world is his strangle-hold about his own neck, the hold which is depriving him of the very life he so longs to attain. And there is no way out, no way of letting go, which he can take by effort, by a decision of the will. . . . But who is it that wants to get out?

There comes a moment when this consciousness of the inescapable trap in which we are at once the trapper and the trapped reaches a breaking point. One might almost say that it "matures" or "ripens," and suddenly there is what the *Lankavatara Sutra* calls a "turning about in the deepest seat of consciousness." In this moment all sense of constraint drops away, and the cocoon which the silkworm spun around himself opens to let him go forth winged as a moth. The peculiar anxiety which Kierkegaard has rightly seen to lie at the very roots of the ordinary man's soul is no longer there. Contrivances, ideals, ambitions, and self-propitiations are no longer necessary, since it is now possible to live spontaneously without trying to be spontaneous. Indeed, there is no alternative, since it is now seen that there never was any self to bring the self under its control.

Reduced to the bare essentials, such is the inner process which the Sunyavada is trying to set in motion with its philosophy of total negation. Thus the greater part of Nagarjuna's work was a carefully logical and systematic refutation of every philosoph-

ical position to be found in the India of his time.[9] Granting that
its object is an inner experience, Western students have always
had difficulty in understanding how such a purely negative point
of view could have any creative consequences. It must therefore
be repeated that the negations apply, not to reality itself, but to
our ideas of reality. The positive and creative content of the
Sunyavada is not in the philosophy itself, but in the new vision
of reality which is revealed when its work is done, and Nagarjuna
does not spoil this vision by trying to describe it.

The Mahayana does, however, have another term for reality
which is perhaps rather more indicative than *sunya,* the void. This
is the word *tathata,* which we may translate as "suchness," "thus-
ness," or "thatness." Similarly, the Buddhas are called Tathagatas–
they who go, or come, "thus." The Sanskrit word *tat* (our "that")
is probably based on a child's first efforts at speech, when it
points at something and says, "Ta" or "Da." Fathers flatter themselves by imagining that the child is calling them by name–
"Dada" or "Daddy." But perhaps the child is just expressing its
recognition of the world, and saying "That!" When we say just
"That" or "Thus," we are pointing to the realm of nonverbal
experience, to reality as we perceive it directly, for we are trying
to indicate what we see or feel rather than what we think or say.
Tathata therefore indicates the world just as it is, unscreened and
undivided by the symbols and definitions of thought. It points to
the concrete and actual as distinct from the abstract and conceptual. A Buddha is a Tathagata, a "thus-goer," because he is
awakened to this primary, nonconceptual world which no words
can convey, and does not confuse it with such ideas as being or
non-being, good or bad, past or future, here or there, moving or

[9] The reader who is interested in exploring Nagarjuna's philosophy more
deeply should refer to the magnificent work of Professor T. R. V. Murti,
The Central Philosophy of Buddhism. (See Bibliography.) Unhappily, there
are now available only fragmentary translations of Nagarjuna's writings in
English, unless he was indeed the author of the *Prajna-paramita* literature,
for which see Conze (2, 3).

still, permanent or impermanent. As the Bodhisattva Manjusri
speaks of the Tathagata in the *Saptasatika:*

> Suchness (*tathata*) neither becomes nor ceases to become; thus do
> I see the Tathagata. Suchness does not stand at any point or place;
> thus do I see the Tathagata. Suchness is neither past, future, nor
> present; thus do I see the Tathagata. Suchness does not arise from
> the dual or the non-dual; thus do I see the Tathagata. Suchness
> is neither impure nor pure; thus do I see the Tathagata. Suchness
> neither arises nor comes to an end; thus do I see the Tathagata.
> (195) [10]

Because *tathata* is the true state of a Buddha and of all beings
whatsoever, it is also referred to as our true or original nature,
and thus our "Buddha nature." One of the cardinal doctrines of
the Mahayana is that all beings are endowed with Buddha nature, and so have the possibility of becoming Buddhas. Because
of the identity of Buddha nature and *tathata,* the term "Buddha"
is frequently used of reality itself and not just of the awakened
man. It so comes about that in the Mahayana a Buddha is often
seen as a personification of reality, forming the basis of those
popular cults in which the Buddhas seem to be worshiped as
gods. I say "seem to be" because even Mahayana Buddhism has
no real equivalent of Judaeo-Christian theism, with its strict
identification of God with the moral principle. Furthermore, the
various Buddhas who are so venerated–Amitabha, Vairocana,
Amitayus, Ratnasambhava, etc.–are always personifications of
one's own true nature.

Here, too, lies the basis of the Buddhism of faith, of the
Sukhavati or Pure Land school, in which it is held that all efforts
to become a Buddha are merely the false pride of the ego. All that
is necessary is to repeat the formula *namo-amitabhaya* (literally,
"the Name of Amitabha" or "Hail, Amitabha") in the faith that
this alone is sufficient to bring about one's rebirth in the Pure

---

[10] "Suchness is neither past, future, nor present," for when it is seen that
there is neither past nor future there is no more a present, since the idea
of the present has meaning only in relation to past and future.

Land over which Amitabha presides. In this Pure Land all the obstacles which stand in the way of becoming a Buddha in this world are removed, so that rebirth in the Pure Land is virtually equivalent to becoming a Buddha. The repetition of the Name is held to be effective because, in ages past, Amitabha vowed that he would not enter into supreme Buddhahood unless rebirth in the Pure Land were assured for all beings who invoked his name. Because he subsequently entered the state of Buddhahood, the vow is effectively fulfilled.

Even Nagarjuna was in sympathy with this doctrine, for it is obviously a popular and more graphic way of saying that since one's own true nature is already the Buddha nature, one does not have to do anything to make it so. On the contrary, to seek to become Buddha is to deny that one is already Buddha—and this is the sole basis upon which Buddhahood can be realized! In short, to become a Buddha it is only necessary to have the faith that one is a Buddha already. Shinran, the great Japanese exponent of the Pure Land, went even so far as to say that it was only necessary to repeat the Name, for he saw that the attempt to make an act of faith was too artificial, and led one to doubt one's own faith.

Pure Land Buddhism is clearly an outgrowth of the Bodhisattva doctrine that the proper work of the liberated man is the liberation of all other beings by *upaya* or "skillful means." By *prajna* or intuitive wisdom he sees into the nature of reality, and this in turn awakens *karuna* or compassion for all who are still in the bonds of ignorance. At its deepest level *karuna* means something rather more than compassion for the ignorance of others. For we saw that the Bodhisattva's return into the world of *samsara* was based on the principle that *samsara* is in fact *nirvana*, and that "the void is precisely form." If *prajna* is to see that "form is void," *karuna* is to see that "the void is form." It is therefore an "affirmation" of the everyday world in its natural "suchness," and this is one of the features of the Mahayana most strongly emphasized in Zen. Indeed, it makes nonsense of the idea that Buddhism is always a philosophy of world-denial, in which the uniqueness of forms has no importance. It was because of *karuna* that Mahayana Buddhism became the principal inspiration of Chinese art in the Sung and Yüan dynasties, an art which stressed natural forms rather than religious symbols. For by *karuna* it is seen that the dissolution of forms into the void is in no way different from the particular characteristics of the forms themselves. The life of things is only conventionally separable from their death; in reality the dying is the living.

The perception that each single form, just as it is, is the void and that, further, the uniqueness of each form arises from the fact that it exists in relation to every other form is the basis of the Dharmadhatu ("Dharma realm") doctrine of the enormous *Avatamsaka Sutra*. This voluminous work is probably the final culmination of Indian Mahayana, and one of its central images is a vast network of gems or crystals, like a spider's web at dawn, in which each gem reflects all the others. This net of gems is the Dharmadhatu, the universe, the realm of innumerable *dharmas* or "thing-events."

Chinese commentators worked out a fourfold classification of the Dharmadhatu which became of considerable importance for Zen late in the T'ang dynasty. Their classification of the "Four Dharma Realms" [b] was as follows:

1. *Shih*,[c] the unique, individual "thing-events" of which the universe is composed.

2. *Li*,[d] the "principle" or ultimate reality underlying the multiplicity of things.

3. *Li shih wu ai*,[e] "between principle and thing no obstruction," which is to say that there is no incompatibility between *nirvana* and *samsara*, void and form. The attainment of the one does not involve the annihilation of the other.

4. *Shih shih wu ai*,[f] "between thing and thing no obstruction," which is to say that each "thing-event" involves every other, and that the highest insight is simply the perception of them in their natural "suchness." At this level every "thing-event" is seen

to be self-determinative, self-generating, or spontaneous, for to be quite naturally what it is, to be *tatha*–just "thus"–is to be free and without obstruction.

The doctrine of the Dharmadhatu is, approximately, that the proper harmony of the universe is realized when each "thing-event" is allowed to be freely and spontaneously itself, without interference. Stated more subjectively, it is saying, "Let everything be free to be just as it is. Do not separate yourself from the world and try to order it around." There is a subtle distinction between this and mere *laissez faire*, which may be suggested by the way in which we move our various limbs. Each one moves by itself, from within. To walk, we do not pick up our feet with our hands. The individual body is therefore a system of *shih shih wu ai*, and a Buddha realizes that the whole universe is his body, a marvelously interrelated harmony organized from within itself rather than by interference from outside.

Mahayana philosophy thinks of the Buddha's body as three-fold, as the *Trikaya* or "Triple Body." His body, considered either as the multitude of "thing-events" or as his particular human forms, is termed the *Nirmanakaya*, or "Body of Transformation." The particular human forms are such historic and prehistoric Buddhas as Gautama, Kasyapa, or Kanakamuni, and since these appear "in the flesh" the *Nirmanakaya* includes, in principle, the entire universe of form. There is next the *Sambhogakaya*, or "Body of Enjoyment." This is the sphere of *prajna*, wisdom, and *karuna*, compassion, the latter looking down to the world of form, and the former looking up to the realm of the void. *Sambhogakaya* might also be called the "Body of Realization" since it is in this "body" that a Buddha realizes that he is a Buddha. Finally there is the *Dharmakaya*, the "Dharma Body," which is the void, the *sunya* itself.

Nagarjuna did not discuss the way in which the void appears as form, the *Dharmakaya* as the *Nirmanakaya*, feeling, perhaps, that this would be completely unintelligible to those who had not actually realized awakening. For the Buddha himself had compared such inquiries to the foolishness of a man shot with an arrow, who would not permit it to be taken out of his flesh until he had been told all the details of his assailant's appearance, family, and motivations. Nevertheless, Nagarjuna's successors, the brothers Asanga and Vasubandhu (*c.* 280–360), who worked out the type of Mahayana philosophy generally known as Yogacara, made some attempt to discuss this particular problem.

According to the Yogacara the world of form is *cittamatra*– "mind only"–or *vijnaptimatra*–"representation only." This view seems to have a very close resemblance to Western philosophies of subjective idealism, in which the external and material world is regarded as a projection of the mind. However, there seem to be some differences between the two points of view. Here, as always, the Mahayana is not so much a theoretical and speculative construction as an account of an inner experience, and a means of awakening the experience in others. Furthermore, the word *citta* is not precisely equivalent to our "mind." Western thought tends to define mind by opposition to matter, and to consider matter not so much as "measure" as the solid stuff which is measured. Measure itself, abstraction, is for the West more of the nature of mind, since we tend to think of mind and spirit as more abstract than concrete.

But in Buddhist philosophy *citta* does not stand over against a conception of solid stuff. The world has never been considered in terms of a primary substance shaped into various forms by the action of mind or spirit. Such an image is not in the history of Buddhist thought, and thus the problem of how impalpable mind can influence solid matter has never arisen. Wherever we should speak of the material or physical or substantial world, Buddhism employs the term *rupa,* which is not so much our "matter" as "form." There is no "material substance" underlying *rupa* unless it be *citta* itself!

The difficulty of making equations and comparisons between Eastern and Western ideas is that the two worlds do not start with the same assumptions and premises. They do not have the same basic categorizations of experience. When, therefore, the world has never been divided into mind and matter, but rather into mind and form, the word "mind" cannot mean quite the same thing in both instances. The word "man," for example, does not have quite the same meaning when contrasted with "woman" as when contrasted with "animal."

A simplified, and somewhat rough, way of stating the difference is that Western idealists have begun to philosophize from a world consisting of mind (or spirit), form, and matter, whereas the Buddhists have begun to philosophize from a world of mind and form.

The Yogacara does not, therefore, discuss the relation of forms of matter to mind; it discusses the relation of forms to mind, and concludes that they are forms *of* mind. As a result, the term "mind" (*citta*) becomes logically meaningless. But because the main concern of Buddhism is with a realm of experience which is nonlogical and meaningless, in the sense that it does not symbolize or signify anything other than itself, there is no objection to "meaningless" terms.

From the logical standpoint the proposition "Everything is mind" says no more than that everything is everything. For if there is nothing which is not mind, the word belongs to no class, and has no limits, no definition. One might as well use "blah"— which is almost exactly what Buddhism does with the nonsense word *tathata*. For the function of these nonsense terms is to draw our attention to the fact that logic and meaning, with its inherent duality, is a property of thought and language but not of the actual world. The nonverbal, concrete world contains no classes and no symbols which signify or mean anything other than themselves. Consequently it contains no duality. For duality arises only when we classify, when we sort our experiences into mental boxes, since a box is no box without an inside and an outside.

Mental boxes are probably formed in our minds long before formal thought and language supply labels to identify them. We have begun to classify as soon as we notice differences, regularities and irregularities, as soon as we make associations of any kind. But–if the word "mental" means anything at all–this act of classification is certainly mental, for to notice differences and to associate them with one another is something more than simply to respond to sense contacts. Yet if classes are a product of the mind, of noticing, association, thought, and language, the world *considered simply as all classes of objects* is a product of the mind.

This is, I think, what the Yogacara means by the assertion that the world is mind-only (*cittamatram lokam*). It means that external and internal, before and after, heavy and light, pleasant and painful, moving and still are all ideas, or mental classifications. Their relation to the concrete world is the same as that of words. Thus the world that we know, when understood as the world as classified, is a product of the mind, and as the sound "water" is not actually water, the classified world is not the real world.

The problem of "what" the mind is can now be seen to be the same as the problem of "what" the real world is. It cannot be answered, for every "what" is a class, and we cannot classify the classifier. Is it not, then, merely absurd to speak of the mind, the *citta*, at all if there is no way of saying what it is? On the contrary, the mathematician Kurt Gödel has given us a rigorous proof of the fact that every logical system must contain a premise which it cannot define without contradicting itself.[11] The Yogacara takes *citta* as its premise and does not define it, since *citta* is here the equivalent of *sunya* and *tathata*. For the mind

is beyond all philosophical views, is apart from discrimination, it is not attainable, nor is it ever born: I say there is nothing but Mind. It is not an existence, nor is it a non-existence; it is indeed beyond both existence and non-existence. . . . Out of Mind spring innumerable things, conditioned by discrimination (i.e., classifica-

[11] For a general account see E. Nagel and J. R. Newman, "Gödel's Proof," *Scientific American*, CXCVI. 6 (June, 1956), pp. 71–86.

tion) and habit-energy; these things people accept as an external
world. . . . What appears to be external does not exist in reality;
it is indeed Mind that is seen as multiplicity; the body, property,
and abode—all these, I say, are nothing but Mind.[12]

Within this undefined continuum of *citta* the Yogacara describes eight kinds of *vijnana*, or "discriminating consciousness."
There is a consciousness appropriate to each of the five senses;
there is the sixth sense-consciousness (*mano-vijnana*), unifying
the other five so that what is touched or heard may be related to
what is seen; there is *manas*, center of the mind's discriminative
and classifying activity; and finally there is the "store-consciousness" (*alaya-vijnana*), the supra-individual mind which contains
the seeds of all possible forms.

The "store-consciousness" is almost equivalent to the *citta*
itself, and is supra-individual because it stands prior to every
differentiation. It is not to be conceived as a sort of ghostly gas
permeating all beings, since space and extension are likewise
here only in potentiality. In other words, the "store-consciousness"
is that from which the formal world arises spontaneously or
playfully (*vikridita*). For the Mahayana does not make the
mistake of trying to account for the production of the world
from the mind by a series of necessary causes. Whatever is linked
by causal necessity is *of* the world of *maya*, not beyond it. Speaking somewhat poetically, the world illusion comes out of the
Great Void for no reason, purposelessly, and just because there is
no necessity for it to do so. For the "activity" of the Void is playful or *vikridita* because it is not motivated action (*karma*).

Thus, as the Yogacara describes it, the production of the formal
world arises spontaneously from the "store-consciousness," flows
up into the *manas*, where the primordial differentiations are

[12] *Lankavatara Sutra*, 154, 29–30, 32–33. In Suzuki (2), p. 242. I have
cited the *Lankavatara* for both Madhyamika and Yogacara viewpoints, since
either both schools have used the *sutra* or else it is a work of the latter in-
corporating views of the former. Since historical order is here a matter of
conjecture, I have simply chosen sources which seem to express the ideas in
question most effectively.

made, passes thence into the six sense-consciousnesses, which in turn produce the sense organs or "gates" (*ayatana*) through which it finally projects the classified external world.

The Buddhist *yoga* therefore consists in reversing the process, in stilling the discriminative activity of the mind, and letting the categories of *maya* fall back into potentiality so that the world may be seen in its unclassified "suchness." Here *karuna* awakens, and the Bodhisattva lets the projection arise again, having become consciously identified with the playful and purposeless character of the Void.

THE RISE AND DEVELOPMENT OF ZEN

The qualities which distinguish Zen or Ch'an from other types of Buddhism are rather elusive when it comes to putting them in words, yet Zen has a definite and unmistakable "flavor." Although the name Zen is *dhyana,* or meditation, other schools of Buddhism emphasize meditation as much as, if not more than, Zen–and at times it seems as if the practice of formal meditation were not necessary to Zen at all. Nor is Zen peculiar in "having nothing to say," in insisting that the truth cannot be put into words, for this is already the Madhyamika as well as the teaching of Lao-tzu.

> *Those who know do not speak;*
> *Those who speak do not know.* (56)

Perhaps the special flavor of Zen is best described as a certain directness. In other schools of Buddhism, awakening or *bodhi* seems remote and almost superhuman, something to be reached only after many lives of patient effort. But in Zen there is always the feeling that awakening is something quite natural, something startlingly obvious, which may occur at any moment. If it involves a difficulty, it is just that it is much too simple. Zen is also direct in its way of teaching, for it points directly and openly to the truth, and does not trifle with symbolism.

Direct pointing (*chih-chih* [a]) is the open demonstration of Zen by nonsymbolic actions or words, which usually appear to the uninitiated as having to do with the most ordinary secular affairs, or to be completely crazy. In answer to a question about Buddhism, the master makes a casual remark about the weather, or performs some simple action which seems to have nothing to do with philosophical or spiritual matters. However, it is difficult to find many instances of this method before the middle of the T'ang dynasty, by which time Zen was already well established. But it is certainly consistent with the emphasis of the earlier masters on immediate awakening in the midst of everyday affairs.

No one has been able to find any trace of a specific Dhyana School in Indian Buddhism, though because of our lack of historical materials this is no evidence that it did not exist. If the characteristic note of Zen is immediate or instantaneous awakening (*tun wu* [b]) without passing through preparatory stages, there are certainly evidences of this principle in India. The *Lankavatara Sutra* states that there are both gradual and sudden (*yugapat*) ways of awakening, the former by purification of the tainted outflows or projections (*ashrava*) of the mind, and the latter by *paravritti*–an instantaneous "turning about" within the depths of consciousness whereby dualistic views are cast off. It is likened to a mirror immediately reflecting whatever forms and images appear before it.[1] There is, too, a clear connection between the idea of immediate awakening and the teaching of the *Vajracchedika*, or "Diamond Cutter Sutra," on the fact that to attain awakening is not to attain anything. In other words, if *nirvana* is actually here and now so that to seek it is to lose it, a realization through progressive stages is hardly appropriate. One would have to see into it in the present moment, directly.

Although its origins are probably later than those of Zen in China, there is also a tradition of this kind in Tantric Buddhism, and there is nothing to indicate that there was a reverse influence from Chinese Zen. Parallels to Zen sayings may be seen in a tenth-century Tantric work by Saraha:

If it [the Truth] is already manifest, what's the use of meditation?
And if it is hidden, one is just measuring darkness. (20)

[1] *Lankavatara Sutra*, II. 14, in Suzuki (3), pp. 49–51. According to tradition this was the favorite *sutra* of Bodhidharma, the semi-legendary founder of Zen in China. Its connection with Zen is fully discussed in Suzuki (2), pp. 44–63.

Mantras and tantras, meditation and concentration,
They are all a cause of self-deception.
Do not defile in contemplation thought that is pure in its own nature,
But abide in the bliss of yourself and cease those torments. (23)
Whatever you see, that is it,
In front, behind, in all the ten directions.
Even today let your master make an end of delusion! (28)
The nature of the sky is originally clear,
But by gazing and gazing the sight becomes obscured. (34) [2]

Tibetan Buddhism likewise comprises a tradition of the Short Path, considered as a swift and steep ascent to *nirvana* for those who have the necessary courage, though a doctrine more suggestive of the Zen emphasis on immediacy and naturalness is found in the "Six Precepts" of Tilopa:

> *No thought, no reflection, no analysis,*
> *No cultivation, no intention;*
> *Let it settle itself.*[3]

Immediate release without any special contrivance or intention is also implied in the Tantric idea of *sahaja*, the "easy" or "natural" state of the liberated sage.

This is not the place to discuss the real meaning of immediate awakening and naturalness, but these instances are cited to show that the tradition of a direct path existed outside China, suggest-

[2] *Saraha's Treasury of Songs*, translated by David Snellgrove in Conze (2), pp. 224–39.
[3] The original is:

   Mi-mno, mi-bsam, mi-dpyad-ching,
   Mi-bsgom, mi-sems, rang-babs-bzhag.

The translation is based upon an elucidation of the passage given me by Mr. Alex Wayman of the University of California. *Mi-mno* is approximately equivalent to the Zen terms *wu-hsin* or *wu-nien*, "no-mind" or "no-thought." *Bsam* is the equivalent of the Sanskrit *cintana*, i.e., discursive thinking about what has been heard, and *dpyad* of *mimamsa*, or "philosophical analysis." *Bsgom* is probably *bhavana* or the Chinese *hsiu*, "to cultivate," "to practice," or "intense concentration." *Sems* is *cetana* or *szu*, with the sense of intention or volition. *Rang-babs-bzhag* is literally "self-settle-establish," and "self-settle" would seem to be an almost exact equivalent of the Taoist *tzu-jan*, "self-so," "spontaneous," or "natural."

ing some original source in Indian Buddhism. An obvious reason for the lack of materials would be that a principle of this kind, so easily open to misinterpretation, might have been kept as a "secret doctrine," discussed openly only in later times. Zen tradition does indeed maintain that immediate awakening is not communicated by the *sutras*, but has been passed down directly from master to pupil. This does not necessarily imply anything so "esoteric" as an experience conveyed by telepathy, but something much less sensational. Thus when Hindu pandits insist that wisdom is not to be gained from the scriptures but only from a teacher or *guru*, it means that the actual texts–such as the *Yoga-sutra*–contain only the headings of the doctrine, and that its full explanation requires someone who has learned the oral tradition. To this it should hardly be necessary to add that since the tradition is primarily an experience, words can communicate it no more and no less than any other experience.

However, it is not really necessary to suppose that there was ever a specific Dhyana School in India. The creation of Zen would seem to be sufficiently explained by the exposure of Taoists and Confucians to the main principles of Mahayana Buddhism. Therefore the appearance of trends very close to Zen can be seen almost as soon as the great Mahayana *sutras* became available in China–that is to say, with the work of the great Indian scholar-monk Kumarajiva. Kumarajiva was translating the *sutras* in Ku-tsang and Ch'ang-an between 384 and 413, at which time one of his outstanding students was the young monk Seng-chao (384–414), who had started out in life as a copyist of the Confucian and Taoist texts.

Seng-chao had been converted to Buddhism as a result of reading the *Vimalakirti Sutra*–a text which has exercised considerable influence upon Zen. Although Seng-chao became a monk, this *sutra* is the story of a layman, Vimalakirti, who excelled all the Buddha's disciples in the depth of his understanding. He had surpassed all the other disciples and Bodhisattvas by answering a question as to the nature of the nondual reality with a "thunderous silence"–an example frequently followed by Zen masters. Vimalakirti "thunderingly silent" is, too, a favorite theme of Zen artists. But the main importance of this *sutra* for China and for Zen was the point that perfect awakening was consistent with the affairs of everyday life, and that, indeed, the highest attainment was to "enter into awakening without exterminating the defilements [*klesa*]."

There was an appeal here to both the Confucian and the Taoist mentality. The Confucian stress on the importance of family life would not easily sympathize with a rigorously monastic type of Buddhism. Though the Chinese Buddhist masters were normally monks, they had large numbers of advanced lay students, and Zen, in particular, has always attached great importance to the expression of Buddhism in formally secular terms–in arts of every type, in manual labor, and in appreciation of the natural universe. Confucian and Taoist alike would be especially agreeable to the idea of an awakening which did not involve the extermination of human passions, as *klesa* may also be translated. We have already noted the peculiar trust in human nature which both these philosophies professed. However, not exterminating the passions does not mean letting them flourish untamed. It means letting go of them rather than fighting them, neither repressing passion nor indulging it. For the Taoist is never violent, since he achieves his ends by noninterference (*wu-wei*), which is a kind of psychological *judo*.

Seng-chao's writings, as well as his commentary on the *Vimalakirti Sutra*, are full of Taoist quotations and phrases, for he seemed to be following the example of less important, though earlier, monks such as Hui-yüan (334–416) and Tao-an (312–385) in using "extension of the idea" (*ko-i* °) for explaining Buddhism through Taoist parallels. So much did this suggest an equivalence between the two traditions that by the end of the fifth century Liu Ch'iu could say:

From the K'un-lun mountains eastward the (Taoist) term "Great Oneness" is used. From Kashmir westward the (Buddhist) term *sambodhi* is used. Whether one looks longingly toward "non-being" (*wu*) or cultivates "emptiness" (*sunyata*), the principle involved is the same.[4]

Two of Seng-chao's doctrines would seem to have had some importance for the later development of Zen—his view of time and change, and his idea that "*prajna* is not knowledge." The chapter on "The Immutability of Things" in his *Book of Chao* is so original and so startlingly similar to the section on time in the first volume of Dogen's *Shobogenzo*, that the celebrated Japanese Zen philosopher can hardly have been unfamiliar with it.

Past things are in the past and do not go there from the present, and present things are in the present, and do not go there from the past. . . . Rivers which compete with one another to inundate the land do not flow. The "wandering air" that blows about is not moving. The sun and moon, revolving in their orbits, do not turn around.[5]

In the same way Dogen pointed out that firewood does not become ashes and life does not become death, just as the winter does not become the spring. Every moment of time is "self-contained and quiescent."[6]

Seng-chao also discussed the seeming paradox that *prajna* is a kind of ignorance. Because the ultimate reality has no qualities and is not a thing, it cannot become an object of knowledge. Therefore *prajna*, direct insight, knows the truth by not knowing.

Wisdom knows not, yet it illumines the deepest profundity. Spirit calculates not, yet it responds to the necessities of the given moment. Because it calculates not, spirit shines in lonely glory in what is beyond the world. Because it knows not, Wisdom illumines the

[4] Quoted by Fung Yu-lan (1), vol. 2, p. 240, from Seng-yu, *Ch'u San-tsang Chi-chi*, 9.

[5] Liebenthal (1), p. 49.

[6] The same idea was used even before Dogen by the Zen master Ma-tsu (*d.* 788): "So with former thoughts, later thoughts, and thoughts in between: the thoughts follow one another without being linked together. Each one is absolutely tranquil." *Ku-tsun-hsü Yü-lu*, 1. 4.

Mystery (*hsüan*) beyond mundane affairs. Yet though Wisdom lies outside affairs, it never lacks them. Though Spirit lies beyond the world, it stays ever within it.[7]

Here is one of the main links between Taoism and Zen, for the style and terminology of the *Book of Chao* is Taoist throughout though the subject matter is Buddhist. The sayings of the early Zen masters, such as Hui-neng, Shen-hui, and Huang-po, are full of these very ideas—that truly to know is not to know, that the awakened mind responds immediately, without calculation, and that there is no incompatibility between Buddhahood and the everyday life of the world.

Even closer to the standpoint of Zen was Seng-chao's fellow student Tao-sheng (360–434), the first clear and unequivocal exponent of the doctrine of instantaneous awakening. If *nirvana* is not to be found by grasping, there can be no question of approaching it by stages, by the slow process of the accumulation of knowledge. It must be realized in a single flash of insight, which is *tun wu*, or, in Japanese, *satori*, the familiar Zen term for sudden awakening. Hsieh Ling-yün [8] in his discussion of Tao-sheng's doctrine even suggests that instantaneous awakening is more appropriate to the Chinese mentality than to the Indian, and lends weight to Suzuki's description of Zen as the Chinese "revolution" against Indian Buddhism. Tao-sheng's doctrine, however unusual and startling, must have found considerable acceptance. It is mentioned again, more than a century later, in a work by Hui-yüan (523–592), who also associates it with the master Hui-tan who lived until about 627.

The importance of these early precursors of Zen is that they provide a clue to the historical beginnings of the movement if we cannot accept the traditional story that it arrived in China in 520, with the Indian monk Bodhidharma. Modern scholars such

[7] Liebenthal (1), pp. 71–72.
[8] 385–433. His *Discussion of Essentials* (*Pien Tsung Lun*) is our principal source of information about Tao-sheng's ideas. See Fung Yu-lan (1), vol. 2, pp. 274–84.

as Fung Yu-lan and Pelliot have cast serious doubts upon the truth of this tradition. They suggest that the Bodhidharma story was a pious invention of later times, when the Zen School needed historical authority for its claim to be a direct transmission of experience from the Buddha himself, outside the *sutras*. For Bodhidharma is represented as the twenty-eighth of a somewhat fanciful list of Indian Patriarchs, standing in a direct line of "apostolic succession" from Gautama.[9]

At this stage of the inquiry it is hard to say whether the views of these scholars are to be taken seriously, or whether they are but another instance of an academic fashion for casting doubt upon the historicity of religious founders. The traditional story which the Zen School gives of its own origin is that Bodhidharma arrived in Canton from India around the year 520, and proceeded to the court of the Emperor Wu of Liang, an enthusiastic patron of Buddhism. However, Bodhidharma's doctrine and his abrupt attitude did not appeal to the Emperor, so that he withdrew for some years to a monastery in the state of Wei, and spent his time "gazing at the wall" until at last he found a suitable disciple in Hui-k'o, who subsequently became the Second Patriarch of Zen in China.[10]

There is, of course, nothing improbable in the arrival of a great Buddhist master from India at this period. Kumarajiva had arrived shortly before 400, Bodhiruci just after 500, and Paramartha was at the court of Liang about the same time as Bodhidharma. Is it really surprising that there should be no surviving record of his existence until little more than a hundred years after his time? These were not the days of newspapers and "Who's Whos," and even in our own excessively documented times people with important contributions to our knowledge and culture

[9] Hu Shih (1) and T'ang Yung-t'ing have suggested that Bodhidharma was in China at the earlier date of 420 to 479. See also Fung Yu-lan (1), vol. 2, pp. 386–90, Pelliot (1), and Dumoulin (2).

[10] The traditional sources are Tao-hsüan's *Sung-kao Seng-chuan* (Taisho 2061), composed between 645 and 667, and Tao-yüan's *Ching Te Ch'uan Teng Lu* (Taisho 2076), written about 1004.

can remain unrecognized and unrecorded until years after their death. Here again, it seems that we may as well accept the story of Bodhidharma until there is some really overwhelming evidence against it, recognizing that the ideas of Seng-chao, Tao-sheng, and others could also have been tributaries to the stream of Zen.

One of the reasons for suspecting the Bodhidharma story is that Zen is so Chinese in style that an Indian origin seems improbable. Yet the very Taoistic Seng-chao was a pupil of Kumarajiva, as was Tao-sheng, and the writings attributed to Bodhidharma and his successors until Hui-neng (638–713) show the clear transition from an Indian to a Chinese view of *dhyana*.[11]

The absence of any record of a Dhyana School in Indian Buddhist literature, or of Bodhidharma in connection with it, is perhaps due to the fact that there was never any Dhyana or Zen School even in China until some two hundred years after Bodhidharma's time. On the other hand, there would have been an almost universal practice of *dhyana*–that is, or *ts'o-ch'an* [d] (Japanese, *za-zen*) or sitting meditation–among Buddhist monks, and the special instructors who supervised this practice were called *dhyana* masters, no matter what their school or sect. There were likewise *vinaya* masters, or instructors in monastic discipline, and *dharma* masters, or instructors in doctrine. Zen became a distinct school only as it promulgated a view of *dhyana* which differed sharply from the generally accepted practice.[12]

Zen tradition represents Bodhidharma as a fierce-looking fellow with a bushy beard and wide-open, penetrating eyes–in which, however, there is just the hint of a twinkle. A legend says that he once fell asleep in meditation and was so furious that he cut

[11] Works attributed to Bodhidharma will be found in Suzuki (1), vol. 1, pp. 165–70, and Senzaki and McCandless (1), pp. 73–84. The style is always Indian and lacks Taoist "flavor."

[12] Hui-neng's *Tan Ching*, for example, records several instances of the Sixth Patriarch's interviews with *dhyana* masters who obviously did not belong to his own "sudden school" of *dhyana*. Furthermore, it was not until the time of Po-chang (720–814), or even later, that the Zen School had monasteries of its own. See Dumoulin and Sasaki (1), p. 13.

off his eyelids, and falling to the ground they arose as the first tea plant. Tea has thereafter supplied Zen monks with a protection against sleep, and so clarifies and invigorates the mind that it has been said, "The taste of Zen [ch'an] and the taste of tea [ch'a] are the same." Another legend holds that Bodhidharma sat so long in meditation that his legs fell off. Hence the delightful symbolism of those Japanese Daruma dolls which represent Bodhidharma as a legless roly-poly so weighted inside that he always stands up again when pushed over. A popular Japanese poem says of the Daruma doll:

> Jinsei nana korobi
> Ya oki.
> *Such is life—*
> *Seven times down,*
> *Eight times up!*

Bodhidharma's alleged interview with the Emperor Wu of Liang is typical of his abrupt and direct manner. For the Emperor described all that he had done to promote the practice of Buddhism, and asked what merit he had gained thereby—taking the popular view that Buddhism is a gradual accumulation of merit through good deeds, leading to better and better circumstances in future lives, and finally to *nirvana*. But Bodhidharma replied, "No merit whatever!" This so undermined the Emperor's idea of Buddhism that he asked, "What, then, is the sacred doctrine's first principle?" Bodhidharma replied, "It's just empty; there's nothing sacred." "Who, then, are you," said the Emperor, "to stand before us?" "I don't know." [13] *e*

After this interview, so unsatisfactory from the Emperor's point of view, Bodhidharma retired to a monastery in Wei, where he is said to have spent nine years in a cave, "gazing at the wall" (*pi-kuan* [1]). Suzuki holds that this is not to be taken literally, and that the expression refers to Bodhidharma's inner state, his

[13] *Ch'uan Teng Lu,* 3.

exclusion of all grasping thoughts from his mind.[14] Thus Bodhidharma remained, until he was approached by the monk Shen-
kuang, afterwards Hui-k'o (486–593, maybe!), who was to become Bodhidharma's successor as the Second Patriarch.

Hui-k'o again and again asked Bodhidharma for instruction,
but was always refused. Yet he continued to sit in meditation
outside the cave, waiting patiently in the snow in the hope
that Bodhidharma would at last relent. In desperation he finally
cut off his left arm and presented it to Bodhidharma as a token
of his agonized sincerity. At this Bodhidharma at last asked
Hui-k'o what he wanted.

"I have no peace of mind [hsin]," said Hui-k'o. "Please pacify
my mind."

"Bring out your mind here before me," replied Bodhidharma,
"and I will pacify it!"

"But when I seek my own mind," said Hui-k'o, "I cannot find
it."

"There!" snapped Bodhidharma, "I have pacified your
mind!" [15] g

At this moment Hui-k'o had his awakening, his *tun-wu* or
satori, so that this interchange purports to be the first instance
of what became the characteristic Zen method of instruction–
the *wen-ta* ʰ (Japanese, *mondo*) or "question-and-answer," sometimes loosely called the "Zen story." The greater part of Zen literature consists of these anecdotes, many of them much more
puzzling than this, and their aim is always to precipitate some
type of sudden realization in the questioner's mind, or to test the
depth of his insight. For this reason, such anecdotes cannot be
"explained" without spoiling their effect. In some respects they
are like jokes which do not produce their intended effect of
laughter when the "punch line" requires further explanation.
One must see the point immediately, or not at all.

[14] Suzuki (1), vol. 1, pp. 170–71.
[15] *Wu-men kuan*, 41.

It should, furthermore, be understood that the main character of these anecdotes is only rarely symbolic, and then, usually, in a rather secondary way, as when the dialogue contains allusions which are obvious to both parties. But such commentators as Gernet (3) are, I feel, mistaken in supposing that the main point is the communication of some Buddhist principle by means of a symbol. The *satori* which so frequently follows these interchanges is by no means a mere comprehension of the answer to a riddle. For whatever the Zen master says or does is a direct and spontaneous utterance of "suchness," of his Buddha nature, and what he gives is no symbol but the very thing. Zen communication is always "direct pointing," in line with the traditional four-phrase summary of Zen:

> Outside teaching; apart from tradition.
> Not founded on words and letters.
> Pointing directly to the human mind.
> Seeing into one's nature and attaining Buddhahood.[16] '

The successor to Hui-k'o is said to have been Seng-ts'an (*d.* 606), and the story of their initial interview is of the same form as between Hui-k'o and Bodhidharma, except that where Hui-k'o asked for "peace of mind," Seng-ts'an asked to be "cleansed of faults." To him there is attributed a celebrated poem called the *Hsin-hsin Ming*, the "Treatise on Faith in the Mind." [17] If Seng-ts'an was indeed its author, this poem is the first clear and comprehensive statement of Zen. Its Taoist flavor is apparent in the opening lines,

> *The perfect Tao is without difficulty,*
> *Save that it avoids picking and choosing.*

[16] In modern Chinese the first two characters mean something like "worldly" or "outside the fold." In the present context they are usually taken to mean that the truth of Zen cannot be expressed in any form of doctrine, or that a teacher can do no more than show how to get it for oneself. However, the marvelous ambiguity of Chinese might intentionally allow both meanings. Consider the predominantly "secular" form of Zen expression, and such sayings as "Wash out your mouth every time you say, 'Buddha!'"

[17] Translations will be found in Suzuki (1), vol. 1, p. 182, and a revision in Suzuki (6), p. 91. Another by Arthur Waley is in Conze (2) p. 295.

And again,

> Follow your nature and accord with the Tao;
> Saunter along and stop worrying.
> If your thoughts are tied you spoil what is genuine. . . .
> Don't be antagonistic to the world of the senses,
> For when you are not antagonistic to it,
> It turns out to be the same as complete Awakening.
> The wise person does not strive (wu-wei);
> The ignorant man ties himself up. . . .
> If you work on your mind with your mind,
> How can you avoid an immense confusion? [18] *j*

Not only is the poem full of such Taoist terms as *wu-wei* and *tzu-jan* (spontaneity), but its whole attitude is that of letting one's mind alone and trusting it to follow its own nature—in contrast to the more typically Indian attitude of bringing it under rigid control and shutting out the experience of the senses.

The Fourth Patriarch, following Seng-ts'an, is believed to have been Tao-hsin (579–651). When he came to Seng-ts'an he asked, "What is the method of liberation?"

"Who binds you?" replied Seng-ts'an.

"No one binds me."

"Why then," asked Seng-ts'an, "should you seek liberation?" [19] *k* And this was Tao-hsin's *satori*. The *Ch'uan Teng Lu* records a fascinating encounter between Tao-hsin and the sage Fa-yung, who lived in a lonely temple on Mount Niu-t'ou, and was so holy that the birds used to bring him offerings of flowers. As the two men were talking, a wild animal roared close by, and Tao-hsin jumped. Fa-yung commented, "I see it is still with you!" —referring, of course, to the instinctive "passion" (*klesa*) of fright. Shortly afterwards, while he was for a moment unobserved, Tao-hsin wrote the Chinese character for "Buddha" on the rock where Fa-yung was accustomed to sit. When Fa-yung

[18] The last two lines carry the same point as Hui-k'o's interview with Bodhidharma.
[19] *Ch'uan Teng Lu*, 3.

returned to sit down again, he saw the sacred Name and hesi-
tated to sit. "I see," said Tao-hsin, "it is still with you!" At this
remark Fa-yung was fully awakened . . . and the birds never
brought any more flowers.

The Fifth Patriarch—and here we begin to enter a more reliable
chapter of history—was Hung-jan (601–675). At his first meeting
with Hung-jan the Patriarch asked:

"What is your name [*hsing*]?"

"I have a nature [*hsing*]," replied Hung-jan punning, "but it's
no usual nature."

"What is this name?" inquired the Patriarch, missing the pun.

"It's Buddha nature."

"You have no name, then?"

"That's because it's an empty nature." [20]

Hung-jan was apparently the first of the Patriarchs to have any
large following, for it is said that he presided over a group of
some five hundred monks in a monastery on the Yellow Plum
Mountain (Wang-mei Shan) at the eastern end of modern
Hupeh. He is, however, much overshadowed by his immediate
successor, Hui-neng (637–713), whose life and teaching mark
the definitive beginning of a truly Chinese Zen—of Zen as it
flourished during what was later called "the epoch of Zen
activity," the latter two hundred years of the T'ang dynasty,
from about 700 to 906.

One must not overlook Hui-neng's contemporaries, for he
lived at a time which was most creative for Chinese Buddhism
as a whole. The great translator and traveler Hsüan-tsang had
returned from India in 645, and was expounding the *vijnaptimatra* ("representation-only") doctrines of the Yogacara in
Ch'ang-an. His former student Fa-tsang (643–712) was developing the important school of the Hua-yen (Japanese, Kegon)
based on the *Avatamsaka Sutra,* and which later provided Zen
with a formal philosophy. Nor must we forget that not so long
before these two men, Chih-k'ai (538–597) had written his re-

20 *Ch'uan Teng Lu,* 3.

markable treatise on the *Mahayana Method of Cessation and Contemplation*,[21] containing the fundamental teaching of the T'ien-t'ai School, which is in many ways close to Zen. Much of Chih-k'ai's treatise foreshadows in both content and terminology the doctrines of Hui-neng and some of his immediate successors.

Hui-neng is said to have had his first awakening when, almost as a boy, he happened to overhear someone reading the *Vajracchedika*. He set out almost at once for Hung-jan's monastery at Wang-mei to have his understanding confirmed and to receive further instruction. We should note (for future reference) that his original *satori* occurred spontaneously, without the benefit of a master, and that his biography represents him as an illiterate peasant from the neighborhood of Canton. Apparently Hung-jan immediately recognized the depth of his insight, but fearing that his humble origins might make him unacceptable in a community of scholarly monks, the Patriarch put him to work in the kitchen compound.

Some time later, the Patriarch announced that he was looking for a successor to whom he might transmit his office, together with the robe and begging bowl (said to have been handed down from the Buddha) which were its insignia. This honor was to be conferred upon the person who submitted the best poem, expressing his understanding of Buddhism. The chief monk of the community was then a certain Shen-hsiu, and all the others naturally assumed that the office would go to him and so made no attempt to compete.

Shen-hsiu, however, was in doubt as to his own understanding, and decided to submit his poem anonymously, claiming authorship only if the Patriarch approved of it. During the night, then, he posted the following lines in the corridor near the Patriarch's quarters:

> *The body is the Bodhi Tree;*
> *The mind like a bright mirror standing.*

[21] *Ta-ch'eng Chih-kuan Fa-men,* Taisho 1924.

Take care to wipe it all the time,
And allow no dust to cling.[1]

The following morning, the Patriarch read the poem and ordered incense to be burned before it, saying that all who put it into practice would be enabled to realize their true nature. But when Shen-hsiu came to him in private and claimed authorship, the Patriarch declared that his understanding was still far from perfect.

On the following day, another poem appeared beside the first:

There never was a Bodhi Tree,
Nor bright mirror standing.
Fundamentally, not one thing exists,
So where is the dust to cling? [m]

The Patriarch knew that only Hui-neng could have written this, but to avoid jealousy he rubbed out the poem with his shoe, and summoned Hui-neng to his room secretly, by night. Here he conferred the Patriarchate, the robe, and the bowl upon him, and told him to flee into the mountains until the hurt feelings of the other monks had subsided and the time was ripe for him to begin his public teaching.[22]

A comparison of the two poems shows at once the distinctive flavor of Hui-neng's Zen. Shen-hsiu's poem reflects what was apparently the general and popular view of *dhyana* practice in Chinese Buddhism. It was obviously understood as the discipline of sitting meditation (*ts'o-ch'an*), in which the mind was "purified" by an intense concentration which would cause all thoughts and attachments to cease. Taken rather literally, many Buddhist and Taoist texts would substantiate this view–that the highest

---

[22] *T'an-ching*, 1. The full title of the work which records the life and teaching of Hui-neng is the *Platform-Sutra of the Sixth Patriarch*, or *Liu-tsu T'an-ching*, Taisho 2008. For translations, see Bibliography under Wong Mou-lam and Rousselle.

state of consciousness is a consciousness empty of all contents, all ideas, feelings, and even sensations. Today in India this is a very prevalent notion of *samadhi*. But our own experience with Christianity should make this type of literalism, even in high circles, rather familiar.

Hui-neng's position was that a man with an empty consciousness was no better than "a block of wood or a lump of stone." He insisted that the whole idea of purifying the mind was irrelevant and confusing, because "our own nature is fundamentally clear and pure." In other words, there is no analogy between consciousness or mind and a mirror that can be wiped. The true mind is "no-mind" (*wu-hsin*), which is to say that it is not to be regarded as an object of thought or action, as if it were a thing to be grasped and controlled. The attempt to work on one's own mind is a vicious circle. To try to purify it is to be contaminated with purity. Obviously this is the Taoist philosophy of naturalness, according to which a person is not genuinely free, detached, or pure when his state is the result of an artificial discipline. He is just imitating purity, just "faking" clear awareness. Hence the unpleasant self-righteousness of those who are deliberately and methodically religious.

Hui-neng's teaching is that instead of trying to purify or empty the mind, one must simply let go of the mind–because the mind is nothing to be grasped. Letting go of the mind is also equivalent to letting go of the series of thoughts and impressions (*nien*) which come and go "in" the mind, neither repressing them, holding them, nor interfering with them.

> Thoughts come and go of themselves, for through the use of wisdom there is no blockage. This is the *samadhi* of *prajna,* and natural liberation. Such is the practice of "no-thought" [*wu-nien*]. But if you do not think of anything at all, and immediately command thoughts to cease, this is to be tied in a knot by a method, and is called an obtuse view. (2) [n]

Of the usual view of meditation practice he said:

> To concentrate on the mind and to contemplate it until it is still is a disease and not *dhyana*. To restrain the body by sitting up for a long time—of what benefit is this towards the Dharma? (8) *o*

And again:

> If you start concentrating the mind on stillness, you will merely produce an unreal stillness. . . . What does the word "meditation" [*ts'o-ch'an*] mean? In this school it means no barriers, no obstacles; it is beyond all objective situations whether good or bad. The word "sitting" [*ts'o*] means not to stir up thoughts in the mind. (5) *p*

In counteracting the false *dhyana* of mere empty-mindedness, Hui-neng compares the Great Void to space, and calls it great, not just because it is empty, but because it contains the sun, moon, and stars. True *dhyana* is to realize that one's own nature is like space, and that thoughts and sensations come and go in this "original mind" like birds through the sky, leaving no trace. Awakening, in his school, is "sudden" because it is for quick-witted rather than slow-witted people. The latter must of necessity understand gradually, or more exactly, after a long time, since the Sixth Patriarch's doctrine does not admit of stages or growth. To be awakened at all is to be awakened completely, for, having no parts or divisions, the Buddha nature is not realized bit by bit.

His final instructions to his disciples contain an interesting clue to the later development of the *mondo* or "question-answer" method of teaching:

> If, in questioning you, someone asks about being, answer with non-being. If he asks about non-being, answer with being. If he asks about the ordinary man, answer in terms of the sage. If he asks about the sage, answer in terms of the ordinary man. By this method of opposites mutually related there arises an understanding of the Middle Way. For every question that you are asked, respond in terms of its opposite. (10) *q*

Hui-neng died in 713, and with his death the institution of the Patriarchate ceased, for the genealogical tree of Zen put forth branches. Hui-neng's tradition passed to five disciples: Huai-jang

(*d.* 775), Ch'ing-yüan (*d.* 740), Shen-hui (668–770), Hsüan-chüeh
(665–713), and Hui-chung (677–744).[23] The spiritual descend-
ants of Huai-jang and Hsing-ssu live on today as the two principal schools of Zen in Japan, the Rinzai and the Soto. In the
two centuries following the death of Hui-neng the proliferation
of lines of descent and schools of Zen is quite complex, and we
need do no more than consider some of the more influential individuals.[24]

The writings and records of Hui-neng's successors continue to
be concerned with naturalness. On the principle that "the true
mind is no-mind," and that "our true nature is no (special)
nature," it is likewise stressed that the true practice of Zen is no

[23] A state of total confusion prevails among writers on Zen as to the naming
of the great T'ang masters. For example, Shen-hui's full name is Ho-tse
Shen-hui, of which the Japanese pronunciation is Kataku Jinne. Shen-hui
is his monastic name, and Ho-tse designates his locality. Japanese writers
usually refer to him as Jinne, using the personal monastic name. On the
other hand, Hsüan-chüeh is Yung-chia Hsüan-chüeh, in Japanese Yoka
Genkaku. But the Japanese writers usually employ his locality name, Yoka!
On the whole, Suzuki uses locality names and Fung Yu-lan monastic names.
Suzuki sometimes gives the Japanese form, and sometimes the Chinese, but
uses a somewhat different way of romanizing the Chinese than Fung (or
rather Bodde, the translator). Lin-chi I-hsüan (Rinzai Gigen) appears in
Suzuki mostly as Rinzai and sometimes as Lin-chi, but in Fung he is Yi-
hsüan! Dumoulin and Sasaki make some attempt at consistency by using
only the Japanese forms, but then it is impossible at first sight to distinguish
Chinese from Japanese individuals. Thus anyone who studies Zen from
other than the original sources is confronted with a situation which makes
historical clarity extremely difficult. Suzuki has been so widely read that
most Western students of Zen are familiar with his usage, however in-
consistent, and I do not want to confuse them further by such an attempt at
consistency as calling Hui-neng by his locality name, Ta-chien. All I can
offer is an index giving all the names. To make matters worse, there is
also much confusion with respect to dates. For Shen-hui, Fung gives 686–
760, Gernet 668–760, and Dumoulin and Sasaki 668–770.
[24] This period is treated in detail in Dumoulin and Sasaki (1). Demiéville
(2) has translated a Tun-huang ms. (Pelliot 4646) concerning a debate
held at Lhasa *c.* 792–794 between a master of the Sudden Ch'an School
and a group of Indian Buddhist scholars. The Ch'an master is identified
only by the name "Mahayana" and there is apparently nothing to link him
with the tradition descending from Hui-neng. His doctrine seems to be
somewhat more quietistic than that of the Sixth Patriarch. The fact that the
Indian scholars were astonished and repelled by his teaching suggests its
purely Chinese origin.

practice, that is, the seeming paradox of being a Buddha without intending to be a Buddha. According to Shen-hui:

> If one has this knowledge, it is contemplation [*samadhi*] without contemplating, wisdom [*prajna*] without wisdom, practice without practicing. (4. 193)
> All cultivation of concentration is wrong-minded from the start. For how, by cultivating concentration, could one obtain concentration? (1. 117)
> If we speak of working with the mind, does this working consist in activity or inactivity of the mind? If it is inactivity, we should be no different from vulgar fools. But if you say that it is activity, it is then in the realm of grasping, and we are bound up by the passions [*klesa*]. What way, then, should we have of gaining deliverance? The *sravakas* cultivate emptiness, dwell in emptiness, and are bound by it. They cultivate concentration, dwell in concentration, and are bound by it. They cultivate tranquillity, dwell in tranquillity, and are bound by it. . . . If working with the mind is to discipline one's mind, how could this be called deliverance? (1. 118) [25]

In the same vein Hsüan-chüeh begins his celebrated poem, the *Song of Realizing the Tao* (*Cheng-tao Ke*):

> *See you not that easygoing Man of Tao, who has abandoned learning and does not strive* [wu-wei]?
> *He neither avoids false thoughts nor seeks the true,*
> *For ignorance is in reality the Buddha nature,*
> *And this illusory, changeful, empty body is the Dharma body.*[26] r

The following story is told of Huai-jang, initiating into Zen his great successor Ma-tsu (*d.* 788), who was at the time practicing sitting meditation at the monastery of Ch'uan-fa.

"Your reverence," asked Huai-jang, "what is the objective of sitting in meditation?"

"The objective," answered Ma-tsu, "is to become a Buddha."

[25] *Shen-hui Ho-chang I-chi.* The Chinese text has been edited by Hu Shih, Shanghai, 1930.
[26] I.e., the Dharmakaya, for which see above, p. 71. Full translations of the *Cheng-tao Ke* (Japanese, *Shodoka*) will be found in Suzuki (6) and Senzaki and McCandless (1).

Thereupon Huai-jang picked up a floor-tile and began to polish it on a rock.

"What are you doing, master?" asked Ma-tsu.

"I am polishing it for a mirror," said Huai-jang.

"How could polishing a tile make a mirror?"

"How could sitting in meditation make a Buddha?" [27] *

Ma-tsu was the first Zen master celebrated for "strange words and extraordinary behavior," and is described as one who walked like a bull and glared like a tiger. When a monk asked him, "How do you get into harmony with the Tao?" Ma-tsu replied, "I am already out of harmony with the Tao!" He was the first to answer questions about Buddhism by hitting the questioner, or by giving a loud shout—"Ho!" [28] † Sometimes, however, he was more discursive, and one of his lectures takes up the problem of discipline thus:

> The Tao has nothing to do with discipline. If you say that it is attained by discipline, when the discipline is perfected it can again be lost (or, finishing the discipline turns out to be losing the Tao). . . . If you say that there is no discipline, this is to be the same as ordinary people.[29] ᵘ

Hsing-ssu's disciple Shih-t'ou (700–790), in the line of Soto Zen, was even more forthright:

> My teaching which has come down from the ancient Buddhas is not dependent on meditation (*dhyana*) or on diligent application of any kind. When you attain the insight as attained by the Buddha, you realize that mind is Buddha and Buddha is mind, that mind, Buddha, sentient beings, *bodhi* and *klesa* are of one and the same substance while they vary in names.[30]

His interesting name "Stone-head" is attributed to the fact that he lived on top of a large rock near the monastery of Hengchou.

[27] *Ch'uan Teng Lu,* 5.
[28] *Ku-tsun-hsü Yü-lu,* 1. 6.
[29] *Ibid.,* 1. 4.
[30] In Suzuki (6), p. 123.

With Ma-tsu's disciple Nan-ch'üan (748–834) and his successor Chao-chou (778–897), the teaching of Zen became peculiarly lively and disturbing. The *Wu-men kuan* (14) tells how Nan-ch'üan interrupted a dispute among his monks as to the ownership of a cat by threatening to cleave the animal with his spade if none of the monks could say a "good word"–that is, give an immediate expression of his Zen. There was dead silence, so the master cut the cat in two. Later in the day Nan-ch'üan recounted the incident to Chao-chou, who at once put his shoes on his head and left the room. "If you had been here," said Nan-ch'üan, "the cat would have been saved!"

Chao-chou is said to have had his awakening after the following incident with Nan-ch'üan:

Chao-chou asked, "What is the Tao?"

The master replied, "Your ordinary [i.e., natural] mind is the Tao."

"How can one return into accord with it?"

"By intending to accord you immediately deviate." *v*

"But without intention, how can one know the Tao?"

"The Tao," said the master, "belongs neither to knowing nor not knowing. Knowing is false understanding; not knowing is blind ignorance. If you really understand the Tao beyond doubt, it's like the empty sky. Why drag in right and wrong?" [31]

When Chao-chou was asked whether a dog has Buddha nature –which is certainly the usual Mahayana doctrine–he gave the one word "No!" (*Wu,*[w] Japanese, *Mu*).[32] When a monk asked him for instruction he merely inquired whether he had eaten his gruel, and then added, "Go wash your bowl!" [33] When asked about the spirit which remains when the body has decomposed, he remarked, "This morning it's windy again." [34]

Ma-tsu had another notable disciple in Po-chang (720–814),

---

[31] *Wu-men kuan*, 19.

[32] *Ibid.*, 1.

[33] *Ibid.*, 7.

[34] *Chao-chou Yü-lu*, in *Ku-tsun-hsü Yü-lu*, 3. 13.

who is said to have organized the first purely Zen community
of monks and to have laid down its regulations on the principle
that "a day of no working is a day of no eating." Since his time
a strong emphasis on manual work and some degree of self-
support has been characteristic of Zen communities. It might
be remarked here that these are not exactly monasteries in the
Western sense. They are rather training schools, from which one
is free to depart at any time without censure. Some members
remain monks for their whole lives; others become secular priests
in charge of small temples; still others may return into lay life.[35]
To Po-chang is attributed the famous definition of Zen, "When
hungry, eat; when tired, sleep." He is said to have had his *satori*
when Ma-tsu shouted at him and left him deaf for three days,
and to have been in the habit of pointing out the Zen life to his
disciples with the saying, "Don't cling; don't seek." For when
asked about seeking for the Buddha nature he answered, "It's
much like riding an ox in search of the ox."

Po-chang's student Huang-po (*d.* 850) is also of considerable
importance in this period. Not only was he the teacher of the
great Lin-chi, but he was also the author of the *Ch'uan Hsin Fa
Yao*, or "Treatise on the Essentials of the Doctrine of Mind."
The content of this work is essentially the same body of doctrine
as is found in Hui-neng, Shen-hui, and Ma-tsu, but it contains
some passages of remarkable clarity as well as some frank and
careful answers to questions at the end.

By their very seeking for it [the Buddha nature] they produce the
contrary effect of losing it, for that is using the Buddha to seek for
the Buddha, and using mind to grasp mind. Even though they do
their utmost for a full *kalpa*, they will not be able to attain to
it. (1)
    If those who study the Tao do not awake to this mind substance,

[35] The somewhat misleading word "monk" seems to be the inevitable translation of *seng*,[x] though *yun shui*,[y] "cloud and water," is a common and re-
vealingly picturesque term for the Zen student, who "drifts like a cloud and
flows like water." But I am at a loss to find a concise English expression for
this term.

they will create a mind over and above mind, seek the Buddha outside themselves and remain attached to forms, practices and performances–all of which is harmful and not the way to supreme knowledge. (3) [36]

Much of it is devoted to a clarification of what is meant by the Void, and by the terms "no-mind" (*wu-hsin*) and "no-thought" (*wu-nien*), all of which are carefully distinguished from literal blankness or nothingness. The use of Taoist language and ideas is found throughout the text:

Fearing that none of you would understand, they [the Buddhas] gave it the name Tao, but you must not base any concept upon that name. So it is said that "when the fish is caught the trap is forgotten." (From Chuang-tzu.) When body and mind achieve spontaneity, the Tao is reached and universal mind can be understood. (29) . . . In former times, men's minds were sharp. Upon hearing a single sentence, they abandoned study and so came to be called "the sages who, abandoning learning, rest in spontaneity." In these days, people only seek to stuff themselves with knowledge and deductions, placing great reliance on written explanations and calling all this the practice. (30) [37]

It appears, however, that Huang-po's personal instruction of his disciples was not always so explanatory. Lin-chi (Japanese, Rinzai, *d.* 867) could never get a word out of him. Every time he attempted to ask a question Huang-po struck him, until in desperation he left the monastery and sought the advice of another master, Ta-yü, who scolded him for being so ungrateful for Huang-po's "grandmotherly kindness." This awakened Lin-chi, who again presented himself before Huang-po. This time, however, it was Lin-chi who did the striking, saying, "There is not much in Huang-po's Buddhism after all!" [38]

The record of Lin-chi's teaching, the *Lin-chi Lu* (Japanese, *Rinzai Roku*), shows a character of immense vitality and original-

[36] In Chu Ch'an (1), pp. 16 and 18. Another partial translation appears in Suzuki (6), pp. 132–40.
[37] In Chu Ch'an (1), pp. 42–43.
[38] *Ch'uan Teng Lu,* 12.

ity, lecturing his students in informal and often somewhat "racy" language. It is as if Lin-chi were using the whole strength of his personality to force the student into immediate awakening. Again and again he berates them for not having enough faith in themselves, for letting their minds "gallop around" in search of something which they have never lost, and which is "right before you at this very moment." Awakening for Lin-chi seems primarily a matter of "nerve"–the courage to "let go" without further delay in the unwavering faith that one's natural, spontaneous functioning is the Buddha mind. His approach to conceptual Buddhism, to the students' obsession with stages to be reached and goals to be attained, is ruthlessly iconoclastic.

> Why do I talk here? Only because you followers of the Tao go galloping around in search of the mind, and are unable to stop it. On the other hand, the ancients acted in a leisurely way, appropriate to circumstances (as they arose). O you followers of the Tao— when you get my point of view you will sit in judgment on top of the . . . Buddhas' heads. Those who have completed the ten stages will seem like underlings, and those who have arrived at Supreme Awakening will seem as if they had cangues around their necks. The Arhans and Pratyeka-buddhas are like a dirty privy. Bodhi and nirvana are like hitching-posts for a donkey.[39]

On the importance of the "natural" or "unaffected" (wu-shih [z]) life he is especially emphatic:

> There is no place in Buddhism for using effort. Just be ordinary and nothing special. Relieve your bowels, pass water, put on your clothes, and eat your food. When you're tired, go and lie down. Ignorant people may laugh at me, but the wise will understand. . . . As you go from place to place, if you regard each one as your own home, they will all be genuine, for when circumstances come you must not try to change them. Thus your usual habits of feeling, which make karma for the Five Hells, will of themselves become the Great Ocean of Liberation.[40]

And on creating karma through seeking liberation–

[39] Lin-chi Lu in Ku-tsun-hsü Yü-lu, 1. 4, pp. 5–6.
[40] Ibid., p. 7.

Outside the mind there is no Dharma, and inside also there is nothing to be grasped. What is it that you seek? You say on all sides that the Tao is to be practiced and put to the proof. Don't be mistaken! If there is anyone who can practice it, this is entirely *karma* making for birth-and-death. You talk about being perfectly disciplined in your six senses and in the ten thousand ways of conduct, but as I see it all this is creating *karma*. To seek the Buddha and to seek the Dharma is precisely making *karma* for the hells.[41] *aa*

In Ma-tsu, Nan-ch'üan, Chao-chou, Huang-po, and Lin-chi we can see the "flavor" of Zen at its best. Taoist and Buddhist as it is in its original inspiration, it is also something more. It is so earthy, so matter-of-fact, and so direct. The difficulty of translating the records of these masters is that their style of Chinese is neither classical nor modern, but rather the colloquial speech of the T'ang dynasty. Its "naturalness" is less refined, less obviously beautiful than that of the Taoist sages and poets; it is almost rough and common. I say "almost" because the expression is not really correct. We are at a loss for parallels from other cultures for comparison, and the Western student can best catch its flavor through observing the works of art which it was subsequently to inspire. The best image might be a garden consisting of no more than an expanse of raked sand, as a ground for several unhewn rocks overgrown with lichens and moss, such as one may see today in the Zen temples of Kyoto. The media are the simplest imaginable; the effect is as if man had hardly touched it, as if it had been transported unchanged from the seashore; but in practice only the most sensitive and experienced artist can achieve it. This sounds, of course, as though "Zen flavor" were a studied and affected primitivism. Sometimes it is. But the genuine Zen flavor is when a man is almost miraculously natural without intending to be so. His Zen life is not to make himself but to *grow* that way.

Thus it should be obvious that the "naturalness" of these T'ang masters is not to be taken just literally, as if Zen were merely to

[41] *Ibid.*, p. 11.

glory in being a completely ordinary, vulgar fellow who scatters ideals to the wind and behaves as he pleases–for this would in itself be an affectation. The "naturalness" of Zen flourishes only when one has lost affectedness and self-consciousness of every description. But a spirit of this kind comes and goes like the wind, and is the most impossible thing to institutionalize and preserve.

Yet in the late T'ang dynasty the genius and vitality of Zen was such that it was coming to be the dominant form of Buddhism in China, though its relation to other schools was often very close. Tsung-mi (779–841) was simultaneously a Zen master and the Fifth Patriarch of the Hua-yen School, representing the philosophy of the *Avatamsaka Sutra*. This extremely subtle and mature form of Mahayana philosophy was employed by T'ung-shan (807–869) in developing the doctrine of the Five Ranks (*wu-wei* [bb]), concerning the fivefold relationship of the absolute (*cheng* [cc]) and the relative (*p'ien* [dd]), and was related by his student Ts'ao-shan (840–901) to the philosophy of the *I Ching*, the *Book of Changes*. Fa-yen (885–958) and Fen-yang (947–1024) were also influential masters who made a deep study of the Hua-yen, and to this day it constitutes as it were the intellectual aspect of Zen. On the other hand, such masters as Te-chao (891–972) and Yen-shou (904–975) maintained close relations with the T'ien-t'ai and Pure Land Schools.

In 845 there was a brief but vigorous persecution of Buddhism by the Taoist Emperor Wu-tsung. Temples and monasteries were destroyed, their lands confiscated, and the monks compelled to return to lay life. Fortunately, his enthusiasm for Taoist alchemy soon involved him in experiments with the "Elixir of Immortality," and from partaking of this concoction he shortly died. Zen had survived the persecution better than any other school, and now entered into a long era of imperial and popular favor. Hundreds of monks thronged its wealthy monastic institutions, and the fortunes of the school so prospered and its numbers so increased that the preservation of its spirit became a very serious problem.

Popularity almost invariably leads to a deterioration of quality, and as Zen became less of an informal spiritual movement and more of a settled institution, it underwent a curious change of character. It became necessary to "standardize" its methods and to find means for the masters to handle students in large numbers. There were also the special problems which arise for monastic communities when their membership increases, their traditions harden, and their novices tend more and more to be mere boys without natural vocation, sent for training by their pious families. The effect of this last factor upon the development of institutional Zen can hardly be underestimated. For the Zen community became less an association of mature men with spiritual interests, and more of an ecclesiastical boarding school for adolescent boys.

Under such circumstances the problem of discipline became paramount. The Zen masters were forced to concern themselves not only with the way of liberation from convention, but also with the instilling of convention, of ordinary manners and morals, in raw youths. The mature Western student who discovers an interest in Zen as a philosophy or as a way of liberation must be careful to keep this in mind, for otherwise he may be unpleasantly startled by monastic Zen as it exists today in Japan. He will find that Zen is a discipline enforced with the big stick. He will find that, although it is still an effective way of liberation at its "upper end," its main preoccupation is with a disciplinary regimen which "trains character" in the same way as the old-fashioned British public school or the Jesuit novitiate. But it does the job remarkably well. The "Zen type" is an extremely fine type—as types go—self-reliant, humorous, clean and orderly to a fault, energetic though unhurried, and "hard as nails" without lack of keen aesthetic sensibility. The general impression of these men is that they have the same sort of balance as the Daruma doll: they are not rigid, but no one can knock them down.

Still another crucial problem arises when a spiritual institution comes into prosperity and power—the very human problem of competition for office and of who has the right to be a master.

Concern for this problem is reflected in the writing of the *Ch'uan Teng Lu*, or "Record of the Transmission of the Lamp," by Taoyüan in about 1004. For one of the main objects of this work was to establish a proper "apostolic succession" for the Zen tradition, so that no one could claim authority unless his *satori* had been approved by someone who had been approved . . . right back to the time of the Buddha himself.

Nothing, however, is more difficult than establishing proper qualifications in the imponderable realm of spiritual insight. Where the candidates are few the problem is not so grave, but where one master is responsible for some hundreds of students the process of teaching and testing requires standardization. Zen solved this problem with remarkable ingenuity, employing a means which not only provided a test of competence but–what was much more–a means of transmitting the Zen experience itself with a minimum of falsification.

This extraordinary invention was the system of the *kung-an* ᵉᵉ (Japanese, *koan*) or "Zen problem." Literally, this term means a "public document" or "case" in the sense of a decision creating a legal precedent. Thus the *koan* system involves "passing" a series of tests based on the *mondo* or anecdotes of the old masters. One of the beginning *koans* is Chao-chou's answer *"Wu"* or "No" to the question as to whether a dog has Buddha nature. The student is expected to show that he has experienced the meaning of the *koan* by a specific and usually nonverbal demonstration which he has to discover intuitively.[42]

The period of prosperity which came with the tenth and eleventh centuries was attended by a sense of "loss of spirit," which in turn gave rise to much study of the great T'ang masters. Their anecdotes were subsequently collected in such anthologies as the *Pi-yen Lu* (1125) and the *Wu-men kuan* (1229). The use of these anecdotes for the *koan* method was originated by Yüan-wu (1063–1135) and his disciple Ta-hui (1089–1163), in

[42] For a fuller description see below, p. 159. In its Japanese form *Koan*, the syllables are pronounced separately–*Ko-an*.

the tenth or eleventh generation of descent from Lin-chi. However, something which already began to resemble it was employed by Huang-lung (1002–1069) in order to cope with his particularly large following. He devised three test-questions known as "Huang-lung's Three Barriers"–

> *Question:* Everybody has a place of birth. Where is your place of birth?
> *Answer:* Early this morning I ate white rice gruel. Now I'm hungry again.
>
> *Question:* How is my hand like the Buddha's hand?
> *Answer:* Playing the lute under the moon.
>
> *Question:* How is my foot like a donkey's foot?
> *Answer:* When the white heron stands in the snow it has a different color.[43]

No doubt the answers given were the original replies to the questions, but later the problem becomes both the question and its answer, for the student is expected to see into the relationship between the two, which, to say the least, is none too obvious. For the moment, it is enough to say that every *koan* has a "point" which is some aspect of Zen experience, that its point is often concealed by being made very much more apparent than one would expect, and that *koans* are concerned not only with the primary awakening to the Void but also with its subsequent expression in life and thought.

The *koan* system was developed in the Lin-chi (Rinzai) School of Zen, but not without opposition. The Soto School felt that it was much too artificial. Whereas the *koan* advocates used this technique as a means for encouraging that overwhelming "feeling of doubt" (*i ching* [ff]) which they felt to be essential as a prerequisite for *satori,* the Soto School argued that it lent itself too easily to that very seeking for *satori* which thrusts it away, or –what is worse–induces an artificial *satori.* Adherents of the Rinzai School sometimes say that the intensity of the *satori* is

---

[43] *Jen-t'ien Yen-mu,* 2.

proportionate to the intensity of the feeling of doubt, of blind seeking, which precedes it, but for Soto this suggests that such a *satori* has a dualistic character, and is thus no more than an artificial emotional reaction. Thus the Soto view was that proper *dhyana* lay in motiveless action (*wu-wei*), in "sitting just to sit," or "walking just to walk." The two schools therefore came to be known respectively as *k'an-hua* Zen (observing the anecdote Zen) and *mo-chao* Zen (silently illumined Zen).

The Rinzai School of Zen was introduced into Japan in 1191 by the Japanese T'ien-t'ai monk Eisai (1141–1215), who established monasteries at Kyoto and Kamakura under imperial patronage. The Soto School was introduced in 1227 by the extraordinary genius Dogen (1200–1253), who established the great monastery of Eiheiji, refusing, however, to accept imperial favors. It should be noted that Zen arrived in Japan shortly after the beginning of the Kamakura Era, when the military dictator Yoritomo and his *samurai* followers had seized power from the hands of the then somewhat decadent nobility. This historical coincidence provided the military class, the *samurai*, with a type of Buddhism which appealed to them strongly because of its practical and earthy qualities and because of the directness and simplicity of its approach. Thus there arose that peculiar way of life called *bushido*, the Tao of the warrior, which is essentially the application of Zen to the arts of war. The association of the peace-loving doctrine of the Buddha with the military arts has always been a puzzle to Buddhists of other schools. It seems to involve the complete divorce of awakening from morality. But one must face the fact that, in its essence, the Buddhist experience is a liberation from conventions of every kind, including the moral conventions. On the other hand, Buddhism is not a revolt against convention, and in societies where the military caste is an integral part of the conventional structure and the warrior's role an accepted necessity Buddhism will make it possible for him to fulfill that role as a Buddhist. The medieval cult of chivalry should be no less of a puzzle to the peace-loving Christian.

The contribution of Zen to Japanese culture has by no means been confined to *bushido*. It has entered into almost every aspect of the people's life–their architecture, poetry, painting, gardening, their athletics, crafts, and trades; it has penetrated the everyday language and thought of the most ordinary folk. For by the genius of such Zen monks as Dogen, Hakuin, and Bankei, by such poets as Ryokan and Basho, and by such a painter as Sesshu, Zen has been made extraordinarily accessible to the common mind.

Dogen, in particular, made an incalculable contribution to his native land. His immense work, the *Shobogenzo* ("Treasury of the Eye of the True Doctrine"), was written in the vernacular and covered every aspect of Buddhism from its formal discipline to its profoundest insights. His doctrine of time, change, and relativity is explained with the aid of the most provoking poetic images, and it is only regrettable that no one has yet had the time and talent to translate this work into English. Hakuin (1685–1768) reconstituted the *koan* system, and is said to have trained no less than eighty successors in Zen. Bankei (1622–1693) found a way of presenting Zen with such ease and simplicity that it seemed almost too good to be true. He spoke to large audiences of farmers and country folk, but no one "important" seems to have dared to follow him.[44]

Meanwhile, Zen continued to prosper in China until well into the Ming dynasty (1368–1643), when the divisions between the various schools of Buddhism began to fade, and the popularity of the Pure Land School with its "easy way" of invoking the Name of Amitabha began to be fused with *koan* practice and at last to absorb it. A few Zen communities seem to have survived to the present day, but, so far as I have been able to study

[44] Because my purpose is only to give enough of the history of Zen to serve as a background for its doctrine and practice, I am not entering into any full discussion of its history in Japan. The work of Dogen, Hakuin, Bankei, and others will be discussed in another context.

them, their emphasis inclines either to Soto or to the more "occultist" preoccupations of Tibetan Buddhism. In either case, their view of Zen seems to be involved with a somewhat complex and questionable doctrine of man's psychic anatomy, which would appear to derive from Taoist alchemical ideas.[45]

The history of Chinese Zen raises one problem of great fascination. Both Rinzai and Soto Zen as we find them in Japanese monasteries today put enormous emphasis on za-zen or sitting meditation, a practice which they follow for many hours of the day–attaching great importance to the correctness of posture and the way of breathing which it involves. To practice Zen is, to all intents and purposes, to practice za-zen, to which the Rinzai School adds sanzen, the periodic visits to the master (roshi) for presenting one's view of the koan. However, the Shen-hui Ho-chang I-chi records the following conversation between Shen-hui and a certain Ch'eng:

The Master asked Dhyana Master Ch'eng: "What method must be practiced to see into one's own nature?"

"It is first of all necessary to apply oneself to the practice of sitting cross-legged in samadhi. Once samadhi is obtained, one must, by means of samadhi, awaken prajna in oneself. By prajna one is able to see into one's own nature."

(Shen-hui:) "When one practices samadhi, isn't this a deliberate activity of the mind?"

(Ch'eng:) "Yes."

(Shen-hui:) "Then this deliberate activity of the mind is an activity of restricted consciousness, and how can it bring seeing into one's own nature?"

(Ch'eng:) "To see into one's own nature, it is necessary to practice samadhi. How could one see it otherwise?"

(Shen-hui:) "All practice of samadhi is fundamentally a wrong view. How, by practicing samadhi, could one attain samadhi?" (1. 111)

[45] An example of this fusion may be seen in the *T'ai I Chin Hua Tsung Chih*, a treatise of the Ming or perhaps Ch'ing dynasty, for which see Wilhelm (1).

We have already mentioned the incident between Ma-tsu and Huai-jang, in which the latter compared sitting in meditation to polishing a tile for a mirror. On another occasion Huai-jang said:

> To train yourself in sitting meditation [*za-zen*] is to train yourself to be a sitting Buddha. If you train yourself in *za-zen*, (you should know that) Zen is neither sitting nor lying. If you train yourself to be a sitting Buddha, (you should know that) the Buddha is not a fixed form. Since the Dharma has no (fixed) abode, it is not a matter of making choices. If you (make yourself) a sitting Buddha this is precisely killing the Buddha. If you adhere to the sitting position, you will not attain the principle (of Zen).[46] *gg*

This seems to be the consistent doctrine of all the T'ang masters from Hui-neng to Lin-chi. Nowhere in their teachings have I been able to find any instruction in or recommendation of the type of *za-zen* which is today the principal occupation of Zen monks.[47] On the contrary, the practice is discussed time after time in the apparently negative fashion of the two quotations just cited.

It could be assumed that *za-zen* was so much the normal rule of the Zen monk's life that our sources do not bother to discuss it, and that their teachings are designed solely for advanced students who have so mastered *za-zen* that the time has come to go beyond it. This, however, does not agree too well with the references to the enormous clerical and lay audiences attending some of the discourses, since it would be somewhat fantastic to suppose that China was swarming with accomplished yogis. The discourses frequently begin by saying, in a rather brief and off-hand fashion, that these teachings are for those who are well

---

[46] *Ku-tsun-hsü Yü-lu*, 1. 1, p. 2.

[47] It is true that a text known as the *T'so-chan I*, or "Directions for Za-zen," is incorporated in the *Po-chang Ching-kuei*—the regulations for the Zen community attributed to Po-chang (720–814)—and that the regulations themselves prescribe times for meditation. However, we can find no edition of this work prior to 1265 (Suzuki), and it may even be as late as 1338 (Dumoulin). The existing version shows the influence of the Shingon sect, which is akin to Tibetan Lamaism and came to China during the eighth century.

Bodhidharma. By Hakuin Zenji (1683-1768).
Yamamoto Collection. *Photo courtesy of Oakland Art Museum.*

Two views of the rock and sand garden at Ryoanji, Kyoto.

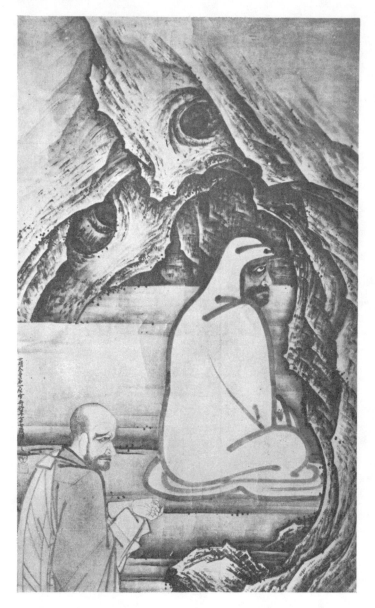

Bodhidharma and Hui-k'e. By Sesshu (1420-1506).

Haboku Landscape. By Sesshu (1420-1506). Tokyo Museum.

trained in the Buddhist virtues. But this could mean no more than that they are for mature people who have mastered the ordinary social and moral conventions, and are therefore not in danger of using Buddhism as a pretext for rebellion against the common decencies.

Alternatively, it could be assumed that the type of *za-zen* under criticism is *za-zen* practiced for a purpose, to "get" Buddhahood, instead of "sitting just to sit." This would concur with the Soto objection to the Rinzai School with its method of cultivating the state of "great doubt" by means of the *koan*. While the Soto is not quite fair to the Rinzai in this respect, this would certainly be a plausible interpretation of the early masters' doctrine. However, there are several references to the idea that prolonged sitting is not much better than being dead. There is, of course, a proper place for sitting—along with standing, walking, and lying—but to imagine that sitting contains some special virtue is "attachment to form." Thus in the *T'an-ching* Hui-neng says:

> *A living man who sits and does not lie down;*
> *A dead man who lies down and does not sit!*
> *After all these are just dirty skeletons.* (8) [hh]

Even in Japanese Zen one occasionally encounters a Zen practice which lays no special emphasis upon *za-zen*, but rather stresses the use of one's ordinary work as the means of meditation. This was certainly true of Bankei,[48] and this principle underlies the common use of such arts as "tea ceremony," flute playing, brush drawing, archery, fencing, and *ju-jutsu* as ways of practicing Zen. Perhaps, then, the exaggeration of *za-zen* in later times is part and parcel of the conversion of the Zen monastery into a boys' training school. To have them sit still for hours on end under the watchful eyes of monitors with sticks is certainly a sure method of keeping them out of mischief.

[48] See Suzuki (10), pp. 176–80.

Yet however much *za-zen* may have been exaggerated in the Far East, a certain amount of "sitting just to sit" might well be the best thing in the world for the jittery minds and agitated bodies of Europeans and Americans–provided they do not use it as a method for turning themselves into Buddhas.

PART TWO

PRINCIPLES AND PRACTICE

One

"Empty and Marvelous"

The opening words of the oldest Zen poem say that

> *The perfect Way [Tao] is without difficulty,*
> *Save that it avoids picking and choosing.*
> *Only when you stop liking and disliking*
> *Will all be clearly understood.*
> *A split hair's difference,*
> *And heaven and earth are set apart!*
> *If you want to get the plain truth,*
> *Be not concerned with right and wrong.*
> *The conflict between right and wrong*
> *Is the sickness of the mind.*[1] [a]

The point is not to make an effort to silence the feelings and cultivate bland indifference. It is to see through the universal illusion that what is pleasant or good may be wrested from what is painful or evil. It was a first principle in Taoism that

> *When everyone recognizes beauty as beautiful,*
> *   there is already ugliness;*
> *When everyone recognizes goodness as good,*
> *   there is already evil.*
> *"To be" and "not to be" arise mutually;*
> *Difficult and easy are mutually realized;*
> *Long and short are mutually contrasted;*
> *High and low are mutually posited; . . .*
> *Before and after are in mutual sequence.*[2]

To see this is to see that good without evil is like up without down, and that to make an ideal of pursuing the good is like try-

[1] Seng-ts'an, *Hsin-hsin Ming.*
[2] *Tao Te Ching,* 2.

115

ing to get rid of the left by turning constantly to the right. One is therefore compelled to go round in circles.[8]

The logic of this is so simple that one is tempted to think it over-simple. The temptation is all the stronger because it upsets the fondest illusion of the human mind, which is that in the course of time everything may be made better and better. For it is the general opinion that were this not possible the life of man would lack all meaning and incentive. The only alternative to a life of constant progress is felt to be a mere existence, static and dead, so joyless and inane that one might as well commit suicide. The very notion of this "only alternative" shows how firmly the mind is bound in a dualistic pattern, how hard it is to think in any other terms than good or bad, or a muddy mixture of the two.

Yet Zen is a liberation from this pattern, and its apparently dismal starting point is to understand the absurdity of choosing, of the whole feeling that life may be significantly improved by a constant selection of the "good." One must start by "getting the feel" of relativity, and by knowing that life is not a situation from which there is anything to be grasped or gained—as if it were something which one approaches from outside, like a pie or a barrel of beer. To succeed is always to fail—in the sense that the more one succeeds in anything, the greater is the need to go on succeeding. To eat is to survive to be hungry.

The illusion of significant improvement arises in moments of contrast, as when one turns from the left to the right on a hard bed. The position is "better" so long as the contrast remains, but before long the second position begins to feel like the first. So one acquires a more comfortable bed and, for a while, sleeps in peace. But the solution of the problem leaves a strange vacuum in one's consciousness, a vacuum soon filled by the sensation of another intolerable contrast, hitherto unnoticed, and just as urgent, just as frustrating as the problem of the hard bed. The vacuum arises

---

[8] Believe it or not, there is actually a politician in San Francisco who so detests the political Left Wing that he will not make a left turn with his car.

because the sensation of comfort can be maintained only in relation to the sensation of discomfort, just as an image is visible to
the eye only by reason of a contrasting background. The good
and the evil, the pleasant and the painful are so inseparable, so
identical in their difference–like the two sides of a coin–that

> *Fair is foul, and foul is fair,*

or, in the words of a poem in the *Zenrin Kushu:* [4]

> *To receive trouble is to receive good fortune;*
> *To receive agreement is to receive opposition.*[b]

Another puts it more vividly:

> *At dusk the cock announces dawn;*
> *At midnight, the bright sun.*[c]

Zen does not, for this reason, take the attitude that it is so
futile to eat when hungry that one may as well starve, nor is it so
inhuman as to say that when we itch we should not scratch.
Disillusionment with the pursuit of the good does not involve the
evil of stagnation as its necessary alternative, for the human situation is like that of "fleas on a hot griddle." None of the alternatives offer a solution, for the flea who falls must jump, and the
flea who jumps must fall. Choosing is absurd because there is no
choice.

To the dualistic mode of thought it will therefore seem that the
standpoint of Zen is that of fatalism as opposed to free choice.
When Mu-chou was asked, "We dress and eat every day, and
how do we escape from having to put on clothes and eat food?"
he answered, "We dress; we eat." "I don't understand," said the

---

[4] The *Zenrin Kushu* is an anthology of some five thousand two-line poems,
compiled by Toyo Eicho (1429–1504). Its purpose was to provide Zen
students with a source-book of verses from which to select couplets expressing the theme of a newly solved *koan.* Many masters require such a verse
as soon as the proper answer to the *koan* has been given. The couplets have
been drawn from a vast variety of Chinese sources–Buddhist, Taoist, classical literature, popular songs, etc.

monk. "If you don't understand, put on your clothes and eat your food." [5][d] On being asked how to escape from the "heat," another master directed the questioner to the place where it is neither hot nor cold. When asked to explain himself he replied, "In summer we sweat; in winter we shiver." Or, as a poem puts it:

When cold, we gather round the hearth before the blazing fire;
When hot, we sit on the bank of the mountain stream in the bamboo
grove.[6][e]

And from this point of view one can

See the sun in the midst of the rain;
Scoop clear water from the heart of the fire.[f]

But the viewpoint is not fatalistic. It is not simply submission to the inevitability of sweating when it is hot, shivering when it is cold, eating when hungry, and sleeping when tired. Submission to fate implies someone who submits, someone who is the helpless puppet of circumstances, and for Zen there is no such person. The duality of subject and object, of the knower and the known, is seen to be just as relative, as mutual, as inseparable as every other. We do not sweat *because* it is hot; the sweating is the heat. It is just as true to say that the sun is light because of the eyes as to say that the eyes see light because of the sun. The viewpoint is unfamiliar because it is our settled convention to think that heat comes first and then, by causality, the body sweats. To put it the other way round is startling, like saying "cheese and bread" instead of "bread and cheese." Thus the *Zenrin Kushu* says:

Fire does not wait for the sun to be hot,
Nor the wind for the moon, to be cool.

This shocking and seemingly illogical reversal of common sense may perhaps be clarified by the favorite Zen image of "the moon in the water." The phenomenon moon-in-the-water is likened to

[5]*Mu-chou Lu,* in *Ku-tsun-hsü Yü-lu,* 2. 6.
[6] *Zenrin Ruishu,* 2.

human experience. The water is the subject, and the moon the object. When there is no water, there is no moon-in-the-water, and likewise when there is no moon. But when the moon rises the water does not wait to receive its image, and when even the tiniest drop of water is poured out the moon does not wait to cast its reflection. For the moon does not intend to cast its reflection, and the water does not receive its image on purpose. The event is caused as much by the water as by the moon, and as the water manifests the brightness of the moon, the moon manifests the clarity of the water. Another poem in the *Zenrin Kushu* says:

> *Trees show the bodily form of the wind;*
> *Waves give vital energy to the moon.[9]*

To put it less poetically–human experience is determined as much by the nature of the mind and the structure of its senses as by the external objects whose presence the mind reveals. Men feel themselves to be victims or puppets of their experience because they separate "themselves" from their minds, thinking that the nature of the mind-body is something involuntarily thrust upon "them." They think that they did not ask to be born, did not ask to be "given" a sensitive organism to be frustrated by alternating pleasure and pain. But Zen asks us to find out "who" it is that "has" this mind, and "who" it was that did not ask to be born before father and mother conceived us. Thence it appears that the entire sense of subjective isolation, of being the one who was "given" a mind and to whom experience happens, is an illusion of bad semantics–the hypnotic suggestion of repeated wrong thinking. For there is no "myself" apart from the mind-body which gives structure to my experience. It is likewise ridiculous to talk of this mind-body as something which was passively and involuntarily "given" a certain structure. It *is* that structure, and before the structure arose there was no mind-body.

Our problem is that the power of thought enables us to construct symbols of things apart from the things themselves. This includes the ability to make a symbol, an idea of ourselves apart from ourselves. Because the idea is so much more comprehensible than the reality, the symbol so much more stable than the fact, we learn to identify ourselves with our idea of ourselves. Hence the subjective feeling of a "self" which "has" a mind, of an inwardly isolated subject to whom experiences involuntarily happen. With its characteristic emphasis on the concrete, Zen points out that our precious "self" is just an idea, useful and legitimate enough if seen for what it is, but disastrous if identified with our real nature. The unnatural awkwardness of a certain type of self-consciousness comes into being when we are aware of conflict or contrast between the idea of ourselves, on the one hand, and the immediate, concrete feeling of ourselves, on the other.

When we are no longer identified with the idea of ourselves, the entire relationship between subject and object, knower and known, undergoes a sudden and revolutionary change. It becomes a real relationship, a mutuality in which the subject creates the object just as much as the object creates the subject. The knower no longer feels himself to be independent of the known; the experiencer no longer feels himself to stand apart from the experience. Consequently the whole notion of getting something "out" of life, of seeking something "from" experience, becomes absurd. To put it in another way, it becomes vividly clear that in concrete fact I have no other self than the totality of things of which I am aware. This is the Hua-yen (Kegon) doctrine of the net of jewels, of *shih shih wu ai* (Japanese, *ji ji mu ge*), in which every jewel contains the reflection of all the others.

The sense of subjective isolation is also based on a failure to see the relativity of voluntary and involuntary events. This relativity is easily felt by watching one's breath, for by a slight change of viewpoint it is as easy to feel that "I breathe" as that "It breathes me." We feel that our actions are voluntary when they follow a decision, and involuntary when they happen without decision. But if decision itself were voluntary, every decision would have to be preceded by a decision to decide—an infinite regression which fortunately does not occur. Oddly enough, if we had to decide to decide, we would not be free to decide. We are free to decide because decision "happens." We just decide without having the faintest understanding of how we do it. In fact, it is neither voluntary nor involuntary. To "get the feel" of this relativity is to find another extraordinary transformation of our experience as a whole, which may be described in either of two ways. I feel that I am deciding everything that happens, or, I feel that everything, including my decisions, is just happening spontaneously. For a decision–the freest of my actions–just happens like hiccups inside me or like a bird singing outside me.

Such a way of seeing things is vividly described by a modern Zen master, the late Sokei-an Sasaki:

> One day I wiped out all the notions from my mind. I gave up all desire. I discarded all the words with which I thought and stayed in quietude. I felt a little queer–as if I were being carried into something, or as if I were touching some power unknown to me . . . and Ztt! I entered. I lost the boundary of my physical body. I had my skin, of course, but I felt I was standing in the center of the cosmos. I spoke, but my words had lost their meaning. I saw people coming towards me, but all were the same man. All were myself! I had never known this world. I had believed that I was created, but now I must change my opinion: I was never created; I was the cosmos; no individual Mr. Sasaki existed.[7]

It would seem, then, that to get rid of the subjective distinction between "me" and "my experience"–through seeing that my idea of myself is not myself–is to discover the actual relationship between myself and the "outside" world. The individual, on the one hand, and the world, on the other, are simply the abstract limits or terms of a concrete reality which is "between" them, as the concrete coin is "between" the abstract, Euclidean surfaces of its two sides. Similarly, the reality of all "inseparable opposites"–life and death, good and evil, pleasure and pain, gain and loss–is that "between" for which we have no words.

[7] "The Transcendental World," *Zen Notes*, vol. 1, no. 5. First Zen Institute of America. New York, 1954.

Man's identification with his idea of himself gives him a specious and precarious sense of permanence. For this idea is relatively fixed, being based upon carefully selected memories of his past, memories which have a preserved and fixed character. Social convention encourages the fixity of the idea because the very usefulness of symbols depends upon their stability. Convention therefore encourages him to associate his idea of himself with equally abstract and symbolic roles and stereotypes, since these will help him to form an idea of himself which will be definite and intelligible. But to the degree that he identifies himself with the fixed idea, he becomes aware of "life" as something which flows past him–faster and faster as he grows older, as his idea becomes more rigid, more bolstered with memories. The more he attempts to clutch the world, the more he feels it as a process in motion.

On one occasion Ma-tsu and Po-chang were out for a walk, when they saw some wild geese flying past.

"What are they?" asked Ma-tsu.

"They're wild geese," said Po-chang.

"Where are they going?" demanded Ma-tsu.

Po-chang replied, "They've already flown away."

Suddenly Ma-tsu grabbed Po-chang by the nose and twisted it so that he cried out in pain.

"How," shouted Ma-tsu, "could they ever have flown away?"

This was the moment of Po-chang's awakening.[8]

The relativity of time and motion is one of the principal themes of Dogen's Shobogenzo, where he writes:

> If we watch the shore while we are sailing in a boat, we feel that the shore is moving. But if we look nearer to the boat itself, we know then that it is the boat which moves. When we regard the universe in confusion of body and mind, we often get the mistaken belief that our mind is constant. But if we actually practice (Zen) and come back to ourselves, we see that this was wrong.
>
>   When firewood becomes ashes, it never returns to being firewood. But we should not take the view that what is latterly ashes was

8 *Pi-yen Chi.*

formerly firewood. What we should understand is that, according
to the doctrine of Buddhism, firewood stays at the position of firewood. . . . There are former and later stages, but these stages
are clearly cut.

It is the same with life and death. Thus we say in Buddhism
that the Un-born is also the Un-dying. Life is a position of time.
Death is a position of time. They are like winter and spring, and
in Buddhism we do not consider that winter *becomes* spring, or
that spring *becomes* summer.[9]

Dogen is here trying to express the strange sense of timeless
moments which arises when one is no longer trying to resist the
flow of events, the peculiar stillness and self-sufficiency of the
succeeding instants when the mind is, as it were, going along
with them and not trying to arrest them. A similar view is expressed thus by Ma-tsu:

A *sutra* says, "It is only a group of elements which come together
to make this body." When it arises, only these elements arise. When
it ceases, only these elements cease. But when these elements arise,
do not say, "I am arising," and when they cease, do not say, "I
am ceasing." So, too, with our former thoughts, later thoughts, and
intervening thoughts (or, experiences): the thoughts follow one
another without being linked together. Each one is absolutely
tranquil.[10] [h]

Buddhism has frequently compared the course of time to the
apparent motion of a wave, wherein the actual water only moves
up and down, creating the illusion of a "piece" of water moving
over the surface. It is a similar illusion that there is a constant
"self" moving through successive experiences, constituting a link
between them in such a way that the youth becomes the man
who becomes the graybeard who becomes the corpse.

Connected, then, with the pursuit of the good is the pursuit of
the future, the illusion whereby we are unable to be happy without a "promising future" for the symbolic self. Progress towards

[9] *Shobogenzo*, fasc. 1. For this translation I am indebted to my colleague
Professor Sabro Hasegawa.
[10] *Ku-tsun-hsü Yü-lu*, 1. 2. 4.

the good is therefore measured in terms of the prolongation of human life, forgetting that nothing is more relative than our sense of the length of time. A Zen poem says:

> *The morning glory which blooms for an hour*
> *Differs not at heart from the giant pine,*
> *Which lives for a thousand years.*

Subjectively, a gnat doubtless feels that its span of a few days is a reasonably long lifetime. A tortoise, with its span of several hundred years, would feel subjectively the same as the gnat. Not so long ago the life expectancy of the average man was about forty-five years. Today it is from sixty-five to seventy years, but subjectively the years are faster, and death, when it comes, is always all too soon. As Dogen said:

> *The flowers depart when we hate to lose them;*
> *The weeds arrive while we hate to watch them grow.*

This is perfectly natural, perfectly human, and no pulling and stretching of time will make it otherwise.

On the contrary, the measuring of worth and success in terms of time, and the insistent demand for assurances of a promising future, make it impossible to live freely both in the present and in the "promising" future when it arrives. For there is never anything but the present, and if one cannot live there, one cannot live anywhere. The *Shobogenzo* says:

When a fish swims, he swims on and on, and there is no end to the water. When a bird flies, he flies on and on, and there is no end to the sky. From the most ancient times there was never a fish who swam out of the water, nor a bird who flew out of the sky. Yet when the fish needs just a little water, he uses just a little; and when he needs lots, he uses lots. Thus the tips of their heads are always at the outer edge (of their space). If ever a bird flies beyond that edge, he dies, and so also with the fish. From the water the fish makes his life, and from the sky, the bird. But this life is made by the bird and the fish. At the same time, the bird and the fish are made by life. Thus there are the fish, the water, and life, and all three create each other.

Yet if there were a bird who first wanted to examine the size of the sky, or a fish who first wanted to examine the extent of the water—and then try to fly or to swim, they will never find their own ways in the sky or water.[11]

This is not a philosophy of not looking where one is going; it is a philosophy of not making where one is going so much more important than where one is that there will be no point in going.

The life of Zen begins, therefore, in a disillusion with the pursuit of goals which do not really exist—the good without the bad, the gratification of a self which is no more than an idea, and the morrow which never comes. For all these things are a deception of symbols pretending to be realities, and to seek after them is like walking straight into a wall upon which some painter has, by the convention of perspective, suggested an open passage. In short, Zen *begins* at the point where there is nothing further to seek, nothing to be gained. Zen is most emphatically not to be regarded as a system of self-improvement, or a way of becoming a Buddha. In the words of Lin-chi, "If a man seeks the Buddha, that man loses the Buddha."

For all ideas of self-improvement and of becoming or getting something in the future relate solely to our abstract image of ourselves. To follow them is to give ever more reality to that image. On the other hand, our true, nonconceptual self is already the Buddha, and needs no improvement. In the course of time it may grow, but one does not blame an egg for not being a chicken; still less does one criticize a pig for having a shorter neck than a giraffe. A *Zenrin* poem says:

In the landscape of spring there is neither high nor low;
The flowering branches grow naturally, some long, some short.[4]

When Ts'ui-wei was asked about the meaning of Buddhism, he answered: "Wait until there is no one around, and I will tell you." Some time later the monk approached him again, saying: "There is nobody here now. Please answer me." Ts'ui-wei led him out

[11] *Shobogenzo*, fasc. 1. Read to the author by Sabro Hasegawa.

into the garden and went over to the bamboo grove, saying nothing. Still the monk did not understand, so at last Ts'ui-wei said: "Here is a tall bamboo; there is a short one!" [12] Or, as another *Zenrin* verse puts it:

> A long thing is the long Body of Buddha;
> A short thing is the short Body of Buddha.[j]

What is therefore to be gained from Zen is called *wu-shih* (Japanese, *buji*) or "nothing special," for as the Buddha says in the *Vajracchedika:*

I obtained not the least thing from unexcelled, complete awakening, and for this very reason it is called "unexcelled, complete awakening." (22)

The expression *wu-shih* also has the sense of the perfectly natural and unaffected, in which there is no "fuss" or "business." The attainment of *satori* is often suggested by the old Chinese poem:

> Mount Lu in misty rain; the River Che at high tide.
> When I had not been there, no rest from the pain of longing!
> I went there and returned. . . . It was nothing special:
> Mount Lu in misty rain; the River Che at high tide.

According to the famous saying of Ch'ing-yüan:

Before I had studied Zen for thirty years, I saw mountains as mountains, and waters as waters. When I arrived at a more intimate knowledge, I came to the point where I saw that mountains are not mountains, and waters are not waters. But now that I have got its very substance I am at rest. For it's just that I see mountains once again as mountains, and waters once again as waters.[13] [k]

The difficulty of Zen is, of course, to shift one's attention from the abstract to the concrete, from the symbolic self to one's true nature. So long as we merely talk about it, so long as we turn over ideas in our minds about "symbol" and "reality," or keep repeating, "I am not my idea of myself," this is still mere abstrac-

[12] *Ch'uan Teng Lu,* 15.
[13] *Ch'uan Teng Lu,* 22.

tion. Zen created the method (*upaya*) of "direct pointing" in order to escape from this vicious circle, in order to thrust the real immediately to our notice. When reading a difficult book it is of no help to think, "I *should* concentrate," for one thinks about concentration instead of what the book has to say. Likewise, in studying or practicing Zen it is of no help to think about Zen. To remain caught up in ideas and words about Zen is, as the old masters say, to "stink of Zen."

For this reason the masters talk about Zen as little as possible, and throw its concrete reality straight at us. This reality is the "suchness" (*tathata*) of our natural, nonverbal world. If we see this just as it is, there is nothing good, nothing bad, nothing inherently long or short, nothing subjective and nothing objective. There is no symbolic self to be forgotten, and no need for any idea of a concrete reality to be remembered.

A monk asked Chao-chou, "For what reason did the First Patriarch come from the West?" (This is a formal question, asking for the central point of Bodhidharma's teaching, i.e., of Zen itself.)

Chao-chou answered: "The cypress tree in the yard."

"Aren't you trying," said the monk, "to demonstrate it by means of an objective reality?"

"I *am* not!" retorted the master.

"For what reason, then, did the First Patriarch come from the West?"

"The cypress tree in the yard!" [14]

Notice how Chao-chou whips the monk out of his conceptualization about the answer. When T'ung-shan was asked, "What is the Buddha?" he answered, "Three pounds of flax!" Upon this Yüan-wu comments:

Various answers have been given by different masters to the question, "What is the Buddha?" . . . None, however, can excel T'ung-shan's "three pounds (*chin*) of flax" as regards its irrationality which cuts off all passage of speculation. Some comment that

[14] *Chao-chou Lu* in *Ku-tsun-hsü Yü-lu*, 3. 13.

T'ung-shan was weighing flax at the moment, hence the answer.
. . . Still others think that as the questioner was not conscious of
the fact that he himself was the Buddha, T'ung-shan answered him
in this indirect way. Such are all like corpses, for they are utterly
unable to comprehend the living truth. There are still others who
take the "three pounds of flax" as the Buddha. What wild and
fantastic remarks they make! [15]

The masters are resolute in cutting short all theorizing and
speculation about these answers. "Direct pointing" entirely fails
in its intention if it requires or stimulates any conceptual
comment.

Fa-yen asked the monk Hsüan-tzu why he had never asked him
any questions about Zen. The monk explained that he had already attained his understanding from another master. Pressed
by Fa-yen for an explanation, the monk said that when he had
asked his teacher, "What is the Buddha?" he had received the
answer, "Ping-ting T'ung-tzu comes for fire!"

"A good answer!" said Fa-yen. "But I'm sure you don't understand it."

"Ping-ting," explained the monk, "is the god of fire. For him to
be seeking for fire is like myself, seeking the Buddha. I'm the
Buddha already, and no asking is needed."

"Just as I thought!" laughed Fa-yen. "You didn't get it."

The monk was so offended that he left the monastery, but
later repented of himself and returned, humbly requesting instruction.

"You ask me," said Fa-yen.

"What is the Buddha?" inquired the monk.

"Ping-ting T'ung-tzu comes for fire!" [16]

The point of this *mondo* is perhaps best indicated by two
poems submitted by the Pure Land Buddhist Ippen Shonin to the
Zen master Hoto, translated by Suzuki from the *Sayings of Ippen*.
Ippen was one of those who studied Zen to find a *rapprochement*

[15] *Pi-yen Chi*, 12, in Suzuki (1), vol. 2, pp. 71–72.
[16] *Ch'uan Teng Lu*, 25.

between Zen and the Pure Land School, with its practice of repeating the Name of Amitabha. In Japanese, the formula is *"Namu Amida Butsu!"* Ippen first presented this verse:

> When the Name is uttered,
> Neither the Buddha nor the self
> There is:
> Na-mu-a-mi-da-bu-tsu–
> The voice alone is heard.

Hoto, however, felt that this did not quite express the point, but gave his approval when Ippen submitted a second verse:

> When the Name is uttered,
> Neither the Buddha nor the self
> There is:
> Na-mu-a-mi-da-bu-tsu,
> Na-mu-a-mi-da-bu-tsu! [17]

Po-chang had so many students that he had to open a second monastery. To find a suitable person as its master, he called his monks together and set a pitcher before them, saying:

"Without calling it a pitcher, tell me what it is."

The head monk said, "You couldn't call it a piece of wood."

At this the monastery cook kicked the pitcher over and walked away. The cook was put in charge of the new monastery.[18] One of Nan-ch'üan's lectures is worth quoting here:

During the period (*kalpa*) before the world was manifested there were no names. The moment the Buddha arrives in the world there are names, and so we clutch hold of forms. In the great Tao there is absolutely nothing secular or sacred. If there are names, everything is classified in limits and bounds. Therefore the old man West of the River (i.e., Ma-tsu) said: "It is not mind; it is not Buddha; it is not a thing." [19] *l*

This, of course, reflects the doctrine of the *Tao Te Ching* that

[17] Suzuki (1), vol. 2, p. 263.
[18] *Wu-men kuan*, 40. However, as Wu-men comments, he fell right into Po-chang's trap, because he exchanged an easy job for a difficult one!
[19] *Nan-ch'üan Yü-lu* in *Ku-tsun-hsü Yü-lu*, 3. 12.

The nameless is the origin of heaven and earth;
Naming is the mother of the ten thousand things. (1)

But Lao-tzu's "nameless" and Nan-ch'üan's "*kalpa* of the void" before the manifestation of the world are not prior to the conventional world of things in time. They are the "suchness" of the world just as it is now, and to which the Zen masters are directly pointing. Po-chang's cook was living wide awake in that world, and answered the master's problem in its concrete and nameless terms.

A monk asked Ts'ui-wei, "For what reason did the First Patriarch come from the West?"

Ts'ui-wei answered, "Pass me that chin-rest."

As soon as the monk passed it, Ts'ui-wei hit him with it.[20]

Another master was having tea with two of his students when he suddenly tossed his fan to one of them, saying, "What's this?" The student opened it and fanned himself. "Not bad," was his comment. "Now you," he went on, passing it to the other student, who at once closed the fan and scratched his neck with it. This done, he opened it again, placed a piece of cake on it, and offered it to the master. This was considered even better, for when there are no names the world is no longer "classified in limits and bounds."

There is, no doubt, some parallel between these demonstrations and the viewpoint of Korzybskian semantics. There is the same stress on the importance of avoiding confusion between words and signs, on the one hand, and the infinitely variable "unspeakable" world, on the other. Class demonstrations of semantic principles often resemble types of *mondo*. Professor Irving Lee, of Northwestern University, used to hold up a matchbox before his class, asking "What's this?" The students would usually drop squarely into the trap and say, "A matchbox!" At this Professor Lee would say, "No, no! It's *this*–" throwing the matchbox at the class, and adding, "*Matchbox* is a noise. Is *this* a noise?"

However, it would seem that Korzybski still thought of the

[20] *Pi-yen Lu*, 20. The chin-rest is the *ch'an-pan*, a board for supporting the chin during long meditation.

"unspeakable" world as a multiplicity of infinitely differentiated events. For Zen, the world of "suchness" is neither one nor many, neither uniform nor differentiated. A Zen master might hold up his hand—to someone insisting that there are real differences in the world—and say, "Without saying a word, point to the difference between my fingers." At once it is clear that "sameness" and "difference" are abstractions. The same would have to be said of all categorizations of the concrete world—even "concrete" itself —for such terms as "physical," "material," "objective," "real," and "existential" are extremely abstract symbols. Indeed, the more one tries to define them, the more meaningless they turn out to be.

The world of "suchness" is void and empty because it teases the mind out of thought, dumfounding the chatter of definition so that there is nothing left to be said. Yet it is obvious that we are not confronted with literal nothingness. It is true that, when pressed, every attempt to catch hold of our world leaves us empty-handed. Furthermore, when we try to be sure at least of ourselves, the knowing, catching subjects, we disappear. We cannot find any self apart from the mind, and we cannot find any mind apart from those very experiences which the mind—now vanished—was trying to grasp. In R. H. Blyth's arresting metaphor, when we were just about to swat the fly, the fly flew up and sat on the swatter. In terms of immediate perception, when we look for things there is nothing but mind, and when we look for mind there is nothing but things. For a moment we are paralyzed, because it seems that we have no basis for action, no ground under foot from which to take a jump. But this is the way it always was, and in the next moment we find ourselves as free to act, speak, and think as ever, yet in a strange and miraculous new world from which "self" and "other," "mind" and "things" have vanished. In the words of Te-shan:

> Only when you have no thing in your mind and no mind in things are you vacant and spiritual, empty and marvelous.[21] m

[21] *Lien-teng Hui-yao*, 22. This is Ruth Sasaki's elegant translation in Dumoulin and Sasaki (1), p. 48, where she points out that in this context "spiritual" connotes a state beyond expression in words.

The marvel can only be described as the peculiar sensation of freedom in action which arises when the world is no longer felt to be some sort of obstacle standing over against one. This is not freedom in the crude sense of "kicking over the traces" and behaving in wild caprice. It is the discovery of freedom in the most ordinary tasks, for when the sense of subjective isolation vanishes, the world is no longer felt as an intractable object.

Yün-men once said, "Our school lets you go any way you like. It kills and it brings to life–either way."

A monk then asked, "How does it kill?"

The master replied, "Winter goes and spring comes."

"How," asked the monk, "is it when winter goes and spring comes?"

The master said, "Shouldering a staff you wander this way and that, East or West, South or North, knocking at the wild stumps as you please." [22] *

The passing of the seasons is not passively suffered, but "happens" as freely as one wanders in the fields, knocking at old stumps with a stick. In the context of Christianity this might be interpreted as feeling that one has become omnipotent, that one is God, directing everything that happens. However, it must be remembered that in Taoist and Buddhist thought there is no conception of a God who deliberately and consciously governs the universe. Lao-tzu said of the Tao:

> To its accomplishments it lays no claim.
> It loves and nourishes all things,
> but does not lord it over them. (34)
> The Tao, without doing anything (wu-wei),
> leaves nothing undone. (37)

To use the imagery of a Tibetan poem, every action, every event comes of itself from the Void "as from the surface of a clear lake there leaps suddenly a fish." When this is seen to be as true of

[22] Yün-men Kuang-lu, in Ku-tsun-hsü Yü-lu, 4. 16.

the deliberate and the routine as of the surprising and the unforeseen, one can agree with the Zen poet P'ang-yun:

> *Miraculous power and marvelous activity—*
> *Drawing water and hewing wood!* [23] o

[23] *Ch'uan Teng Lu*, 8.

"SITTING QUIETLY, DOING NOTHING"

In both life and art the cultures of the Far East appreciate nothing more highly than spontaneity or naturalness (*tzu-jan*). This is the unmistakable tone of sincerity marking the action which is not studied and contrived. For a man rings like a cracked bell when he thinks and acts with a split mind—one part standing aside to interfere with the other, to control, to condemn, or to admire. But the mind, or the true nature, of man cannot actually be split. According to a *Zenrin* poem, it is

> *Like a sword that cuts, but cannot cut itself;*
> *Like an eye that sees, but cannot see itself.*[a]

The illusion of the split comes from the mind's attempt to be both itself and its idea of itself, from a fatal confusion of fact with symbol. To make an end of the illusion, the mind must stop trying to act upon itself, upon its stream of experiences, from the standpoint of the idea of itself which we call the ego. This is expressed in another *Zenrin* poem as

> *Sitting quietly, doing nothing,*
> *Spring comes, and the grass grows by itself.*[b]

This "by itself" is the mind's and the world's natural way of action, as when the eyes see by themselves, and the ears hear by themselves, and the mouth opens by itself without having to be forced apart by the fingers. As the *Zenrin* says again:

> *The blue mountains are of themselves blue mountains;*
> *The white clouds are of themselves white clouds.*[c]

In its stress upon naturalness, Zen is obviously the inheritor of Taoism, and its view of spontaneous action as "marvelous activity" (*miao-yung* [d]) is precisely what the Taoists meant by the word *te*—"virtue" with an overtone of magical power. But neither in Taoism nor in Zen does it have anything to do with magic in the merely sensational sense of performing superhuman "miracles." The "magical" or "marvelous" quality of spontaneous action is, on the contrary, that it is perfectly human, and yet shows no sign of being contrived.

Such a quality is peculiarly subtle (another meaning of *miao*), and extremely hard to put into words. The story is told of a Zen monk who wept upon hearing of the death of a close relative. When one of his fellow students objected that it was most unseemly for a monk to show such personal attachment he replied, "Don't be stupid! I'm weeping because I want to weep." The great Hakuin was deeply disturbed in his early study of Zen when he came across the story of the master Yen-t'ou, who was said to have screamed at the top of his voice when murdered by a robber.[1] Yet this doubt was dissolved at the moment of his *satori*, and in Zen circles his own death is felt to have been especially admirable for its display of human emotion. On the other hand, the abbot Kwaisen and his monks allowed themselves to be burned alive by the soldiers of Oda Nobunaga, sitting calmly in the posture of meditation. Such contradictory "naturalness" seems most mysterious, but perhaps the clue lies in the saying of Yün-men: "In walking, just walk. In sitting, just sit. Above all, don't wobble." For the essential quality of naturalness is the sincerity of the undivided mind which does not dither between alternatives. So when Yen-t'ou screamed, it was such a scream that it was heard for miles around.

But it would be quite wrong to suppose that this natural sincerity comes about by observing such a platitude as "Whatsoever thy hand findeth to do, do it with all thy might." When Yen-t'ou screamed, he was not screaming *in order* to be natural, nor did he first make up his mind to scream and then implement the decision with the full energy of his will. There is a total con-

[1] *Ch'uan Teng Lu*, 26.

tradiction in planned naturalness and intentional sincerity. This
is to overlay, not to discover, the "original mind." Thus to try
to be natural is an affectation. To try not to try to be natural is
also an affectation. As a *Zenrin* poem says:

> *You cannot get it by taking thought;*
> *You cannot seek it by not taking thought.*[e]

But this absurdly complex and frustrating predicament arises
from a simple and elementary mistake in the use of the mind.
When this is understood, there is no paradox and no difficulty.
Obviously, the mistake arises in the attempt to split the mind
against itself, but to understand this clearly we have to enter
more deeply into the "cybernetics" of the mind, the basic pattern
of its self-correcting action.

It is, of course, part of the very genius of the human mind
that it can, as it were, stand aside from life and reflect upon it,
that it can be aware of its own existence, and that it can criticize
its own processes. For the mind has something resembling a
"feed-back" system. This is a term used in communications engi-
neering for one of the basic principles of "automation," of
enabling machines to control themselves. Feed-back enables a
machine to be informed of the effects of its own action in such
a way as to be able to correct its action. Perhaps the most familiar
example is the electrical thermostat which regulates the heating
of a house. By setting an upper and a lower limit of desired temperature, a thermometer is so connected that it will switch the
furnace on when the lower limit is reached, and off when the
upper limit is reached. The temperature of the house is thus kept
within the desired limits. The thermostat provides the furnace
with a kind of sensitive organ–an extremely rudimentary analogy
of human self-consciousness.[2]

---

[2] I do not wish to press the analogy between the human mind and servo-
mechanisms to the point of saying that the mind-body is "nothing but"
an extremely complicated mechanical automaton. I only want to go so
far as to show that feed-back involves some problems which are similar
to the problems of self-consciousness and self-control in man. Otherwise,

The proper adjustment of a feed-back system is always a complex mechanical problem. For the original machine, say, the furnace, is adjusted by the feed-back system, but this system in turn needs adjustment. Therefore to make a mechanical system more and more automatic will require the use of a series of feed-back systems—a second to correct the first, a third to correct the second, and so on. But there are obvious limits to such a series, for beyond a certain point the mechanism will be "frustrated" by its own complexity. For example, it might take so long for the information to pass through the series of control systems that it would arrive at the original machine too late to be useful. Similarly, when human beings think too carefully and minutely about an action to be taken, they cannot make up their minds in time to act. In other words, one cannot correct one's means of self-correction indefinitely. There must soon be a source of information at the end of the line which is the final authority. Failure to trust its authority will make it impossible to act, and the system will be paralyzed.

The system can be paralyzed in yet another way. Every feed-back system needs a margin of "lag" or error. If we try to make a thermostat absolutely accurate—that is, if we bring the upper and lower limits of temperature very close together in an attempt to hold the temperature at a constant 70 degrees—the whole system will break down. For to the extent that the upper and lower limits coincide, the signals for switching off and switching on will coincide! If 70 degrees is both the lower and upper limit the "go" sign will also be the "stop" sign; "yes" will imply "no" and "no" will imply "yes." Whereupon the mechanism will start "trembling," going on and off, on and off, until it shakes itself to pieces. The system is too sensitive and shows symptoms which are startlingly like human anxiety. For when a

mechanism and organism seem to me to be different in principle—that is, in their actual functioning—since the one is made and the other grown. The fact that one can translate some organic processes into mechanical terms no more implies that organism is mechanism than the translation of commerce into arithmetical terms implies that commerce *is* arithmetic.

human being is so self-conscious, so self-controlled that he cannot let go of himself, he dithers or wobbles between opposites. This is precisely what is meant in Zen by going round and round on "the wheel of birth-and-death," for the Buddhist *samsara* is the prototype of all vicious circles.[3]

Now human life consists primarily and originally in action—in living in the concrete world of "suchness." But we have the power to control action by reflection, that is, by thinking, by comparing the actual world with memories or "reflections." Memories are organized in terms of more or less abstract images—words, signs, simplified shapes, and other symbols which can be reviewed very rapidly one after another. From such memories, reflections, and symbols the mind constructs its idea of itself. This corresponds to the thermostat—the source of information about its own past action by which the system corrects itself. The mind-body must, of course, trust that information in order to act, for paralysis will soon result from trying to remember whether we have remembered everything accurately.

But to keep up the supply of information in the memory, the mind-body must continue to act "on its own." It must not cling too closely to its own record. There must be a "lag" or distance between the source of information and the source of action. This does *not* mean that the source of action must hesitate before it accepts the information. It means that it must not identify itself with the source of information. We saw that when the furnace responds too closely to the thermostat, it cannot go ahead without also trying to stop, or stop without also trying to go ahead. This is just what happens to the human being, to the mind, when the desire for certainty and security prompts identification between the mind and its own image of itself. It cannot let go of itself. It feels that it should not do what it is doing, and that it should do what it is not doing. It feels that it should not be what

[3] See the fascinating discussion of analogies between mechanical and logical contradictions and the psychoneuroses by Gregory Bateson in Reusch and Bateson, *Communication: the Social Matrix of Psychiatry,* esp. Chap. 8. (Norton; New York, 1950.)

it is, and be what it isn't. Furthermore, the effort to remain always "good" or "happy" is like trying to hold the thermostat to a constant 70 degrees by making the lower limit the same as the upper.

The identification of the mind with its own image is, therefore, paralyzing because the image is fixed–it is past and finished. But it is a fixed image of oneself in motion! To cling to it is thus to be in constant contradiction and conflict. Hence Yün-men's saying, "In walking, just walk. In sitting, just sit. Above all, don't wobble." In other words, the mind cannot act without giving up the impossible attempt to control itself beyond a certain point. It must let go of itself both in the sense of trusting its own memory and reflection, and in the sense of acting spontaneously, on its own into the unknown.

This is why Zen often seems to take the side of action as against reflection, and why it describes itself as "no-mind" (*wu-hsin*) or "no-thought" (*wu-nien*), and why the masters demonstrate Zen by giving instantaneous and unpremeditated answers to questions. When Yün-men was asked for the ultimate secret of Buddhism, he replied, "Dumpling!" In the words of the Japanese master Takuan:

> When a monk asks, "What is the Buddha?" the master may raise his fist; when he is asked, "What is the ultimate idea of Buddhism?" he may exclaim even before the questioner finishes his sentence, "A blossoming branch of the plum," or "The cypress-tree in the court-yard." The point is that the answering mind does not "stop" anywhere, but responds straightway without giving any thought to the felicity of an answer.[4]

This is allowing the mind to act on its own.

But reflection is also action, and Yün-men might also have said, "In acting, just act. In thinking, just think. Above all, don't wobble." In other words, if one is going to reflect, just reflect–but do not reflect about reflecting. Yet Zen would agree that reflection about reflection is also action–provided that in doing it we

[4] In Suzuki (7), p. 80.

do just that, and do not tend to drift off into the infinite regression of trying always to stand above or outside the level upon which we are acting. Thus Zen is also a liberation from the dualism of thought and action, for it thinks as it acts—with the same quality of abandon, commitment, or faith. The attitude of *wu-hsin* is by no means an anti-intellectualist exclusion of thinking. *Wu-hsin* is action on any level whatsoever, physical or psychic, without trying *at the same moment* to observe and check the action from outside. This attempt to act and think about the action simultaneously is precisely the identification of the mind with its idea of itself. It involves the same contradiction as the statement which states something about itself—"This statement is false."

The same is true of the relationship between feeling and action. For feeling blocks action, and blocks itself as a form of action, when it gets caught in this same tendency to observe or feel itself indefinitely—as when, in the midst of enjoying myself, I examine myself to see if I am getting the utmost out of the occasion. Not content with tasting the food, I am also trying to taste my tongue. Not content with feeling happy, I want to feel myself feeling happy—so as to be sure not to miss anything.

Whether trusting our memories or trusting the mind to act on its own, it comes to the same thing: ultimately we must act and think, live and die, from a source beyond all "our" knowledge and control. But this source is ourselves, and when we see that, it no longer stands over against us as a threatening object. No amount of care and hesitancy, no amount of introspection and searching of our motives, can make any ultimate difference to the fact that the mind is

Like an eye that sees, but cannot see itself.

In the end, the only alternative to a shuddering paralysis is to leap into action regardless of the consequences. Action in this spirit may be right or wrong with respect to conventional standards. But our decisions upon the conventional level must be supported by the conviction that whatever we do, and whatever "happens" to us, is ultimately "right." In other words, we must enter into it without "second thought," without the *arrière-pensée* of regret, hesitancy, doubt, or self-recrimination. Thus when Yün-men was asked, "What is the Tao?" he answered simply, "Walk on! (*ch'ü* [f])."

But to act "without second thought," without double-mindedness, is by no means a mere precept for our imitation. For we cannot realize this kind of action until it is clear beyond any shadow of doubt that it is actually impossible to do anything else. In the words of Huang-po:

> Men are afraid to forget their own minds, fearing to fall through the void with nothing on to which they can cling. They do not know that the void is not really the void but the real realm of the Dharma. . . . It cannot be looked for or sought, comprehended by wisdom or knowledge, explained in words, contacted materially (i.e., objectively) or reached by meritorious achievement. (14) [5]

Now this impossibility of "grasping the mind with the mind" is, when realized, the non-action (*wu-wei*), the "sitting quietly, doing nothing" whereby "spring comes, and the grass grows by itself." There is no necessity for the mind to try to let go of itself, or to try not to try. This introduces further artificialities. Yet, as a matter of psychological strategy, there is no need for trying to avoid artificialities. In the doctrine of the Japanese master Bankei (1622–1693) the mind which cannot grasp itself is called the "Unborn" (*fusho* [g]), the mind which does not arise or appear in the realm of symbolic knowledge.

> A layman asked, "I appreciate very much your instruction about the Unborn, but by force of habit second thoughts [*nien*] keep tending to arise, and being confused by them it is difficult to be in perfect accord with the Unborn. How am I to trust in it entirely?"
> Bankei said, "If you make an attempt to stop the second thoughts which arise, then the mind which does the stopping and the mind which is stopped become divided, and there is no occasion for

[5] In Chu Ch'an (1), p. 29.

peace of mind. So it is best for you simply to believe that originally there is no (possibility of control by) second thoughts. Yet because of karmic affinity, through what you see and what you hear these thoughts arise and vanish temporarily, but are without substance." (2)

"Brushing off thoughts which arise is just like washing off blood with blood. We remain impure because of being washed with blood, even when the blood that was first there has gone—and if we continue in this way the impurity never departs. This is from ignorance of the mind's unborn, unvanishing, and unconfused nature. If we take second thought for an effective reality, we keep going on and on around the wheel of birth-and-death. You should realize that such thought is just a temporary mental construction, and not try to hold or to reject it. Let it alone just as it occurs and just as it ceases. It is like an image reflected in a mirror. The mirror is clear and reflects anything which comes before it, and yet no image sticks in the mirror. The Buddha mind (i.e., the real, unborn mind) is ten thousand times more clear than a mirror, and more inexpressibly marvelous. In its light all such thoughts vanish without trace. If you put your faith in this way of understanding, however strongly such thoughts may arise, they do no harm." (4) [6]

This is also the doctrine of Huang-po, who says again:

If it is held that there is something to be realized or attained apart from mind, and, thereupon, mind is used to seek it, (that implies) failure to understand that mind and the object of its search are one. Mind cannot be used to seek something from mind for, even after the passage of millions of kalpas, the day of success would never come. (10) [7]

One must not forget the social context of Zen. It is primarily a way of liberation for those who have mastered the disciplines of social convention, of the conditioning of the individual by the group. Zen is a medicine for the ill effects of this conditioning, for the mental paralysis and anxiety which come from excessive self-consciousness. It must be seen against the background of

[6] Bankei's *Daiho Shogen Kokushi Hogo*. Japanese text edited by Furata and Suzuki. (Tokyo, 1943.) Translation read to the author by Professor Hasegawa.
[7] In Chu Ch'an (1), p. 24.

societies regulated by the principles of Confucianism, with their heavy stress on propriety and punctilious ritual. In Japan, too, it must be seen in relation to the rigid schooling required in the training of the *samurai* caste, and the emotional strain to which the *samurai* were exposed in times of constant warfare. As a medicine for these conditions, it does not seek to overthrow the conventions themselves, but, on the contrary, takes them for granted—as is easily seen in such manifestations of Zen as the *cha-no-yu* or "tea ceremony" of Japan. Therefore Zen might be a very dangerous medicine in a social context where convention is weak, or, at the other extreme, where there is a spirit of open revolt against convention ready to exploit Zen for destructive purposes.

With this in mind, we can observe the freedom and natural-ness of Zen without loss of perspective. Social conditioning fosters the identification of the mind with a fixed idea of itself as the means of self-control, and as a result man thinks of himself as "I"—the ego. Thereupon the mental center of gravity shifts from the spontaneous or original mind to the ego image. Once this has happened, the very center of our psychic life is identified with the self-controlling mechanism. It then becomes almost impossible to see how "I" can let go of "myself," for I am pre-cisely my habitual effort to hold on to myself. I find myself totally incapable of any mental action which is not intentional, affected, and insincere. Therefore anything I do to give myself up, to let go, will be a disguised form of the habitual effort to hold on. I cannot be intentionally unintentional or purposely spontaneous. As soon as it becomes important for me to be spontaneous, the intention to be so is strengthened; I cannot get rid of it, and yet it is the one thing that stands in the way of its own fulfillment. It is as if someone had given me some medicine with the warning that it will not work if I think of a monkey while taking it.

While I am remembering to forget the monkey, I am in a "double-bind" situation where "to do" is "not to do," and vice versa. "Yes" implies "no," and "go" implies "stop." At this point Zen comes to me and asks, "If you cannot help remembering the monkey, are you doing it on purpose?" In other words, do I have an intention for being intentional, a purpose for being purposive? Suddenly I realize that my very intending is spontaneous, or that my controlling self–the ego–arises from my uncontrolled or natural self. At this moment all the machinations of the ego come to nought; it is annihilated in its own trap. I see that it is actually impossible not to be spontaneous. For what I cannot help doing I am doing spontaneously, but if I am at the same time trying to control it, I interpret it as a compulsion. As a Zen master said, "Nothing is left to you at this moment but to have a good laugh."

In this moment the whole quality of consciousness is changed, and I feel myself in a new world in which, however, it is obvious that I have always been living. As soon as I recognize that my voluntary and purposeful action happens spontaneously "by itself," just like breathing, hearing, and feeling, I am no longer caught in the contradiction of trying to be spontaneous. There is no real contradiction, since "trying" is "spontaneity." Seeing this, the compulsive, blocked, and "tied-up" feeling vanishes. It is just as if I had been absorbed in a tug-of-war between my two hands, and had forgotten that both were mine. No block to spontaneity remains when the trying is seen to be needless. As we saw, the discovery that both the voluntary and involuntary aspects of the mind are alike spontaneous makes an immediate end of the fixed dualism between the mind and the world, the knower and the known. The new world in which I find myself has an extraordinary transparency or freedom from barriers, making it seem that I have somehow become the empty space in which everything is happening.

Here, then, is the point of the oft-repeated assertion that "all beings are in *nirvana* from the very beginning," that "all dualism is falsely imagined," that "the ordinary mind is the Tao" and that there is therefore no meaning in trying to get into accord with it. In the words of the *Cheng-tao Ke:*

> *Like the empty sky it has no boundaries,*
> *Yet it is right in this place, ever profound and clear.*
> *When you seek to know it, you cannot see it.*
> *You cannot take hold of it,*
> *But you cannot lose it.*
> *In not being able to get it, you get it.*
> *When you are silent, it speaks;*
> *When you speak, it is silent.*
> *The great gate is wide open to bestow alms,*
> *And no crowd is blocking the way.* (34)[h]

It was through seeing this that, in the moment of his *satori,* Hakuin cried out, "How wondrous! How wondrous! There is no birth-and-death from which one has to escape, nor is there any supreme knowledge after which one has to strive!" [8] Or in the words of Hsiang-yen:

> *At one stroke I forgot all my knowledge!*
> *There's no use for artificial discipline,*
> *For, move as I will, I manifest the ancient Way.*[9][i]

Paradoxically, nothing is more artificial than the notion of artificiality. Try as one may, it is as impossible to go against the spontaneous Tao as to live in some other time than now, or some other place than here. When a monk asked Bankei what he thought of disciplining oneself to attain *satori,* the master said, "*Satori* stands in contrast to confusion. Since each person is the substance of Buddha, (in reality) there is not one point of confusion. What, then, is one going to achieve by *satori?*" [10]

Seeing, then, that there is no possibility of departing from the Tao, one is like Hsüan-chüeh's "easygoing" man who

[8] *Orategama,* in Suzuki (1), vol. 1, p. 239.
[9] *Wu-teng Hui-yüan,* 9.
[10] *Bankei Kokushi Seppo.* Read to the author by Professor Hasegawa.

Neither avoids false thoughts nor seeks the true,
For ignorance is in reality the Buddha nature,
And this illusory, changeful, empty body is the Dharmakaya.[11]

One stops trying to be spontaneous by seeing that it is unnecessary to try, and then and there it can happen. The Zen masters often bring out this state by the device of evading a question and then, as the questioner turns to go, calling him suddenly by name. As he naturally replies, "Yes?" the master exclaims, "There it is!"

To the Western reader it may seem that all this is a kind of pantheism, an attempt to wipe out conflicts by asserting that "everything is God." But from the standpoint of Zen this is a long way short of true naturalness since it involves the use of the artificial concept—"everything is God" or "everything is the Tao." Zen annihilates this concept by showing that it is as unnecessary as every other. One does not realize the spontaneous life by depending on the repetition of thoughts or affirmations. One realizes it by seeing that no such devices are necessary. Zen describes all means and methods for realizing the Tao as "legs on a snake"—utterly irrelevant attachments.

To the logician it will of course seem that the point at which we have arrived is pure nonsense—as, in a way, it is. From the Buddhist point of view, reality itself has no meaning since it is not a sign, pointing to something beyond itself. To arrive at reality—at "suchness"—is to go beyond *karma*, beyond consequential action, and to enter a life which is completely aimless. Yet to Zen and Taoism alike this is the very life of the universe, which is complete at every moment and does not need to justify itself by aiming at something beyond. In the words of a *Zenrin* poem:

If you don't believe, just look at September, look at October!
The yellow leaves falling, falling, to fill both mountain and river.[j]

To see this is to be like the two friends of whom another *Zenrin* poem says:

[11] *Cheng-tao Ke, 1.*

Meeting, they laugh and laugh—
The forest grove, the many fallen leaves! ᵏ

To the Taoist mentality, the aimless, empty life does not suggest anything depressing. On the contrary, it suggests the freedom of clouds and mountain streams, wandering nowhere, of flowers in impenetrable canyons, beautiful for no one to see, and of the ocean surf forever washing the sand, to no end.

Furthermore, the Zen experience is more of a conclusion than a premise. It is never to be used as the first step in a line of ethical or metaphysical reasoning, since conclusions draw to it rather than from it. Like the Beatific Vision of Christianity, it is a "which than which there is no whicher"—the true end of man—not a thing to be used for some other end. Philosophers do not easily recognize that there is a point where thinking—like boiling an egg—must come to a stop. To try to formulate the Zen experience as a proposition—"everything is the Tao"—and then to analyze it and draw conclusions from it is to miss it completely. Like the Crucifixion, it is "to the Jews [the moralists] a stumblingblock and to the Greeks [the logicians] foolishness." To say that "everything is the Tao" almost gets the point, but just at the moment of getting it, the words crumble into nonsense. For we are here at a limit at which words break down because they always imply a meaning beyond themselves—and here there is no meaning beyond.

Zen does not make the mistake of using the experience "all things are of one Suchness" as the premise for an ethic of universal brotherhood. On the contrary, Yüan-wu says:

> If you are a real man, you may by all means drive off with the farmer's ox, or grab the food from a starving man.[12] ˡ

This is only to say that Zen lies beyond the ethical standpoint, whose sanctions must be found, not in reality itself, but in the mutual agreement of human beings. When we attempt to universalize or absolutize it, the ethical standpoint makes it im-

[12] Comment on *Pi-yen Lu*, 3.

possible to exist, for we cannot live for a day without destroying the life of some other creature.

If Zen is regarded as having the same function as a religion in the West, we shall naturally want to find some logical connection between its central experience and the improvement of human relations. But this is actually putting the cart before the horse. The point is rather that some such experience or way of life as this is the object of improved human relations. In the culture of the Far East the problems of human relations are the sphere of Confucianism rather than Zen, but since the Sung dynasty (959–1278) Zen has consistently fostered Confucianism and was the main source of the introduction of its principles into Japan. It saw their importance for creating the type of cultural matrix in which Zen could flourish without coming into conflict with social order, because the Confucian ethic is admittedly human and relative, not divine and absolute.

Although profoundly "inconsequential," the Zen experience has consequences in the sense that it may be applied in any direction, to any conceivable human activity, and that wherever it is so applied it lends an unmistakable quality to the work. The characteristic notes of the spontaneous life are *mo chih ch'u* [m] or "going ahead without hesitation," *wu-wei*, which may here be understood as purposelessness, and *wu-shih*, lack of affectation or simplicity.

While the Zen experience does not imply any specific course of action, since it has no purpose, no motivation, it turns unhesitatingly to anything that presents itself to be done. *Mo chih ch'u* is the mind functioning without blocks, without "wobbling" between alternatives, and much of Zen training consists in confronting the student with dilemmas which he is expected to handle without stopping to deliberate and "choose." The response to the situation must follow with the immediacy of sound issuing from the hands when they are clapped, or sparks from a flint when struck. The student unaccustomed to this type of response will at first be confused, but as he gains faith in his "original" or spontaneous mind he will not only respond with ease, but the responses themselves will acquire a startling appropriateness. This is something like the professional comedian's gift of unprepared wit which is equal to any situation.

The master may begin a conversation with the student by asking a series of very ordinary questions about trivial matters, to which the student responds with perfect spontaneity. But suddenly he will say, "When the bath-water flows down the drain, does it turn clockwise or counter-clockwise?" As the student stops at the unexpectedness of the question, and perhaps tries to remember which way it goes, the master shouts, "Don't think! Act! This way–" and whirls his hand in the air. Or, perhaps less helpfully, he may say, "So far you've answered my questions quite naturally and easily, but where's your difficulty now?"

The student, likewise, is free to challenge the master, and one can imagine that in the days when Zen training was less formal the members of Zen communities must have had enormous fun laying traps for each other. To some extent this type of relationship still exists, despite the great solemnity of the *sanzen* interview in which the *koan* is given and answered. The late Kozuki Roshi was entertaining two American monks at tea when he casually asked, "And what do you gentlemen know about Zen?" One of the monks flung his closed fan straight at the master's face. All in the same instant the master inclined his head slightly to one side, the fan shot straight through the paper *shoji* behind him, and he burst into a ripple of laughter.

Suzuki has translated a long letter from the Zen master Takuan on the relationship of Zen to the art of fencing, and this is certainly the best literary source of what Zen means by *mo chih ch'u*, by "going straight ahead without stopping." [13] Both Takuan and Bankei stressed the fact that the "original" or "unborn" mind is constantly working miracles even in the most ordinary person. Even though a tree has innumerable leaves, the mind takes them

[13] Suzuki (7), pp. 73–87. Excerpts from this letter also appear in Suzuki (1), vol. 3, pp. 318–19.

in all at once without being "stopped" by any one of them. Explaining this to a visiting monk, Bankei said, "To prove that your mind is the Buddha mind, notice how all that I say here goes into you without missing a single thing, even though I don't try to push it into you." [14] When heckled by an aggressive Nichiren monk who kept insisting that he couldn't understand a word, Bankei asked him to come closer. The monk stepped forward. "Closer still," said Bankei. The monk came forward again. "How well," said Bankei, "you understand me!" [15] In other words, our natural organism performs the most marvelously complex activities without the least hesitation or deliberation. Conscious thought is itself founded upon its whole system of spontaneous functioning, for which reason there is really no alternative to trusting oneself completely to its working. Oneself *is* its working.

Zen is not merely a cult of impulsive action. The point of *mo chih ch'u* is not to eliminate reflective thought but to eliminate "blocking" in both action and thought, so that the response of the mind is always like a ball in a mountain stream—"one thought after another without hesitation." There is something similar to this in the psychoanalytic practice of free association, employed as a technique to get rid of obstacles to the free flow of thought from the "unconscious." For there is a tendency to confuse "blocking"—a purely obstructive mechanism—with thinking out an answer, but the difference between the two is easily noticed in such a purely "thinking out" process as adding a column of figures. Many people find that at certain combinations of numbers, such as 8 and 5 or 7 and 6, a feeling of resistance comes up which halts the process. Because it is always annoying and disconcerting, one tends also to block at blocking, so that the state turns into the kind of wobbling dither characteristic of the snarled feed-back system. The simplest cure is to feel free to block, so that one does not block at blocking. When one feels

[14] *Bankei Kokushi Seppo.* Read to the author by Professor Hasegawa.
[15] In Suzuki (10), p. 123.

free to block, the blocking automatically eliminates itself. It is like riding a bicycle. When one starts falling to the left, one does not resist the fall (i.e., the block) by turning to the right. One turns the wheel to the left–and the balance is restored. The principle here is, of course, the same as getting out of the contradiction of "trying to be spontaneous" through accepting the "trying" as "spontaneous," through not resisting the block.

"Blocking" is perhaps the best translation of the Zen term *nien* [*] as it occurs in the phrase *wu-nien*, "no-thought" or, better, "no second thought." Takuan points out that this is the real meaning of "attachment" in Buddhism, as when it is said that a Buddha is free from worldly attachments. It does not mean that he is a "stone Buddha" with no feelings, no emotions, and no sensations of hunger or pain. It means that he does not block at anything. Thus it is typical of Zen that its style of action has the strongest feeling of commitment, of "follow-through." It enters into everything wholeheartedly and freely without having to keep an eye on itself. It does not confuse spirituality with thinking about God while one is peeling potatoes. Zen spirituality is just to peel the potatoes. In the words of Lin-chi:

> When it's time to get dressed, put on your clothes. When you must walk, then walk. When you must sit, then sit. Don't have a single thought in your mind about seeking for Buddhahood. . . . You talk about being perfectly disciplined in your six senses and in all your actions, but in my view all this is making *karma*. To seek the Buddha (nature) and to seek the Dharma is at once to make *karma* which leads to the hells. To seek (to be) Bodhisattvas is also making *karma*, and likewise studying the *sutras* and commentaries. Buddhas and Patriarchs are people without such artificialities. . . . It is said everywhere that there is a Tao which must be cultivated and a Dharma which must be realized. What Dharma do you say must be realized, and what Tao cultivated? What do you lack in the way you are functioning right now? What will you add to where you are? [16] [°]

As another *Zenrin* poem says:

[16] *Lin-chi Lu* in *Ku-tsun-hsü Yü-lu*, 1. 4. 6, 11–12, 12.

> *There's nothing equal to wearing clothes and eating food.*
> *Outside this there are neither Buddhas nor Patriarchs.*[p]

This is the quality of *wu-shih*, of naturalness without any contrivances or means for being natural, such as thoughts of Zen, of the Tao, or of the Buddha. One does not exclude such thoughts; they simply fall away when seen to be unnecessary. "He does not linger where the Buddha is, and where there is no Buddha he passes right on." [17]
For as the *Zenrin* says again:

> *To be conscious of the original mind, the original nature—*
> *Just this is the great disease of Zen!* [q]

As "the fish swims in the water but is unmindful of the water, the bird flies in the wind but knows not of the wind," so the true life of Zen has no need to "raise waves when no wind is blowing," to drag in religion or spirituality as something over and above life itself. This is why the sage Fa-yung received no more offerings of flowers from the birds after he had had his interview with the Fourth Patriarch, for his holiness no longer "stood out like a sore thumb." Of such a man the *Zenrin* says:

> *Entering the forest he moves not the grass;*
> *Entering the water he makes not a ripple.*[r]

No one notices him because he does not notice himself.

It is often said that to be clinging to oneself is like having a thorn in the skin, and that Buddhism is a second thorn to extract the first. When it is out, both thorns are thrown away. But in the moment when Buddhism, when philosophy or religion, becomes another way of clinging to oneself through seeking a spiritual security, the two thorns become one—and how is it to be taken out? This, as Bankei said, is "wiping off blood with blood." Therefore in Zen there is neither self nor Buddha to which one can cling, no good to gain and no evil to be avoided, no thoughts

---

[17] *Shih Niu T'u*, 8.

to be eradicated and no mind to be purified, no body to perish and no soul to be saved. At one blow this entire framework of abstractions is shattered to fragments. As the *Zenrin* says:

> *To save life it must be destroyed.*
> *When utterly destroyed, one dwells for the first time in peace.*[s]
>
> *One word settles heaven and earth;*
> *One sword levels the whole world.*[t]

Of this "one sword" Lin-chi said:

> If a man cultivates the Tao, the Tao will not work—on all sides evil conditions will head up competitively. But when the sword of wisdom [*prajna*] comes out there's not one thing left.[18] [u]

The "sword of *prajna*" which cuts away abstraction is that "direct pointing" whereby Zen avoids the entanglements of religiosity and goes straight to the heart. Thus when the Governor of Lang asked Yao-shan, "What is the Tao?" the master pointed upwards to the sky and downwards to a water jug beside him. Asked for an explanation, he replied: "A cloud in the sky and water in the jug."

[18] In *Ku-tsun-hsü Yü-lu*, 1. 4. 13.

Three

ZA-ZEN AND THE KOAN

There is a saying in Zen that "original realization is marvelous practice" (Japanese, *honsho myoshu* ª). The meaning is that no distinction is to be made between the realization of awakening (*satori*) and the cultivation of Zen in meditation and action. Whereas it might be supposed that the practice of Zen is a means to the end of awakening, this is not so. For the practice of Zen is not the true practice so long as it has an end in view, and when it has no end in view it is awakening–the aimless, self-sufficient life of the "eternal now." To practice with an end in view is to have one eye on the practice and the other on the end, which is lack of concentration, lack of sincerity. To put it in another way: one does not practice Zen to become a Buddha; one practices it because one is a Buddha from the beginning–and this "original realization" is the starting point of the Zen life. Original realization is the "body" (*t'i* ᵇ) and the marvelous practice the "use" (*yung* ᶜ), and the two correspond respectively to *prajna*, wisdom, and *karuna*, the compassionate activity of the awakened Bodhisattva in the world of birth-and-death.

In the two preceding chapters we discussed the original realization. In this and the one that follows we turn to the practice or activity which flows from it–firstly, to the life of meditation and, secondly, to the life of everyday work and recreation.

We have seen that–whatever may have been the practice of the T'ang masters–the modern Zen communities, both Soto and Rinzai, attach the highest importance to meditation or "sitting Zen" (*za-zen*). It may seem both strange and unreasonable that strong and intelligent men should simply sit still for hours on end. The Western mentality feels that such things are not only unnatural but a great waste of valuable time, however useful as

154

a discipline for inculcating patience and fortitude. Although the West has its own contemplative tradition in the Catholic Church, the life of "sitting and looking" has lost its appeal, for no religion is valued which does not "improve the world," and it is hard to see how the world can be improved by keeping still. Yet it should be obvious that action without wisdom, without clear awareness of the world as it really is, can never improve anything. Furthermore, as muddy water is best cleared by leaving it alone, it could be argued that those who sit quietly and do nothing are making one of the best possible contributions to a world in turmoil.

There is, indeed, nothing unnatural in long periods of quiet sitting. Cats do it; even dogs and other more nervous animals do it. So-called primitive peoples do it—American Indians, and peasants of almost all nations. The art is most difficult for those who have developed the sensitive intellect to such a point that they cannot help making predictions about the future, and so must be kept in a constant whirl of activity to forestall them. But it would seem that to be incapable of sitting and watching with the mind completely at rest is to be incapable of experiencing the world in which we live to the full. For one does not know the world simply in thinking about it and doing about it. One must first experience it more directly, and prolong the experience without jumping to conclusions.

The relevance of za-zen to Zen is obvious when it is remembered that Zen is seeing reality directly, in its "suchness." To see the world as it is concretely, undivided by categories and abstractions, one must certainly look at it with a mind which is not thinking—which is to say, forming symbols—about it. Za-zen is not, therefore, sitting with a blank mind which excludes all the impressions of the inner and outer senses. It is not "concentration" in the usual sense of restricting the attention to a single sense object, such as a point of light or the tip of one's nose. It is simply a quiet awareness, without comment, of whatever happens to be here and now. This awareness is attended by the most vivid sensation of "nondifference" between oneself and the external world, between the mind and its contents—the various sounds, sights, and other impressions of the surrounding environment. Naturally, this sensation does not arise by trying to acquire it; it just comes by itself when one is sitting and watching without any purpose in mind—even the purpose of getting rid of purpose.

In the *sodo* or *zendo*, monks' hall or meditation hall, of a Zen community there is, of course, nothing particularly distracting in the external surroundings. There is a long room with wide platforms down either side where the monks both sleep and meditate. The platforms are covered with *tatami*, thick floor-mats of straw, and the monks sit in two rows facing one another across the room. The silence which prevails is deepened rather than broken by occasional sounds that float up from a near-by village, by the intermittent ringing of soft-toned bells from other parts of the monastery, and by the chatter of birds in the trees. Other than this there is only the feel of the cold, clear mountain air and the "woody" smell of a special kind of incense.

Much importance is attached to the physical posture of *za-zen*. The monks sit on firmly padded cushions with legs crossed and feet soles-upward upon the thighs. The hands rest upon the lap, the left over the right, with palms upward and thumbs touching one another. The body is held erect, though not stiffly, and the eyes are left open so that their gaze falls upon the floor a few feet ahead. The breathing is regulated so as to be slow without strain, with the stress upon the out-breath, and its impulse from the belly rather than the chest. This has the effect of shifting the body's center of gravity to the abdomen so that the whole posture has a sense of firmness, of being part of the ground upon which one is sitting. The slow, easy breathing from the belly works upon the consciousness like bellows, and gives it a still, bright clarity. The beginner is advised to accustom himself to the stillness by doing nothing more than counting his breaths from one to ten, over and over again, until the sensation of sitting without comment becomes effortless and natural.

While the monks are thus seated, two attendants walk slowly back and forth along the floor between the platforms, each carrying a *keisaku* or "warning" stick, round at one end and flattened at the other–a symbol of the Bodhisattva Manjusri's sword of *prajna*. As soon as they see a monk going to sleep, or sitting in an incorrect posture, they stop before him, bow ceremoniously, and beat him on the shoulders. It is said that this is not "punishment" but an "invigorating massage" to take the stiffness out of the shoulder muscles and bring the mind back to a state of alertness. However, monks with whom I have discussed this practice seem to have the same wryly humorous attitude about it which one associates with the usual corporal disciplines of boys' boarding schools. Furthermore, the *sodo* regulations say, "At the time of morning service, the dozing ones are to be severely dealt with the *keisaku*." [1]

At intervals, the sitting posture is interrupted, and the monks fall into ranks for a swift march around the floor between the platforms to keep themselves from sluggishness. The periods of *za-zen* are also interrupted for work in the monastery grounds, cleaning the premises, services in the main shrine or "Buddha hall," and other duties–as well as for meals and short hours of sleep. At certain times of year *za-zen* is kept up almost continuously from 3:30 a.m. until 10 p.m., and these long periods are called *sesshin*, or "collecting the mind." Every aspect of the monks' lives is conducted according to a precise, though not ostentatious, ritual which gives the atmosphere of the *sodo* a slightly military air. The rituals are signaled and accompanied by about a dozen different kinds of bells, clappers, and wooden gongs, struck in various rhythms to announce the times for *za-zen*, meals, services, lectures, or *sanzen* interviews with the master.

[1] In Suzuki (5), p. 99. The regulations also say, "When submitting to the *keisaku*, courteously fold your hands and bow; do not permit any egoistic thoughts to assert themselves and cherish anger." The point seems to be that the *keisaku* has two uses–one for shoulder massage and another, however politely worded, for punishment. It is of interest that Bankei abolished this practice in his own community, on the ground that a man is no less a Buddha when asleep than when awake.

The ritualistic or ceremonious style is so characteristic of Zen that it may need some explanation in a culture which has come to associate it with affectation or superstition. In Buddhism the four principal activities of man–walking, standing, sitting, and lying–are called the four "dignities," since they are the postures assumed by the Buddha nature in its human (*nirmanakaya*) body. The ritualistic style of conducting one's everyday activities is therefore a celebration of the fact that "the ordinary man is a Buddha," and is, furthermore, a style that comes almost naturally to a person who is doing everything with total presence of mind. Thus if in something so simple and trivial as lighting a cigarette one is fully aware, seeing the flame, the curling smoke, and the regulation of the breath as the most important things in the universe, it will seem to an observer that the action has a ritualistic style.

This attitude of "acting as a Buddha" is particularly stressed in the Soto School, where both *za-zen* and the round of daily activities are not at all seen as means to an end but as the actual realization of Buddhahood. As Dogen says in the *Shobogenzo:*

> Without looking forward to tomorrow every moment, you must think only of this day and this hour. Because tomorrow is difficult and unfixed and difficult to know, you must think of following the Buddhist way while you live today. . . . You must concentrate on Zen practice without wasting time, thinking that there is only this day and this hour. After that it becomes truly easy. You must forget about the good and bad of your nature, the strength or weakness of your power.[2]

In *za-zen* there must be no thought either of aiming at *satori* or of avoiding birth-and-death, no striving for anything in future time.

> If life comes, this is life. If death comes, this is death. There is no reason for your being under their control. Don't put any hope in them. This life and death are the life of the Buddha. If you try to throw them away in denial, you lose the life of the Buddha.[3]

[2] *Zuimonki* chapter. In Masunaga (1), p. 42.
[3] *Shoji* chapter. *Ibid.,* p. 44.

The "three worlds" of past, present, and future are not, as is commonly supposed, stretched out to inaccessible distances.

> The so-called past is the top of the heart; the present is the top of the fist; and the future is the back of the brain.[4]

All time is here in this body, which is the body of Buddha. The past exists in its memory and the future in its anticipation, and both of these are now, for when the world is inspected directly and clearly past and future times are nowhere to be found.

This is also the teaching of Bankei:

> You are primarily Buddhas; you are not going to be Buddhas for the first time. There is not an iota of a thing to be called error in your inborn mind. . . . If you have the least desire to be better than you actually are, if you hurry up to the slightest degree in search of something, you are already going against the Unborn.[5]

Such a view of Zen practice is therefore somewhat difficult to reconcile with the discipline which now prevails in the Rinzai School, and which consists in "passing" a graduated series of approximately fifty koan problems. Many of the Rinzai masters are most emphatic about the necessity of arousing a most intense spirit of seeking–a compelling sense of "doubt" whereby it becomes almost impossible to forget the koan one is trying to solve. Naturally, this leads to a good deal of comparison between the degrees of attainment of various individuals, and a very definite and formal recognition is attached to final "graduation" from the process.

Since the formal details of the koan discipline are one of the few actual secrets remaining in the Buddhist world, it is difficult to appraise it fairly if one has not undergone the training. On the other hand, if one has undergone it one is obliged not to talk about it–save in vague generalities. The Rinzai School has always forbidden the publication of formally acceptable answers to the various koan because the whole point of the discipline is to dis-

---

[4] *Kenbutsu* chapter. *Ibid.*, p. 45.
[5] In Suzuki (10), pp. 177–78.

cover them for oneself, by intuition. To know the answers without having so discovered them would be like studying the map without taking the journey. Lacking the actual shock of recognition, the bare answers seem flat and disappointing, and obviously no competent master would be deceived by anyone who gave them without genuine feeling.

There is no reason, however, why the process should actually involve all the silliness about "grades of attainment," about who has "passed" and who has not, or about who is or is not a "genuine" Buddha by these formal standards. All well-established religious institutions are beset by this kind of nonsense, and they generally boil down to a kind of aestheticism, an excessive passion for the cultivation of a special "style" whose refinements distinguish the sheep from the goats. By such standards the liturgical aesthete can distinguish Roman from Anglican Catholic priests, confusing the mannerisms of traditional atmosphere with the supernatural marks of true or false participation in the apostolic succession. Sometimes, however, the cultivation of a traditional style may be rather admirable, as when a school of craftsmen or artists hands down from generation to generation certain trade secrets or technical refinements whereby objects of peculiar beauty are manufactured. Even so, this very easily becomes a rather affected and self-conscious discipline, and at that moment all its "Zen" is lost.

The *koan* system as it exists today is largely the work of Hakuin (1685–1768), a formidable and immensely versatile master, who gave it a systematic organization so that the complete course of Zen study in the Rinzai School is divided into six stages. There are, first, five groups of *koan* [d]:

1. *Hosshin*, or *Dharmakaya koan*, whereby one "enters into the frontier gate of Zen."

2. *Kikan*, or "cunning barrier" *koan*, having to do with the active expression of the state realized in the first group.

3. *Gonsen*, or "investigation of words" *koan*, presumably having to do with the expression of Zen understanding in speech.

4. *Nanto,* or "hard to penetrate" *koan.*

5. *Goi,* or "Five Ranks" *koan,* based on the five relationships of "lord" and "servant" or of "principle" (*li*) and "thing-event" (*shih*), wherein Zen is related to the Hua-yen or *Avatamsaka* philosophy.

The sixth stage is a study of the Buddhist precepts and the regulations of the monk's life (*vinaya*) in the light of Zen understanding.[6]

Normally, this course of training takes about thirty years. By no means all Zen monks complete the whole training. This is required only of those who are to receive their master's *inka* or "seal of approval" so that they themselves may become masters (*roshi*), thoroughly versed in all the "skillful means" (*upaya*) for teaching Zen to others. Like so many other things of this kind, the system is as good as one makes it, and its graduates are both tall Buddhas and short Buddhas. It should not be assumed that a person who has passed a *koan,* or even many *koan,* is necessarily a "transformed" human being whose character and way of life are radically different from what they were before. Nor should it be assumed that *satori* is a single, sudden leap from the common consciousness to "complete, unexcelled awakening" (*anuttara samyak sambodhi*). *Satori* really designates the sudden and intuitive way of seeing into anything, whether it be remembering a forgotten name or seeing into the deepest principles of Buddhism. One seeks and seeks, but cannot find. One then gives up, and the answer comes by itself. Thus there may be many occasions of *satori* in the course of training, great *satori* and little *satori,* and the solution of many of the *koan* depends upon nothing more sensational than a kind of "knack" for understanding the Zen style of handling Buddhist principles.

Western ideas of Buddhist attainments are all too often distorted by the "mysterious East" approach, and by the sensational fantasies so widely circulated in theosophical writings during the

[6] This outline is based on information given in a conference at the American Academy of Asian Studies by Ruth Sasaki.

decades just before and after the turn of the century. Such fantasies were based not upon a first-hand study of Buddhism but on literal readings of mythological passages in the *sutras*, where the Buddhas and Bodhisattvas are embellished with innumerable miraculous and superhuman attributes. Thus there must be no confusion between Zen masters and theosophical "mahatmas"– the glamorous "Masters of Wisdom" who live in the mountain fastnesses of Tibet and practice the arts of occultism. Zen masters are quite human. They get sick and die; they know joy and sorrow; they have bad tempers or other little "weaknesses" of character just like anyone else, and they are not above falling in love and entering into a fully human relationship with the opposite sex. The perfection of Zen is to be perfectly and simply human. The difference of the adept in Zen from the ordinary run of men is that the latter are, in one way or another, at odds with their own humanity, and are attempting to be angels or demons.[7] A *doka* poem by Ikkyu says:

> We eat, excrete, sleep, and get up;
> This is our world.
> All we have to do after that–
> Is to die.[8]

Koan training involves typically Asian concepts of the relation between master and pupil which are quite unlike ours. For in Asian cultures this is a peculiarly sacred relationship in which the master is held to become responsible for the *karma* of the

[7] One can hardly exaggerate the importance of the great Buddhist symbol of the *bhavachakra*, the Wheel Becoming. The angels and demons occupy the highest and lowest positions, the positions of perfect happiness and perfect frustration. These positions lie on the opposite sides of a circle because they lead to each other. They represent not so much literal beings as our own ideals and terrors, since the Wheel is actually a map of the human mind. The human position lies in the middle, i.e., at the left of the Wheel, and it is only from this position that one may become a Buddha. Human birth is therefore regarded as unusually fortunate, but this is not to be confused with the physical event, for one is not actually "born into the human world" until one has fully accepted one's humanity.

[8] Translated by R. H. Blyth in "Ikkyu's Doka," *The Young East*, vol. 2, no. 7. (Tokyo, 1953.)

pupil. The pupil, in turn, is expected to accord absolute obedience and authority to the master, and to hold him in almost higher respect than his own father—and in Asian countries this is saying a great deal. To a young Zen monk the *roshi* therefore stands as a symbol of the utmost patriarchal authority, and he usually plays the role to perfection—being normally a man advanced in years, fierce and "tigerish" in aspect, and, when formally robed and seated for the *sanzen* interview, a person of supreme presence and dignity. In this role he constitutes a living symbol of everything that makes one afraid of being spontaneous, everything that prompts the most painful and awkward self-consciousness. He assumes this role as an *upaya,* a skillful device, for challenging the student to find enough "nerve" to be perfectly natural in the presence of this formidable archetype. If he can do this, he is a free man whom no one on earth can embarrass. It must be borne in mind, too, that in Japanese culture the adolescent and the youth are peculiarly susceptible to ridicule, which is freely used as a means of conforming the young to social convention.

To the normal Asian concept of the master-pupil relationship, Zen adds something of its own in the sense that it leaves the formation of the relationship entirely to the initiative of the pupil. The basic position of Zen is that it has nothing to say, nothing to teach. The truth of Buddhism is so self-evident, so obvious that it is, if anything, concealed by explaining it. Therefore the master does not "help" the student in any way, since helping would actually be hindering. On the contrary, he goes out of his way to put obstacles and barriers in the student's path. Thus Wu-men's comments on the various *koan* in the *Wu-men kuan* are intentionally misleading, the *koan* as a whole are called "wisteria vines" or "entanglements," and particular groups "cunning barriers" (*kikan*) and "hard to penetrate" (*nanto*). This is like encouraging the growth of a hedge by pruning, for obviously the basic intention is to help, but the Zen student does not really know Zen unless he finds it out for himself. The Chinese proverb

"What comes in through the gate is not family treasure" is understood in Zen to mean that what someone else tells you is not your own knowledge. *Satori*, as Wu-men explained, comes only after one has exhausted one's thinking, only when one is convinced that the mind cannot grasp itself. In the words of another of Ikkyu's *doka*:

> A *mind to search elsewhere*
> *For the Buddha,*
> *Is foolishness*
> *In the very centre of foolishness.*

For

> *My self of long ago,*
> *In nature non-existent;*
> *Nowhere to go when dead,*
> *Nothing at all.*[9]

The preliminary *hosshin* type of *koan* begins, therefore, to obstruct the student by sending him off in the direction exactly opposite to that in which he should look. Only it does it rather cleverly, so as to conceal the stratagem. Everyone knows that the Buddha nature is "within" oneself and is not to be sought outside, so that no student would be fooled by being told to seek it by going to India or by reading a certain *sutra*. On the contrary, he is told to look for it in himself! Worse still, he is encouraged to seek it with the whole energy of his being, never giving up his quest by day or night, whether actually in *za-zen* or whether working or eating. He is encouraged, in fact, to make a total fool of himself, to whirl round and round like a dog trying to catch up with its own tail.

Thus normal first *koan* are Hui-neng's "Original Face," Chao-chou's "*Wu*," or Hakuin's "One Hand." At the first *sanzen* interview, the *roshi* instructs the reluctantly accepted student to discover his "original face" or "aspect," that is, his basic nature, as it

[9] R. H. Blyth, *ibid.*, vol. 3, no. 9, p. 14, and vol. 2, no. 2, p. 7.

was before his father and mother conceived him. He is told to return when he has discovered it, and to give some proof of discovery. In the meantime he is under no circumstance to discuss the problem with others or to seek their help. Joining the other monks in the *sodo*, the *jikijitsu* or "head monk" will probably instruct him in the rudiments of *za-zen*, showing him how to sit, and perhaps encouraging him to return to the *roshi* for *sanzen* as soon as possible, and to lose no opportunity for getting the proper view of his *koan*. Pondering the problem of his "original face," he therefore tries and tries to imagine what he was before he was born, or, for that matter, what he now is at the very center of his being, what is the basic reality of his existence apart from his extension in time and space.

He soon discovers that the *roshi* has no patience whatever with philosophical or other wordy answers. For the *roshi* wants to be "shown." He wants something concrete, some solid proof. The student therefore begins to produce such "specimens of reality" as lumps of rock, leaves and branches, shouts, gestures of the hands—anything and everything he can imagine. But all is resolutely rejected until the student, unable to imagine anything more, is brought to his wits' end—at which point he is of course beginning to get on the right track. He "knows that he doesn't know."

When the beginning *koan* is Chao-chou's "*Wu*," the student is asked to find out why Chao-chou answered "*Wu*" or "None" to the question, "Does a dog have the Buddha nature?" The *roshi* asks to be shown this "nothing." A Chinese proverb says that "A single hand does not make a clap," [e] and therefore Hakuin asked, "What is the sound of one hand?" Can you hear what is not making a noise? Can you get any sound out of this one object which has nothing to hit? Can you get any "knowledge" of your own real nature? What an idiotic question!

By such means the student is at last brought to a point of feeling completely stupid—as if he were encased in a huge block of ice, unable to move or think. He just knows nothing; the whole world, including himself, is an enormous mass of pure doubt. Everything he hears, touches, or sees is as incomprehensible as "nothing" or "the sound of one hand." At *sanzen* he is perfectly dumb. He walks or sits all day in a "vivid daze," conscious of everything going on around him, responding mechanically to circumstances, but totally baffled by everything.

After some time in this state there comes a moment when the block of ice suddenly collapses, when this vast lump of unintelligibility comes instantly alive. The problem of who or what it is becomes transparently absurd–a question which, from the beginning, meant nothing whatever. There is no one left to ask himself the question or to answer it. Yet at the same time this transparent meaninglessness can laugh and talk, eat and drink, run up and down, look at the earth and sky, and all this without any sense of there being a problem, a sort of psychological knot, in the midst of it. There is no knot because the "mind seeking to know the mind" or the "self seeking to control the self" has been defeated out of existence and exposed for the abstraction which it always was. And when that tense knot vanishes there is no more sensation of a hard core of selfhood standing over against the rest of the world. In this state, the *roshi* needs only a single look at the student to know that he is now ready to begin his Zen training in earnest.

It is not quite the paradox which it seems to say that Zen training can begin only when it has been finished. For this is simply the basic Mahayana principle that *prajna* leads to *karuna,* that awakening is not truly attained unless it also implies the life of the Bodhisattva, the manifestation of the "marvelous use" of the Void for the benefit of all sentient beings.

At this point the *roshi* begins to present the student with *koan* which ask for impossible feats of action or judgment, such as:

"Take the four divisions of Tokyo out of your sleeve."

"Stop that ship on the distant ocean."

"Stop the booming of the distant bell."

"A girl is crossing the street. Is she the younger or the older sister?"

Such *koan* are rather more obviously "tricky" than the basic introductory problems, and show the student that what are dilemmas for thought present no barriers to action. A paper handkerchief easily becomes the four divisions of Tokyo, and the student solves the problem of the younger or older sister by mincing across the room like a girl. For in her absolute "suchness" the girl is just *that;* she is only relatively "sister," "older," or "younger." One can perhaps understand why a man who had practiced *za-zen* for eight years told R. H. Blyth that "Zen is just a trick of words," for on the principle of extracting a thorn with a thorn Zen is extricating people from the tangle in which they find themselves from confusing words and ideas with reality.

The continued practice of *za-zen* now provides the student with a clear, unobstructed mind into which he can toss the *koan* like a pebble into a pool and simply watch to see what his mind does with it. As he concludes each *koan*, the *roshi* usually requires that he present a verse from the *Zenrin Kushu* which expresses the point of the *koan* just solved. Other books are also used, and the late Sokei-an Sasaki, working in the United States, found that an admirable manual for this purpose was *Alice in Wonderland!* As the work goes on, crucial *koan* alternate with subsidiary *koan* which explore the implications of the former, and give the student a thorough working acquaintance with every theme in the Buddhist view of the universe, presenting the whole body of understanding in such a way that he knows it in his bones and nerves. By such means he learns to respond with it instantly and unwaveringly in the situations of everyday life.

The final group of *koan* are concerned with the "Five Ranks" (*go-i*)—a schematic view of the relations between relative knowledge and absolute knowledge, thing-events (*shih*) and underlying principle (*li*). The originator of the scheme was T'ung-shan (807–869), but it arises from the contacts of Zen with the Hua-yen (Japanese, Kegon) School, and the doctrine of the Five Ranks is closely related to that of the fourfold *Dharma-dhatu*.[10] The Ranks are often represented in terms of the relative positions of lord and servant or host and guest, standing respectively for the underlying principle and the thing-events. Thus we have:

1. The lord looks down at the servant.
2. The servant looks up at the lord.
3. The lord.
4. The servant.
5. The lord and the servant converse together.

Suffice it to say that the first four correspond to the four *Dharmadhatu* of the Hua-yen School, though the relationship is somewhat complex, and the fifth to "naturalness." In other words, one may regard the universe, the *Dharmadhatu*, from a number of equally valid points of view—as many, as one, as both one and many, and as neither one nor many. But the final position of Zen is that it does not take any special viewpoint, and yet is free to take every viewpoint according to the circumstances. In the words of Lin-chi:

> Sometimes I take away the man (i.e., the subject) but do not take away the circumstances (i.e., the object). Sometimes I take away the circumstances but do not take away the man. Sometimes I take away both the man and the circumstances. Sometimes I take away neither the man nor the circumstances.[11]

And sometimes, he might have added, I just do nothing special (*wu-shih*).[12]

Koan training comes to its conclusion in the stage of perfect naturalness of freedom in both the absolute and the relative

[10] For details, see above, pp. 160f.
[11] In *Ku-tsun-hsü Yü-lu*, 1. 4, pp. 3–4.
[12] A detailed but extremely confusing account of the Five Ranks will be found in Dumoulin and Sasaki (1), pp. 25–29.

worlds, but because this freedom is not opposed to the conventional order, but is rather a freedom which "upholds the world" (*lokasamgraha*), the final phase of study is the relationship of Zen to the rules of social and monastic life. As Yun-men once asked, "In such a wide world, why answer the bell and put on ceremonial robes?" [13] Another master's answer in quite a different context applies well here—"If there is any reason for it you may cut off my head!" For the moral act is significantly moral only when it is free, without the compulsion of a reason or necessity. This is also the deepest meaning of the Christian doctrine of free will, for to act "in union with God" is to act, not from the constraint of fear or pride, nor from hope of reward, but with the baseless love of the "unmoved mover."

To say that the *koan* system has certain dangers or drawbacks is only to say that anything can be misused. It is a highly sophisticated and even institutionalized technique, and therefore lends itself to affectation and artificiality. But so does any technique, even when so untechnical as Bankei's method of no method. This, too, can become a fetish. Yet it is important to be mindful of the points at which the drawbacks are most likely to arise, and it would seem that in *koan* training there are two.

The first is to insist that the *koan* is the "only way" to a genuine realization of Zen. Of course, one may beg the question by saying that Zen, over and above the experience of awakening, is precisely the style of handling Buddhism which the *koan* embody. But in this case the Soto School is not Zen, and no Zen is to be found anywhere in the world outside the particular tradition of the Rinzai branch. So defined, Zen has no universality and becomes as exotic and culturally conditioned as No drama or the practice of Chinese calligraphy. From the standpoint of the West, such Zen will appeal only to fanciers of "Nipponery," to romanticists who like to play at being Japanese. Not that there is anything inherently "bad" in such romanticism, for there are no such things as "pure" cultures, and the borrowing of other

[13] *Wu-men kuan*, 16.

people's styles always adds to the variety and spice of life. But Zen is so much more than a cultural refinement.

The second, and more serious, drawback can arise from the opposition of *satori* to the intense "feeling of doubt" which some *koan* exponents so deliberately encourage. For this is to foster a dualistic *satori*. To say that the depth of the *satori* is proportional to the intensity of seeking and striving which precede it is to confuse *satori* with its purely emotional adjuncts. In other words, if one wants to feel exhilaratingly light-footed, it is always possible to go around for some time with lead in one's shoes—and then take them off. The sense of relief will certainly be proportional to the length of time such shoes have been worn, and to the weight of the lead. This is equivalent to the old trick of religious revivalists who give their followers a tremendous emotional uplift by first implanting an acute sense of sin, and then relieving it through faith in Jesus. But such "uplifts" do not last, and it was of such a *satori* that Yün-feng said, "That monk who has any *satori* goes right into hell like a flying arrow." [14]

Awakening almost necessarily involves a sense of relief because it brings to an end the habitual psychological cramp of trying to grasp the mind with the mind, which in turn generates the ego with all its conflicts and defenses. In time, the sense of relief wears off—but not the awakening, unless one has confused it with the sense of relief and has attempted to exploit it by indulging in ecstasy. Awakening is thus only incidentally pleasant or ecstatic, only at first an experience of intense emotional release. But in itself it is just the ending of an artificial and absurd use of the mind. Above and beyond that it is *wu-shih*—nothing special—since the ultimate content of awakening is never a particular object of knowledge or experience. The Buddhist doctrine of the "Four Invisibles" is that the Void (*sunya*) is to a Buddha as water to a fish, air to a man, and the nature of things to the deluded—beyond conception.

[14] *Ku-tsun-hsü Yü-lu*, 41.

It should be obvious that what we are, most substantially and fundamentally, will never be a distinct object of knowledge. Whatever we can know–life and death, light and darkness, solid and empty–will be the relative aspects of something as inconceivable as the color of space. Awakening is not to know what this reality is. As a *Zenrin* poem says:

> *As butterflies come to the newly planted flowers,*
> *Bodhidharma says, "I know not." [g]*

Awakening is to know what reality is not. It is to cease identifying oneself with any object of knowledge whatsoever. Just as every assertion about the basic substance or energy of reality must be meaningless, any assertion as to what "I am" at the very roots of my being must also be the height of folly. Delusion is the false metaphysical premise at the root of common sense; it is the average man's unconscious ontology and epistemology, his tacit assumption that he is a "something." The assumption that "I am nothing" would, of course, be equally wrong since something and nothing, being and non-being, are related concepts, and belong equally to the "known."

One method of muscular relaxation is to begin by increasing tension in the muscles so as to have a clear feeling of what *not* to do.[15] In this sense there is some point in using the initial *koan* as a means of intensifying the mind's absurd effort to grasp itself. But to identify *satori* with the consequent feeling of relief, with the *sense* of relaxation, is quite misleading, for the *satori* is the letting go and not the feeling of it. The conscious aspect of the Zen life is not, therefore, *satori*–not the "original mind"–but everything one is left free to do and to see and feel when the cramp in the mind has been released.

From this standpoint Bankei's simple trust in the "Unborn mind" and even Shinran's view of *Nembutsu* are also entrances to *satori*. To "let go" it is not always necessary to wear out the

[15] See Edmund Jacobson, *Progressive Relaxation.* (Chicago, 1938.)

attempt to grasp until it becomes intolerable. As against this violent way there is also a *judo*–a "gentle way," the way of seeing that the mind, the basic reality, remains spontaneous and ungrasped whether one tries to grasp it or not. One's own doing or not doing drop away by sheer irrelevance. To think that one must grasp or not grasp, let go or not let go, is only to foster the illusion that the ego is real, and that its machinations are an effective obstacle to the Tao. Beside the spontaneous functioning of the "Unborn mind" these efforts or non-efforts are strictly null. In the more imagistic language of Shinran, one has only to hear of the "saving vow" of Amitabha and to say his Name, the *Nembutsu*, even just once without concern as to whether one has faith or not, or as to whether one is desireless or not. All such concern is the pride of the ego. In the words of the Shin-shu mystic Kichibei:

> When all the idea of self-power based upon moral values and disciplinary measures is purged, there is nothing left in you that will declare itself to be the hearer, and just because of this you do not miss anything you hear.[16]

So long as one thinks about listening, one cannot hear clearly, and so long as one thinks about trying or not trying to let go of oneself, one cannot let go. Yet whether one thinks about listening or not, the ears are hearing just the same, and nothing can stop the sound from reaching them.

The advantage of the *koan* method is perhaps that, for general purposes, the other way is too subtle, and too easily subject to misinterpretation—especially by monks who might all too readily use it as an excuse for loafing around the monastery while living off the donations of the devout laity. This is almost certainly why the emphasis of the T'ang masters on "not-seeking" gave way to the more energetic use of the *koan* as a means of exhausting the strength of the egoistic will. Bankei's Zen without method or means offers no basis for a school or institution, since the monks

16 In Suzuki (10), p. 130.

may just as well go their way and take up farming or fishing. As a result no external sign of Zen is left; there is no longer any finger pointing at the moon of Truth—and this is necessary for the Bodhisattva's task of delivering all beings, even though it runs the risk of mistaking the finger for the moon.

Four

ZEN IN THE ARTS

Happily, it is possible for us not only to hear about Zen but also to see it. Since "one showing is worth a hundred sayings," the expression of Zen in the arts gives us one of the most direct ways of understanding it. This is the more so because the art forms which Zen has created are not symbolic in the same way as other types of Buddhist art, or as is "religious" art as a whole. The favorite subjects of Zen artists, whether painters or poets, are what we should call natural, concrete, and secular things. Even when they turn to the Buddha, or to the Patriarchs and masters of Zen, they depict them in a peculiarly down-to-earth and human way. Furthermore, the arts of Zen are not merely or primarily representational. Even in painting, the work of art is considered not only as representing nature but as being itself a work of nature. For the very technique involves the art of artlessness, or what Sabro Hasegawa has called the "controlled accident," so that paintings are formed as naturally as the rocks and grasses which they depict.

This does not mean that the art forms of Zen are left to mere chance, as if one were to dip a snake in ink and let it wiggle around on a sheet of paper. The point is rather that for Zen there is no duality, no conflict between the natural element of chance and the human element of control. The constructive powers of the human mind are no more artificial than the formative actions of plants or bees, so that from the standpoint of Zen it is no contradiction to say that artistic technique is discipline in spontaneity and spontaneity in discipline.

The art forms of the Western world arise from spiritual and philosophical traditions in which spirit is divided from nature, and comes down from heaven to work upon it as an intelligent energy upon an inert and recalcitrant stuff. Thus Malraux speaks always of the artist "conquering" his medium as our explorers and scientists also speak of conquering mountains or conquering space. To Chinese and Japanese ears these are grotesque expressions. For when you climb it is the mountain as much as your own legs which lifts you upwards, and when you paint it is the brush, ink, and paper which determine the result as much as your own hand.

Taoism, Confucianism, and Zen are expressions of a mentality which feels completely at home in this universe, and which sees man as an integral part of his environment. Human intelligence is not an imprisoned spirit from afar but an aspect of the whole intricately balanced organism of the natural world, whose principles were first explored in the *Book of Changes*. Heaven and earth are alike members of this organism, and nature is as much our father as our mother, since the Tao by which it works is originally manifested in the *yang* and the *yin*–the male and female, positive and negative principles which, in dynamic balance, maintain the order of the world. The insight which lies at the root of Far Eastern culture is that opposites are relational and so fundamentally harmonious. Conflict is always comparatively superficial, for there can be no ultimate conflict when the pairs of opposites are mutually interdependent. Thus our stark divisions of spirit and nature, subject and object, good and evil, artist and medium are quite foreign to this culture.

In a universe whose fundamental principle is relativity rather than warfare there is no purpose because there is no victory to be won, no end to be attained. For every end, as the word itself shows, is an extreme, an opposite, and exists only in relation to its other end. Because the world is not going anywhere there is no hurry. One may as well "take it easy" like nature itself, and in the Chinese language the "changes" of nature and "ease" are the same word, *i.*[a] This is a first principle in the study of Zen and of any Far Eastern art: hurry, and all that it involves, is fatal. For there is no goal to be attained. The moment a goal is conceived it becomes impossible to practice the discipline of the art, to master the very rigor of its technique. Under the watchful and critical eye of a master one may practice the writing of Chinese characters for days and days, months and months. But he watches as a gardener watches the growth of a tree, and wants his student to have the attitude of the tree–the attitude of purposeless growth in which there are no short cuts because every stage of the way is both beginning and end. Thus the most accomplished master no more congratulates himself upon "arriving" than the most fumbling beginner.

Paradoxical as it may seem, the purposeful life has no content, no point. It hurries on and on, and misses everything. Not hurrying, the purposeless life misses nothing, for it is only when there is no goal and no rush that the human senses are fully open to receive the world. Absence of hurry also involves a certain lack of interference with the natural course of events, especially when it is felt that the natural course follows principles which are not foreign to human intelligence. For, as we have seen, the Taoist mentality makes, or forces, nothing but "grows" everything. When human reason is seen to be an expression of the same spontaneous balance of *yang* and *yin* as the natural universe, man's action upon his environment is not felt as a conflict, an action from outside. Thus the difference between forcing and growing cannot be expressed in terms of specific directions as to what should or should not be done, for the difference lies primarily in the quality and feeling of the action. The difficulty of describing these things for Western ears is that people in a hurry cannot feel.

The expression of this whole attitude in the arts is perhaps best approached through painting and poetry. Although it may seem that the arts of Zen are confined to the more refined expressions of culture, it should be remembered that almost every profession and craft is known in Japan as a *do*, that is, a Tao or Way, not unlike what used to be known in the West as a "mystery." To some extent, every *do* was at one time a lay method of learning the principles which are embodied in Taoism, Zen, and Confucianism, even as modern Masonry is a survival from times when the craft of the mason was a means of initiation into a spiritual tradition. Even in modern Osaka some of the older merchants follow a *do* or way of commerce based upon *shingaku*–a system of psychology closely related to Zen.

After the persecution of Chinese Buddhism in 845, Zen was for some time not only the dominant form of Buddhism but also the most powerful spiritual influence in the growth of Chinese culture. This influence was at its height during the Southern Sung dynasty (1127–1279), and during this time the Zen monasteries became leading centers of Chinese scholarship. Lay scholars, Confucian and Taoist alike, visited them for periods of study, and Zen monks in turn familiarized themselves with Chinese classical studies. Since writing and poetry were among the chief preoccupations of Chinese scholars, and since the Chinese way of painting is closely akin to writing, the roles of scholar, artist, and poet were not widely separated. The Chinese gentleman-scholar was not a specialist, and it was quite against the nature of the Zen monk to confine his interests and activities to purely "religious" affairs. The result was a tremendous cross-fertilization of philosophical, scholarly, poetic, and artistic pursuits in which the Zen and Taoist feeling for "naturalness" became the dominant note. It was during this same period that Eisai and Dogen came from Japan to return with Zen to their own country, to be followed by an incessant stream of Japanese scholar-monks eager to take home not only Zen but every other aspect of Chinese culture. Shiploads of monks, amounting almost to floating monasteries, plied between China and Japan, carrying not only *sutras* and Chinese classical books, but also tea, silk, pottery, incense, paintings, drugs, musical instruments, and every refinement of Chinese culture–not to mention Chinese artists and craftsmen.

Closest to the feeling of Zen was a calligraphic style of painting, done with black ink on paper or silk–usually a painting and poem in one. Chinese black ink is capable of a great variety of tones, varied by the amount of water, and the ink itself is found in an enormous number of qualities and "colors" of black. The ink comes in a solid stick, and is prepared by pouring a little water into a flat stone dish, upon which the stick is rubbed until the liquid is of the required density. Writing or painting is done with a sharply pointed brush set in a bamboo stem–a brush which is held upright without resting the wrist on the paper, and whose soft hairs give its strokes a great versatility. Since the touch of the brush is so light and fluid, and since it must move continuously over the absorbent paper if the ink is to flow out regularly, its control requires a free movement of the hand and arm as if one were dancing rather than writing on paper. In short, it is a perfect instrument for the expression of unhesitating spontaneity, and a single stroke is enough to "give away" one's character to an experienced observer.

Sumi-e, as the Japanese call this style of painting, may have been perfected as early as the T'ang dynasty by the almost legendary masters Wu Tao-tzu (*c.* 700–760) and Wang-wei (*c.* 698–759). However, the authenticity of works ascribed to them is doubtful, though they may be as early as the ninth century and include a painting so fully characteristic of Zen as the impressionistic waterfall attributed to Wang-wei–a thundering stream of sheer power, suggested by a few slightly curved sweeps of the brush between two masses of rock. The great formative age of this style was undoubtedly the Sung dynasty (959–1279), and is represented by such painters as Hsia-kuei, Ma-yüan, Mu-ch'i, and Liang-k'ai.

The Sung masters were pre-eminently landscape painters, creators of a tradition of "nature painting" which has hardly been surpassed anywhere in the world. For it shows us the life of nature–of mountains, waters, mists, rocks, trees, and birds–as felt by Taoism and Zen. It is a world to which man belongs but which he does not dominate; it is sufficient to itself, for it was not "made for" anyone and has no purpose of its own. As Hsüan-chüeh said:

Over the river, the shining moon; in the pine trees, sighing wind;
All night long so tranquil—why? And for whom? [1] [b]

Sung landscapes are by no means as fantastic and stylized as
Western critics often suggest, for to travel in similar territory, in
mountainous, misty country, is to see them at every turn of the
road, and it is a simple matter for the photographer to take pictures which look exactly like Chinese paintings. One of the most
striking features of the Sung landscape, as of *sumi-e* as a whole,
is the relative emptiness of the picture—an emptiness which appears, however, to be part of the painting and not just unpainted
background. By filling in just one corner, the artist makes the
whole area of the picture alive. Ma-yüan, in particular, was a
master of this technique, which amounts almost to "painting by
not painting," or what Zen sometimes calls "playing the string-
less lute." The secret lies in knowing how to balance form with
emptiness and, above all, in knowing when one has "said"
enough. For Zen spoils neither the aesthetic shock nor the *satori*
shock by filling in, by explanation, second thoughts, and intellectual commentary. Furthermore, the figure so integrally related
to its empty space gives the feeling of the "marvelous Void"
from which the event suddenly appears.

Equally impressive is the mastery of the brush, of strokes
ranging from delicate elegance to rough vitality, from minutely
detailed trees to bold outlines and masses given texture by the
"controlled accidents" of stray brush hairs and uneven inking
of the paper. Zen artists have preserved this technique to the
present day in the so-called *zenga* style of Chinese characters,
circles, bamboo branches, birds, or human figures drawn with
these uninhibited, powerful brush strokes which keep on moving
even when the painting is finished. After Mu-ch'i, perhaps the
greatest master of the rough brush was the Japanese monk Sesshu
(1421–1506), whose formidable technique included the most refined screens of pine trees and birds, mountain landscapes remi-

[1] *Cheng-tao Ke, 24.*

niscent of Hsia-kuei, and almost violently alive landscapes for which he used not only the brush but fistfuls of inked straw to get the right texture of "flying hair lines."

The Western eye is immediately struck by the absence of symmetry in these paintings, by the consistent avoidance of regular and geometrical shapes, whether straight or curved. For the characteristic brush line is jagged, gnarled, irregularly twisting, dashing, or sweeping–always spontaneous rather than predictable. Even when the Zen monk or artist draws a solitary circle–one of the most common themes of *zenga*–it is not only slightly eccentric and out of shape, but the very texture of the line is full of life and verve with the incidental splashes and gaps of the "rough brush." For the abstract or "perfect" circle becomes concrete and natural–a living circle–and, in the same way, rocks and trees, clouds and waters appear to the Chinese eye as most like themselves when most unlike the intelligible forms of the geometer and architect.

Western science has made nature intelligible in terms of its symmetries and regularities, analyzing its most wayward forms into components of a regular and measurable shape. As a result we tend to see nature and to deal with it as an "order" from which the element of spontaneity has been "screened out." But this order is *maya*, and the "true suchness" of things has nothing in common with the purely conceptual aridities of perfect squares, circles, or triangles–except by spontaneous accident. Yet this is why the Western mind is dismayed when ordered conceptions of the universe break down, and when the basic behavior of the physical world is found to be a "principle of uncertainty." We find such a world meaningless and inhuman, but familiarity with Chinese and Japanese art forms might lead us to an altogether new appreciation of this world in its living, and finally unavoidable, reality.

Mu-ch'i and Liang-k'ai did many paintings of the Zen Patriarchs and masters, whom they represented for the most part as abandoned lunatics, scowling, shouting, loafing around, or roaring with laughter at drifting leaves. As favorite themes they adopted, as Zen figures, the two crazy hermits Han-shan and Shih-te, and the enormously rotund folk-god Pu-tai, to complete a marvelous assortment of happy tramps and rogues to exemplify the splendid nonsense and emptiness of the Zen life. Zen and–to some extent–Taoism seem to be the only spiritual traditions which feel secure enough to lampoon themselves, or to feel sufficiently un-self-conscious to laugh not only about their religion but in the midst of it. In these lunatic figures the Zen artists portray something slightly more than a parody of their own *wu-shin* or "mindless" way of life, for as "genius is to madness close allied" there is a suggestive parallel between the meaningless babble of the happy lunatic and the purposeless life of the Zen sage. In the words of a *Zenrin* poem:

> *The wild geese do not intend to cast their reflection;*
> *The water has no mind to receive their image.*

Thus the aimless life is the constant theme of Zen art of every kind, expressing the artist's own inner state of going nowhere in a timeless moment. All men have these moments occasionally, and it is just then that they catch those vivid glimpses of the world which cast such a glow over the intervening wastes of memory– the smell of burning leaves on a morning of autumn haze, a flight of sunlit pigeons against a thundercloud, the sound of an unseen waterfall at dusk, or the single cry of some unidentified bird in the depths of a forest. In the art of Zen every landscape, every sketch of bamboo in the wind or of lonely rocks, is an echo of such moments.

Where the mood of the moment is solitary and quiet it is called *sabi*.[c] When the artist is feeling depressed or sad, and in this peculiar emptiness of feeling catches a glimpse of something rather ordinary and unpretentious in its incredible "suchness," the mood is called *wabi*.[d] When the moment evokes a more intense, nostalgic sadness, connected with autumn and the vanishing away of the world, it is called *aware*.[e] And when the vision is the sudden perception of something mysterious and strange, hinting at an unknown never to be discovered, the mood is called *yugen.*[f] These extremely untranslatable Japanese words denote the four basic moods of *furyu,*[g] that is, of the general atmosphere of Zen "taste" in its perception of the aimless moments of life.

Inspired by the Sung masters, the Japanese produced a whole cluster of superb *sumi* painters whose work ranks today among the most prized treasures of the nation's art–Muso Kokushi (1275–1351), Cho Densu (*d.* 1431), Shubun (1414–1465), Soga Jasoku (*d.* 1483), Sesshu (1421–1506), Miyamoto Musashi (1582–1645), and many others. Notable paintings were also made by the great Zen monks Hakuin and Sengai (1750–1837), the latter showing a flair for abstract painting so startlingly suggestive of the twentieth century that it is easy to understand the interest of so many contemporary painters in Zen.

Toward the beginning of the seventeenth century, Japanese artists developed a still more suggestive and "offhand" style of *sumi-e* called *haiga* as an illustrative accompaniment to *haiku* poems. These were derived from *zenga,* the informal paintings of the Zen monks accompanying verses from the *Zenrin Kushu* and sayings from the various *mondo* and the *sutras. Zenga* and *haiga* represent the most "extreme" form of *sumi* painting–the most spontaneous, artless, and rough, replete with all those "controlled accidents" of the brush in which they exemplify the marvelous meaninglessness of nature itself.

From the earliest times the Zen masters had shown a partiality for short, gnomic poems–at once laconic and direct like their answers to questions about Buddhism. Many of these, like those we have quoted from the *Zenrin Kushu,* contained overt references to Zen and its principles. However, just as T'ung-shan's "Three pounds of flax!" was an answer full of Zen but not about Zen, so the most expressive Zen poetry is that which "says nothing," which, in other words, is not philosophy or commentary *about* life. A monk asked Feng-hsüeh, "When speech and silence are both inadmissible, how can one pass without error?" The master replied:

> *I always remember Kiangsu in March–*
> *The cry of the partridge, the mass of fragrant flowers!* [2] [h]

Here again, as in painting, is the expression of a live moment in its pure "suchness"–though it is a pity to have to say so–and the masters frequently quoted classical Chinese poetry in this way, using couplets or quatrains which pointed, and said no more.

The practice of taking couplets from the old Chinese poems for use as songs was also favored in literary circles, and at the beginning of the eleventh century Fujiwara Kinto compiled an anthology of such excerpts, together with short Japanese *waka* poems, under the title *Roeishu*, the *Collection of Clear Songs*. Such a use of poetry obviously expresses the same type of artistic vision as we find in the paintings of Ma-yüan and Mu-ch'i, the same use of empty space brought to life with a few strokes of the brush. In poetry the empty space is the surrounding silence which a two-line poem requires–a silence of the mind in which one does not "think about" the poem but actually feels the sensation which it evokes–all the more strongly for having said so little.

By the seventeenth century the Japanese had brought this "wordless" poetry to perfection in the *haiku*, the poem of just seventeen syllables which drops the subject almost as it takes it up. To non-Japanese people *haiku* are apt to seem no more than beginnings or even titles for poems, and in translation it is impossible to convey the effect of their sound and rhythm. However, translation can usually convey the image–and this is the important point. Of course there are many *haiku* which seem as stilted as the Japanese paintings on cheap lacquer trays for export. But the non-Japanese listener must remember that a good *haiku* is a pebble thrown into the pool of the listener's mind, evoking associations out of the richness of his own memory. It

[2] *Wu-men Kuan*, 24.

invites the listener to participate instead of leaving him dumb with admiration while the poet shows off.

The development of the *haiku* was largely the work of Basho (1643–1694), whose feeling for Zen wanted to express itself in a type of poetry altogether in the spirit of *wu-shih*–"nothing special." "To write *haiku*," he said, "get a three-foot child"–for Basho's poems have the same inspired objectivity as a child's expression of wonder, and return us to that same feeling of the world as when it first met our astonished eyes.

> Kimi hi take
> Yoki mono miseru
> Yukimarogel
>
> *You light the fire;*
> *I'll show you something nice,–*
> *A great ball of snow!* [3]

Basho wrote his *haiku* in the simplest type of Japanese speech, naturally avoiding literary and "highbrow" language, so creating a style which made it possible for ordinary people to be poets. Bankei, his contemporary, did just the same thing for Zen, for as one of Ikkyu's *doka* poems says:

> *Whatever runs counter*
> *To the mind and will of ordinary people*
> *Hinders the Law of Men*
> *And the Law of Buddha.* [4]

This is in the spirit of Nan-ch'üan's saying, "The ordinary mind is the Tao"–where "ordinary" means "simply human" rather than "merely vulgar." It was thus that the seventeenth century saw an

---

[3] This and all the following translations of *haiku* are the work of R. H. Blyth, and come for the most part from his superb work, the four-volume *Haiku*, which is without any question the best treatment of the subject in English. Blyth has the additional advantage of some experience in Zen training, and as a result his grasp of Chinese and Japanese literature is unusually perceptive. See Blyth (2) in the Bibliography.

[4] R. H. Blyth in "Ikkyu's Doka," *The Young East*, vol. 2, no. 7. (Tokyo, 1953.)

extraordinary popularization of the Zen atmosphere in Japan, reaching down from the monks and *samurai* to farmers and artisans.

The true feeling of *haiku* is "given away" in one of Basho's poems which, however, says just too much to be true *haiku:*

> *How admirable,*
> *He who thinks not, "Life is fleeting,"*
> *When he sees the lightning!*

For the *haiku* sees things in their "suchness," without comment—a view of the world which the Japanese call *sono-mama,* "Just as it is," or "Just so."

> *Weeds in the rice-field,*
> *Cut and left lying just so—*
> *Fertilizer!*

In Zen a man has no mind apart from what he knows and sees, and this is almost expressed by Gochiku in the *haiku:*

> *The long night;*
> *The sound of the water*
> *Says what I think.*

And still more directly—

> *The stars on the pond;*
> *Again the winter shower*
> *Ruffles the water.*

Haiku and *waka* poems convey perhaps more easily than painting the subtle differences between the four moods of *sabi, wabi, aware,* and *yugen.* The quiet, thrilling loneliness of *sabi* is obvious in

> *On a withered branch*
> *A crow is perched,*
> *In the autumn evening.*

But it is less obvious and therefore deeper in

> *With the evening breeze,*
> *The water laps against*
> *The heron's legs.*

> *In the dark forest*
> *A berry drops:*
> *The sound of the water.*

Sabi is, however, loneliness in the sense of Buddhist detachment, of seeing all things as happening "by themselves" in miraculous spontaneity. With this goes that sense of deep, illimitable quietude which descends with a long fall of snow, swallowing all sounds in layer upon layer of softness.

> *Sleet falling;*
> *Fathomless, infinite*
> *Loneliness.*

Wabi, the unexpected recognition of the faithful "suchness" of very ordinary things, especially when the gloom of the future has momentarily checked our ambitiousness, is perhaps the mood of

> *A brushwood gate,*
> *And for a lock–*
> *This snail.*

> *The woodpecker*
> *Keeps on in the same place:*
> *Day is closing.*

> *Winter desolation;*
> *In the rain-water tub,*
> *Sparrows are walking.*

Aware is not quite grief, and not quite nostalgia in the usual sense of longing for the return of a beloved past. *Aware* is the echo of what has passed and of what was loved, giving them a resonance such as a great cathedral gives to a choir, so that they would be the poorer without it.

No one lives at the Barrier of Fuha;
  The wooden penthouse is fallen away;
All that remains
  Is the autumn wind.

The evening haze;
  Thinking of past things,
    How far-off they are!

Aware is the moment of crisis between seeing the transience of the world with sorrow and regret, and seeing it as the very form of the Great Void.

The stream hides itself
  In the grasses
    Of departing autumn.

Leaves falling,
  Lie on one another;
    The rain beats on the rain.

That moment of transition is just about to "cross over" in the *haiku* written by Issa upon the death of his child:

This dewdrop world—
  It may be a dewdrop,
    And yet—and yet—

Since *yugen* signifies a kind of mystery, it is the most baffling of all to describe, and the poems must speak for themselves.

The sea darkens;
  The voices of the wild ducks
    Are faintly white.

The skylark:
  Its voice alone fell,
    Leaving nothing behind.

In the dense mist,
  What is being shouted
    Between hill and boat?

> A trout leaps;
>   Clouds are moving
>   In the bed of the stream.

Or an example of *yugen* in the *Zenrin* poems:

> Wind subsiding, the flowers still fall;
> Bird crying, the mountain silence deepens.[4]

Because Zen training had involved a constant use of these Chinese couplets since at least the end of the fifteenth century, the emergence of *haiku* is hardly surprising. The influence is self-evident in this "*yugen*-in-reverse" *haiku* by Moritake. The *Zenrin* says:

> The shattered mirror will reflect no more;
> The fallen flower will hardly rise to the branch.[4]

And Moritake—

> A fallen flower
>   Returning to the branch?
>   It was a butterfly.

The association of Zen with poetry must inevitably bring up the name of the Soto Zen monk and hermit Ryokan (1758–1831). So often one thinks of the saint as a man whose sincerity provokes the enmity of the world, but Ryokan holds the distinction of being the saint whom everyone loved—perhaps because he was natural, again as a child, rather than good. It is easy to form the impression that the Japanese love of nature is predominantly sentimental, dwelling on those aspects of nature which are "nice" and "pretty"—butterflies, cherry blossoms, the autumn moon, chrysanthemums, and old pine trees.[5] But Ryokan is also the poet of lice, fleas, and being utterly soaked with cold rain.

---

[5] An impression especially sickening to the poetic mood of the middle twentieth century. It comes, however, from a level of *haiku* and other art forms which corresponds to our own greeting-card verse and confectionery-box

> *On rainy days*
> *The monk Ryokan*
> *Feels sorry for himself.*

And his view of "nature" is all of a piece:

> *The sound of the scouring*
> *Of the saucepan blends*
> *With the tree-frogs' voices.*

In some ways Ryokan is a Japanese St. Francis, though much less obviously religious. He is a wandering fool, un-self-consciously playing games with children, living in a lonely hut in the forest where the roof leaks and the wall is hung with poems in his marvelously illegible, spidery handwriting, so prized by Japanese calligraphers. He thinks of the lice on his chest as insects in the grass, and expresses the most natural human feelings–sadness, loneliness, bewilderment, or pity–without a trace of shame or pride. Even when robbed he is still rich, for

> *The thief*
> *Left it behind–*
> *The moon at the window.*

And when there is no money,

> *The wind brings*
> *Fallen leaves enough*
> *To make a fire.*

When life is empty, with respect to the past, and aimless, with respect to the future, the vacuum is filled by the present–normally reduced to a hairline, a split second in which there is no time

art. But consider the almost surrealistic imagery of the following from the Zenrin:

> *On Mount Wu-t'ai the clouds are steaming rice;*
> *Before the ancient Buddha hall, dogs piss at heaven.*

And there are many *haiku* such as this from Issa:

> *The mouth*
> *That cracked a flea*
> *Said,* "Namu Amida Butsu!"

for anything to happen. The sense of an infinitely expanded present is nowhere stronger than in *cha-no-yu,* the art of tea. Strictly, the term means something like "Tea with hot water," and through this one art Zen has exercised an incalculable influence on Japanese life, since the *chajin,* or "man of tea," is an arbiter of taste in the many subsidiary arts which *cha-no-yu* involves–architecture, gardening, ceramics, metalwork, lacquer, and the arrangement of flowers (*ikebana*).

Since *cha-no-yu* has become a conventional accomplishment for young ladies, it has been made the subject of a great deal of sentimental nonsense–associated with brocaded young dolls in moonlit rooms, nervously trying to imitate the most stilted feelings about porcelain and cherry blossom. But in the austere purity of, say, the Soshu Sen School the art of tea is a genuine expression of Zen which requires, if necessary, no further apparatus than a bowl, tea, and hot water. If there is not even that, *chado*–"the way of tea"–can be practiced anywhere and with anything, since it is really the same as Zen.

If Christianity is wine and Islam coffee, Buddhism is most certainly tea. Its quietening, clarifying, and slightly bitter taste gives it almost the same taste as awakening itself, though the bitterness corresponds to the pleasing roughness of "natural texture," and the "middle path" between sweet and sour. Long before the development of *cha-no-yu,* tea was used by Zen monks as a stimulant for meditation, and in this context it was drunk in a mood of unhurried awareness which naturally lent itself to a ritualistic type of action. In summer it refreshed and in winter warmed those wandering hermit-monks who liked to build grass and bamboo huts in the mountain forests, or by rock-filled streams in the gorges. The totally undistracting emptiness and simplicity of the Taoist or Zen hermitage has set the style not only for the special type of house for *cha-no-yu* but for Japanese domestic architecture as a whole.[6]

---

[6] An influence combined with a native style which can still be seen at the ancient Shinto shrine of Ise–a style which strongly suggests the cultures of the southern Pacific islands.

The monastic "tea ceremony" was introduced into Japan by Eisai, and though its form is different from the present *cha-no-yu,* it was nonetheless its origin, and appears to have been adopted for lay use during the fifteenth century. From this the *cha-no-yu* proper was perfected by Sen-no-Rikyu (1518–1591), and from him descend the three main schools of tea now flourishing. Ceremonial tea is not the ordinary leaf tea which is steeped in hot water; it is finely powdered green tea, mixed with hot water by means of a bamboo whisk until it becomes what a Chinese writer called "the froth of the liquid jade." *Cha-no-yu* is most appreciated when confined to a small group, or just two companions, and was especially loved by the old-time *samurai*–as today by harassed businessmen–as a frank escape from the turmoil of the world.[7]

Ideally, the house for *cha-no-yu* is a small hut set apart from the main dwelling in its own garden. The hut is floored with *tatami,* or straw mats, enclosing a fire-pit; the roof is usually thatched with rice straw; and the walls, as in all Japanese homes, are paper *shoji* supported by uprights of wood with a natural finish. One side of the room is occupied by an alcove, or *tokonoma,* the position for a single hanging scroll of painting or calligraphy, together with a rock, a spray of flowers, or some other object of art.

The atmosphere, though formal, is strangely relaxed, and the guests feel free to talk or watch in silence as they wish. The host takes his time to prepare a charcoal fire, and with a bamboo dipper pours water into a squat kettle of soft brown iron. In the same formal but completely unhurried manner, he brings in the other utensils–a plate with a few cakes, the tea bowl and caddy, the whisk, and a larger bowl for leavings. During these preparations a casual conversation continues, and soon the water in the kettle begins to simmer and sigh, so that the guests fall silent to listen. After a while, the host serves tea to the guests one by one

---

[7] Since it is frequently my pleasure to be invited for *cha-no-yu* by Sabro Hasegawa, who has a remarkable intuition for issuing these invitations at the most hectic moments, I can testify that I know no better form of psychotherapy.

from the same bowl, taking it from the caddy with a strip of bamboo bent into a spoon, pouring water from the kettle with the long-handled dipper, whipping it into a froth with the whisk, and laying the bowl before the first guest with its most interesting side towards him.

The bowls used for *cha-no-yu* are normally dull-colored and roughly finished, often unglazed at the base, and on the sides the glaze has usually been allowed to run–an original fortunate mistake which has been seen to offer endless opportunities for the "controlled accident." Specially favored are Korean rice bowls of the cheapest quality, a peasant ware of crude texture from which the tea masters have selected unintentional masterpieces of form. The tea caddy is often of tarnished silver or infinitely deep black lacquer, though sometimes old pottery medicine jars are used–purely functional articles which were again picked out by the masters for their unaffected beauty. A celebrated caddy once smashed to pieces was mended with gold cement, and became the much more treasured for the haphazard network of thin gold lines which then covered its surface. After the tea has been drunk, the guests may ask to inspect all the utensils which have been used, since every one of them has been made or chosen with the utmost care, and often brought out for the occasion because of some feature that would particularly appeal to one of the guests.

Every appurtenance of the *cha-no-yu* has been selected in accordance with canons of taste over which the most sensitive men in Japan have brooded for centuries. Though the choice is usually intuitive, careful measurement of the objects reveals interesting and unexpected proportions–works of spontaneous geometry as remarkable as the spiral shell of the nautilus or the structure of the snow crystal. Architects, painters, gardeners, and craftsmen of all kinds have worked in consultation with the *cha-no-yu* masters, like an orchestra with its conductor, so that their "Zen taste" has passed on into the objects made by the same craftsmen for everyday use. This applies most particularly to ordinary, functional things–kitchen implements, *shoji* paper, soup bowls, common teapots and cups, floor mats, baskets, utilitarian bottles and jars, textiles for everyday clothing, and a hundred other simple artifacts in which the Japanese show their good taste to best advantage.

The "Zen" of the *cha-no-yu* comes out all the more for the purely secular character of the ritual, which has no liturgical character like the Catholic Mass or the elaborate ceremonies of Shingon Buddhism. Though the guests avoid political, financial, or business matters in their conversation, there is sometimes non-argumentative discussion of philosophical matters, though the preferred topics are artistic and natural. It must be remembered that Japanese people take to such subjects as readily and un-self-consciously as we talk of sports or travel, and that their dis-cussion of natural beauty is not the affectation it might be in our own culture. Furthermore, they do not feel in the least guilty about this admitted "escape" from the so-called "realities" of business and worldly competition. Escape from these concerns is as natural and necessary as sleep, and they feel neither com-punction nor awkwardness in belonging for a while to the Taoist world of carefree hermits, wandering through the moun-tains like wind-blown clouds, with nothing to do but cultivate a row of vegetables, gaze at the drifting mist, and listen to the waterfalls. A few, perhaps, find the secret of bringing the two worlds together, of seeing the "hard realities" of human life to be the same aimless working of the Tao as the patterns of branches against the sky. In the words of Hung Tzu-ch'eng:

If the mind is not overlaid with wind and waves, you will always be living among blue mountains and green trees. If your true nature has the creative force of Nature itself, wherever you may go, you will see fishes leaping and geese flying.[8]

The style of garden which goes with Zen and *cha-no-yu* is not, of course, one of those ornate imitation landscapes with bronze cranes and miniature pagodas. The intention of the best Japanese

[8] *Ts'ai-ken T'an*, 291. Hung's book of "vegetable-root talk" is a collection of wandering observations by a sixteenth-century poet whose philosophy was a blend of Taoism, Zen, and Confucianism.

gardens is not to make a realistic illusion of landscape, but simply to suggest the general atmosphere of "mountain and water" in a small space, so arranging the design of the garden that it seems to have been helped rather than governed by the hand of man. The Zen gardener has no mind to impose his own intention upon natural forms, but is careful rather to follow the "intentionless intention" of the forms themselves, even though this involves the utmost care and skill. In fact the gardener never ceases to prune, clip, weed, and train his plants, but he does so in the spirit of being part of the garden himself rather than a directing agent standing outside. He is not interfering with nature because he is nature, and he cultivates as if not cultivating. Thus the garden is at once highly artificial and extremely natural!

This spirit is seen at its best in the great sand and rock gardens of Kyoto, of which the most famous example is the garden of Ryoanji. It consists of five groups of rocks laid upon a rectangle of raked sand, backed by a low stone wall, and surrounded by trees. It suggests a wild beach, or perhaps a seascape with rocky islands, but its unbelievable simplicity evokes a serenity and clarity of feeling so powerful that it can be caught even from a photograph. The major art which contributes to such gardens is *bonseki*, which may well be called the "growing" of rocks. It requires difficult expeditions to the seashore, to mountains and rivers, in search of rock forms which wind and water have shaped into asymmetrical, living contours. These are carted to the garden site, and placed so as to look as if they had grown where they stand, so as to be related to the surrounding space or to the area of sand in the same way as figure to background in Sung paintings. Because the rock must look as if it had always been in the same position, it must have the air of moss-covered antiquity, and, rather than try to plant moss on the rock, the rock is first set for some years in a place where the moss will grow by itself, and thereafter is moved to its final position. Rocks picked out by the sensitive eye of the *bonseki* artist are ranked among Japan's most precious national treasures, but, except to move them, they are untouched by the human hand.

The Zen monks liked also to cultivate gardens which took advantage of an existing natural setting–to arrange rocks and plants along the edges of a stream, creating a more informal atmosphere suggesting a mountain canyon adjoining the monastery buildings. They were always sparing and reserved in their use of color, as were the Sung painters before them, since masses of flowers in sharply varying colors are seldom found in the state of nature. Though not symmetrical, the Japanese garden has a clearly perceptible form; unlike so many English and American flower gardens, they do not resemble a daub in oil colors, and this delight in the form of plants carries over into the art of flower arrangement inside the house, accentuating the shapes of single sprays and leaves rather than bunched colors.

Every one of the arts which have been discussed involves a technical training which follows the same essential principles as training in Zen. The best account of this training thus far available in a Western language is Eugen Herrigel's *Zen in the Art of Archery*, which is the author's story of his own experience under a master of the Japanese bow. To this should be added the already mentioned letter on Zen and swordsmanship (*kendo*) by the seventeenth-century master Takuan, translated by Suzuki in his *Zen Buddhism and Its Influence on Japanese Culture*.

The major problem of each of these disciplines is to bring the student to the point from which he can really begin. Herrigel spent almost five years trying to find the right way of releasing the bowstring, for it had to be done "unintentionally," in the same way as a ripe fruit bursts its skin. His problem was to resolve the paradox of practicing relentlessly without ever "trying," and to let go of the taut string intentionally without intention. His master at one and the same time urged him to keep on working and working, but also to stop making an effort. For the art cannot be learned unless the arrow "shoots itself," unless the string is released *wu-hsin* and *wu-nien*, without "mind" and without blocking, or "choice." After all those years of practice there came a day when it just happened—how, or why, Herrigel never understood.

The same is true in learning to use the brush for writing or painting. The brush must draw by itself. This cannot happen if one does not practice constantly. But neither can it happen if one makes an effort. Similarly, in swordsmanship one must not first decide upon a certain thrust and then attempt to make it, since by that time it will be too late. Decision and action must be simultaneous. This was the point of Dogen's image of firewood and ashes, for to say that firewood does not "become" ashes is to say that it has no intention to be ash before it is actually ash— and then it is no longer firewood. Dogen insisted that the two states were "clearly cut," and in the same way Herrigel's master did not want him to "mix" the two states of stretching and releasing the bow. He instructed him to draw it to the point of fullest tension and stop there without any purpose, any intention in mind as to what to do next. Likewise, in Dogen's view of za-zen one must be sitting "just to sit" and there must not be any intention to have satori.

The sudden visions of nature which form the substance of haiku arise in the same way, for they are never there when one looks for them. The artificial haiku always feels like a piece of life which has been deliberately broken off or wrenched away from the universe, whereas the genuine haiku has dropped off all by itself, and has the whole universe inside it.

Artists and craftsmen of the Far East have, indeed, measured, analyzed, and classified the techniques of the masters to such a degree that by deliberate imitation they can come close to "deceiving, if it were possible, even the elect." By all quantitative standards the work so contrived is indistinguishable from its models, just as bowmen and swordsmen trained by quite other methods can equal the feats of Zen-inspired samurai. But, so far as Zen is concerned, the end results have nothing to do with it. For, as we have seen all along, Zen has no goal; it is a traveling without point, with nowhere to go. To travel is to be alive, but to get somewhere is to be dead, for as our own proverb says, "To travel well is better than to arrive."

A world which increasingly consists of destinations without journeys between them, a world which values only "getting somewhere" as fast as possible, becomes a world without substance. One can get anywhere and everywhere, and yet the more this is possible, the less is anywhere and everywhere worth getting to. For points of arrival are too abstract, too Euclidean to be enjoyed, and it is all very much like eating the precise ends of a banana without getting what lies in between. The point, therefore, of these arts is the doing of them rather than the accomplishments. But, more than this, the real joy of them lies in what turns up unintentionally in the course of practice, just as the joy of travel is not nearly so much in getting where one wants to go as in the unsought surprises which occur on the journey.

Planned surprises are as much of a contradiction as intentional *satori,* and whoever aims at *satori* is after all like a person who sends himself Christmas presents for fear that others will forget him. One must simply face the fact that Zen is all that side of life which is completely beyond our control, and which will not come to us by any amount of forcing or wangling or cunning–stratagems which produce only fakes of the real thing. But the last word of Zen is not an absolute dualism–the rather barren world of controlled action on the one side, and the spontaneous world of uncontrolled surprise on the other. For who controls the controller?

Because Zen does not involve an ultimate dualism between the controller and the controlled, the mind and the body, the spiritual and the material, there is always a certain "physiological" aspect to its techniques. Whether Zen is practiced through *za-zen* or *cha-no-yu* or *kendo,* great importance is attached to the way of breathing. Not only is breathing one of the two fundamental rhythms of the body; it is also the process in which control and spontaneity, voluntary and involuntary action, find their most obvious identity. Long before the origins of the Zen School, both Indian *yoga* and Chinese Taoism practiced "watching the breath," with a view to *letting*–not forcing–it to become as slow and silent as possible. Physiologically and psychologically, the relationship between breathing and "insight" is not yet altogether clear. But if we look at man as process rather than entity, rhythm rather than structure, it is obvious that breathing is something which he does–and thus *is*–constantly. Therefore grasping air with the lungs goes hand-in-hand with grasping at life.

So-called "normal" breathing is fitful and anxious. The air is always being held and not fully released, for the individual seems incapable of "letting" it run its full course through the lungs. He breathes compulsively rather than freely. The technique therefore begins by encouraging a full release of the breath–easing it out as if the body were being emptied of air by a great leaden ball sinking through the chest and abdomen, and settling down into the ground. The returning in-breath is then allowed to follow as a simple reflex action. The air is not actively inhaled; it is just allowed to come–and then, when the lungs are comfortably filled, it is allowed to go out once more, the image of the leaden ball giving it the sense of "falling" out as distinct from being pushed out.

One might go as far as to say that this way of breathing is Zen itself in its physiological aspect. Yet, as with every other aspect of Zen, it is hindered by striving for it, and for this reason beginners in the breathing technique often develop the peculiar anxiety of feeling unable to breathe unless keeping up a conscious control. But just as there is no need to try to be in accord with the Tao, to try to see, or to try to hear, so it must be remembered that the breath will always take care of itself. This is not a breathing "exercise" so much as a "watching and letting" of the breath, and it is always a serious mistake to undertake it in the spirit of a compulsive discipline to be "practiced" with a goal in mind.

This way of breathing is not for special times alone. Like
Zen itself, it is for all circumstances whatsoever, and in this way,
as in others, every human activity can become a form of *za-zen*.
The application of Zen in activity is not restricted to the formal
arts, and, on the other hand, does not absolutely require the
specific "sitting technique" of *za-zen* proper. The late Dr.
Kunihiko Hashida, a lifelong student of Zen and editor of the
works of Dogen, never used formal *za-zen*. But his "Zen practice"
was precisely his study of physics, and to suggest his attitude he
used to say that his lifework was "to science" rather than "to
study science."

In its own way, each one of the arts which Zen has inspired
gives vivid expression to the sudden or instantaneous quality of
its view of the world. The momentariness of *sumi* paintings and
haiku, and the total presence of mind required in *cha-no-yu* and
kendo, bring out the real reason why Zen has always called itself the way of instantaneous awakening. It is not just that *satori*
comes quickly and unexpectedly, all of a sudden, for mere speed
has nothing to do with it. The reason is that Zen is a liberation
from time. For if we open our eyes and see clearly, it becomes
obvious that there is no other time than this instant, and that the
past and the future are abstractions without any concrete reality.

Until this has become clear, it seems that our life is all past and
future, and that the present is nothing more than the infinitesi-
mal hairline which divides them. From this comes the sensation
of "having no time," of a world which hurries by so rapidly that
it is gone before we can enjoy it. But through "awakening to the
instant" one sees that this is the reverse of the truth: it is rather
the past and future which are the fleeting illusions, and the present which is eternally real. We discover that the linear succession
of time is a convention of our single-track verbal thinking, of a
consciousness which interprets the world by grasping little
pieces of it, calling them things and events. But every such grasp
of the mind excludes the rest of the world, so that this type of
consciousness can get an approximate vision of the whole only

through a series of grasps, one after another. Yet the superficiality of this consciousness is seen in the fact that it cannot and does not regulate even the human organism. For if it had to control the heartbeat, the breath, the operation of the nerves, glands, muscles, and sense organs, it would be rushing wildly around the body taking care of one thing after another, with no time to do anything else. Happily, it is not in charge, and the organism is regulated by the timeless "original mind," which deals with life in its totality and so can do ever so many "things" at once.

However, it is not as if the superficial consciousness were one thing, and the "original mind" another, for the former is a specialized activity of the latter. Thus the superficial consciousness can awaken to the eternal present if it stops grasping. But this does not come to pass by trying to concentrate on the present —an effort which succeeds only in making the moment seem ever more elusive and fleeting, ever more impossible to bring into focus. Awareness of the "eternal now" comes about by the same principle as the clarity of hearing and seeing and the proper freedom of the breath. Clear sight has nothing to do with trying to see; it is just the realization that the eyes will take in every detail all by themselves, for so long as they are open one can hardly prevent the light from reaching them. In the same way, there is no difficulty in being fully aware of the eternal present as soon as it is seen that one cannot possibly be aware of anything else—that in concrete fact there *is* no past or future. Making an effort to concentrate on the instantaneous moment implies at once that there are other moments. But they are nowhere to be found, and in truth one rests as easily in the eternal present as the eyes and ears respond to light and sound.

Now this eternal present is the "timeless," unhurried flowing of the Tao—

> Such a tide as, moving, seems to sleep,
> Too full for sound or foam.

As Nan-ch'üan said, to try to accord with it is to deviate from it, though in fact one cannot deviate and there is no one to deviate.

So, too, one cannot get away from the eternal present by trying to attend to it, and this very fact shows that, apart from this present, there is no distinct self that watches and knows it–which is why Hui-k'o could not find his mind when Bodhidharma asked him to produce it. However puzzling this may be, and however many philosophical problems it may raise, one clear look is enough to show its unavoidable truth. There is only this *now*. It does not come from anywhere; it is not going anywhere. It is not permanent, but it is not impermanent. Though moving, it is always still. When we try to catch it, it seems to run away, and yet it is always here and there is no escape from it. And when we turn round to find the self which knows this moment, we find that it has vanished like the past. Therefore the Sixth Patriarch says in the *T'an-ching*:

> In this moment there is nothing which comes to be. In this moment there is nothing which ceases to be. Thus there is no birth-and-death to be brought to an end. Wherefore the absolute tranquillity (of *nirvana*) is this present moment. Though it is at this moment, there is no limit to this moment, and herein is eternal delight. (7) [k]

Yet, when it comes to it, this moment can be called "present" only in relation to past and future, or to someone to whom it is present. But when there is neither past nor future, and no one to whom this moment is present, what is it? When Fa-ch'ang was dying, a squirrel screeched on the roof. "It's just this," he said, "and nothing else."

BIBLIOGRAPHY

The Bibliography is divided into two parts: (1) The principal original sources consulted in the preparation of this book. The Japanese pronunciations are in round brackets. References are to the Japanese edition of the complete Chinese Tripitaka, the *Taisho Daizokyo* in 85 volumes (Tokyo, 1924–1932), and to Nanjio's *Catalogue of the Chinese Translation of the Buddhist Tripitaka* (Oxford, 1883; repr., Tokyo, 1929). (2) A general bibliography of works on Zen in European languages, together with some other works on Indian and Chinese philosophy to which reference has been made in this book. To the best of my knowledge, this section includes every important book or scholarly article on Zen published until the present time, July, 1956.

1. PRINCIPAL SOURCES

Cheng-tao Ke (Shodoka) 證道歌
Song of the Realization of the Way.
Yung-chia Hsüan-chüeh (Yoka Genkaku), 665–713.
Taisho 2014.
Trans. Suzuki (6), Senzaki & McCandless (1).

Ching-te Ch'uan-teng Lu (Keitoku Dento Roku) 景德傳燈錄
Record of the Transmission of the Lamp.
Tao-yüan (Dogen), *c.* 1004.
Taisho 2076. Nanjio 1524.

Daiho Shogen Kokushi Hogo 大法正眼國師法語
Sermons of the National Teacher Daiho Shogen (i.e., Bankei).
Bankei Zenji, 1622–1693.
Ed. Suzuki and Furata. Daito Shuppansha, Tokyo, 1943.

Hsin-hsin Ming (Shinjinmei) 信心銘
Treatise on Faith in the Mind.

203

Seng-ts'an (Sosan), *d.* 606.
Taisho 2010.
Trans. Suzuki (1), vol. 1, and (6), and Waley in Conze (2).

Ku-tsun-hsü Yü-lu (*Kosonshuku Goroku*) 古尊宿語錄
Recorded Sayings of the Ancient Worthies.
Tse (Seki), Sung dynasty.
Fu-hsüeh Shu-chü, Shanghai, n.d. Also in *Dainihon Zoku-
zokyo,* Kyoto, 1905–1912.

Lin-chi Lu (*Rinzai Roku*) 臨濟錄
Record of Lin-chi.
Lin-chi I-hsüan (Rinzai Gigen), *d.* 867.
Taisho 1985. Also in *Ku-tsun-hsü Yü-lu,* fasc. 1.

Liu-tsu T'an-ching (*Rokuso Dangyo*) 六祖壇經
Platform Sutra of the Sixth Patriarch.
Ta-chien Hui-neng (Daikan Eno), 638–713.
Taisho 2008. Nanjio 1525.
Trans. Wong Mou-lam (1) and Rousselle (1).

Pi-yen Lu (*Hekigan Roku*) 碧巖錄
Record of the Green Rock.
Yuan-wu K'o-ch'in (Engo Kokugon), 1063–1135.
Taisho 2003.

Shen-hui Ho-chang I-chi (*Jinne Osho Ishu*) 神會和尚遺集
Collected Traditions of Shen-hui.
Ho-tse Shen-hui (Kataku Jinne), 668–770.
Tun-huang MS, Pelliot 3047 and 3488.
Ed. Hu Shih. Oriental Book Co., Shanghai, 1930.
Trans. Gernet (1).

Shobo Genzo 正法眼藏
The Eye Treasury of the True Dharma.
Dogen Zenji, 1200–1253.
Ed. Kunihiko Hashida. Sankibo Busshorin, Tokyo, 1939.
Also in *Dogen Zenji Zenshu,* pp. 3–472. Shinjusha,
Tokyo, 1940.

Wu-men Kuan (*Mumon Kan*) 無門關
The Barrier Without Gate.
Wu-men Hui-k'ai (Mumon Ekai), 1184–1260.
Taisho 2005.
Trans. Senzaki & Reps (1), Ogata (1), and Dumoulin (1).

2. WORKS IN EUROPEAN LANGUAGES

ANESAKI, M. *History of Japanese Religion*. Kegan Paul, London, 1930.

BENOIT, H. *The Supreme Doctrine*. Pantheon, New York, and Routledge, London, 1955.

BLYTH, R. H. (1) *Zen in English Literature and Oriental Classics*. Hokuseido, Tokyo, 1948.

(2) *Haiku*. 4 vols. Hokuseido, Tokyo, 1949–1952.

(3) *Buddhist Sermons on Christian Texts*. Kokudosha, Tokyo, 1952.

(4) "Ikkyu's Doka," *The Young East*, vols. II. 2 to III. 9. Tokyo, 1952–1954.

CHAPIN, H. B. "The Ch'an Master Pu-tai," *Journal of the American Oriental Society*, vol. LIII, pp. 47–52.

CHU CH'AN (BLOFELD, J.) (1) *The Huang Po Doctrine of Universal Mind*. Buddhist Society, London, 1947.

(2) *The Path to Sudden Attainment*. Buddhist Society, London, 1948.

CH'U TA-KAO *Tao Te Ching*. Buddhist Society, London, 1937.

CONZE, E. (1) *Buddhism: Its Essence and Development*. Cassirer, Oxford, 1953.

(2) *Buddhist Texts Through the Ages*. Edited in conjunction with I. B. Horner, D. Snellgrove, and A. Waley. Cassirer, Oxford, 1954.

(3) *Selected Sayings from the Perfection of Wisdom*. Buddhist Society, London, 1955.

COOMARASWAMY, A. K. "Who Is Satan and Where Is Hell?" *The Review of Religion*, vol. XII. 1, pp. 76–87. New York, 1947.

DEMIÉVILLE, P. (1) *Hobogirin*. 4 fasc. Edited in conjunction with S. Levi and J. Takakusu. Maison Franco-Japonaise, Tokyo, 1928–1931.

(2) *Le Concile de Lhasa*. vol. I. Imprimerie Nationale de France, Paris, 1952.

DUMOULIN, H. (1) "Das Wu-men-kuan oder 'Der Pass ohne Tor,'" *Monumenta Serica*, vol. VIII. 1943.

(2) "Bodhidharma und die Anfänge des Ch'an Buddhismus," *Monumenta Nipponica*, vol. VII. 1951.

DUMOULIN, H., & SASAKI, R. F. *The Development of Chinese Zen after the Sixth Patriarch*. First Zen Institute, New York, 1953.

DUYVENDAK, J. J. L. *Tao Te Ching*. Murray, London, 1954.

ELIOT, SIR C. *Japanese Buddhism*. Arnold, London, 1935.

FIRST ZEN INSTITUTE OF AMERICA. (1) *Cat's Yawn*, 1940–1941. Published in one vol., First Zen Institute, New York, 1947.

(2) *Zen Notes*. First Zen Institute, New York, since January, 1954.

FUNG YU-LAN (1) *A History of Chinese Philosophy*. 2 vols. Tr. Derk Bodde. Princeton, 1953.

(2) *The Spirit of Chinese Philosophy*. Tr. E. R. Hughes. Kegan Paul, London, 1947.

GATENBY, E. V. *The Cloud Men of Yamato*. Murray, London, 1929.

GERNET, J. (1) "Entretiens du Maître de Dhyana Chen-houei du Ho-tsö," *Publications de l'École Française d'Extrême-Orient*, vol. XXXI. 1949.

(2) "Biographie du Maître Chen-houei du Ho-tsö," *Journal Asiatique*, 1951.

(3) "Entretiens du Maître Ling-yeou du Kouei-chan," *Bulletin de l'École Française d'Extrême-Orient*, vol. XLV. 1. 1951.

GILES, H. A. *Chuang-tzu*. Kelly & Walsh, Shanghai, 1926.

GILES, L. *Taoist Teachings*. Translations from Lieh-tzu. Murray, London, 1925.

GROSSE, E. *Die Ostasiatische Tuschmalerei*. Cassirer, Berlin, 1923.

HARRISON, E. J. *The Fighting Spirit of Japan*. Unwin, London, 1913.

HERRIGEL, E. *Zen in the Art of Archery*. Pantheon, New York, 1953.

HUMPHREYS, C. *Zen Buddhism*. Heinemann, London, 1949.

HU SHIH (1) "The Development of Zen Buddhism in China," *Chinese Political and Social Review*, vol. XV. 4. 1932.
(2) "Ch'an (Zen) Buddhism in China, Its History and Method," *Philosophy East and West*, vol. III. 1. Honolulu, 1953.

KEITH, SIR A. B. *Buddhist Philosophy in India and Ceylon*. Oxford, 1923.

LIEBENTHAL, W. "The Book of Chao," *Monumenta Serica*, Monog., XIII. Peking, 1948.

LIN YUTANG *The Wisdom of Lao-tse*. Modern Library, New York, 1948.

LINSSEN, R. *Essais sur le Bouddhisme en général et sur le Zen en particulier*. 2 vols. Editions Etre Libre, Brussels, 1954.

MASUNAGA, R. "The Standpoint of Dogen and His Treatise on Time," *Religion East and West*, vol. I. University of Tokyo, 1955.

MURTI, T. R. V. *The Central Philosophy of Buddhism*. Allen & Unwin, London, 1955.

NEEDHAM, J. *Science and Civilization in China*. 2 vols. (5 vols. to follow). Cambridge University Press, 1954 and 1956.

NUKARIYA, K. *The Religion of the Samurai*. Luzac, London, 1913.

OGATA, S. *Guide to Zen Practice*. A partial translation of the *Mu-mon Kan*. Bukkasha, Kyoto, 1934.

OHASAMA, S., & FAUST, A. *Zen, der lebendige Buddhismus in Japan*. Gotha, 1925.

OKAKURA, K. *The Book of Tea*. Foulis, Edinburgh, 1919.

PELLIOT, P. "Notes sur quelques artistes des Six Dynasties et des T'ang," *T'oung Pao*, vol. XXII. 1923.

ROUSSELLE, E. "Liu-tsu T'an-ching," *Sinica*, vols. V, VI, & XI. 1930, 1931, 1936.

SASAKI, T. *Zen: With Special Reference to Soto Zen.* Soto Sect Headquarters, Tokyo, 1955.

SENGAI *India-Ink Drawings.* Oakland Museum, Oakland, 1956.

SENZAKI, N. *Zen Meditation.* Bukkasha, Kyoto, 1936.

SENZAKI, N., & McCANDLESS, R. *Buddhism and Zen.* Philosophical Library, New York, 1953.

SENZAKI, N., & REPS, P. (1) *The Gateless Gate.* A translation of the *Mu-mon Kan.* Murray, Los Angeles, 1934.

(2) *101 Zen Stories.* McKay, Philadelphia, n.d.

SIREN, O. "Zen Buddhism and Its Relation to Art," *Theosophical Path.* Point Loma, Calif., October, 1934.

SOGEN ASAHINA *Zen.* Sakane, Tokyo, 1954.

SOROKIN, P. (ed). *Forms and Techniques of Altruistic and Spiritual Growth.* Beacon Press, Boston, 1954.

SOYEN SHAKU *Sermons of a Buddhist Abbot.* Open Court, Chicago, 1906.

STCHERBATSKY, TH. *The Conception of Buddhist Nirvana.* Leningrad, 1927.

STEINILBER-OBERLIN, E., & MATSUO, K. *The Buddhist Sects of Japan.* Allen & Unwin, London, 1938.

SUZUKI, D. T. (1) *Essays in Zen Buddhism.* 3 vols. Luzac, London, 1927, 1933, 1934. Repr., Rider, London, 1949, 1950, 1951.

(2) *Studies in the Lankavatara Sutra.* Routledge, London, 1930.

(3) *The Lankavatara Sutra.* Routledge, London, 1932. Repr., 1956.

(4) *Introduction to Zen Buddhism.* Kyoto, 1934. Repr., Philosophical Library, New York, 1949.

(5) *Training of the Zen Buddhist Monk.* Eastern Buddhist Society, Kyoto, 1934.

(6) *Manual of Zen Buddhism.* Kyoto, 1935. Repr., Rider, London, 1950.

(7) *Zen Buddhism and Its Influence on Japanese Culture.* Eastern Buddhist Society, Kyoto, 1938. (Shortly to be reprinted in the Bollingen Series.)

(8) *The Essence of Buddhism.* Buddhist Society, London, 1947.

(9) *The Zen Doctrine of No-Mind.* Rider, London, 1949.

(10) *Living by Zen.* Rider, London, 1950.

(11) *Studies in Zen.* Rider, London, 1955.

(12) "Professor Rudolph Otto on Zen Buddhism," *Eastern Buddhist,* vol. III, pp. 93–116.

(13) "Zen Buddhism on Immortality. An Extract from the Hekiganshu," *Eastern Buddhist,* vol. III, pp. 213–23.

(14) "The Recovery of a Lost MS on the History of Zen in China," *Eastern Buddhist,* vol. IV, pp. 199–298.

(15) "Ignorance and World Fellowship," *Faiths and Fellowship.* Watkins, London, 1937.

(16) "Buddhist Symbolism," *Symbols and Values.* Harper, New York, 1954.

(17) "Zen and Pragmatism," *Philosophy East and West,* vol. IV. 2. Honolulu, 1954.

(18) "The Awakening of a New Consciousness in Zen," *Eranos-Jahrbuch,* vol. XXIII. Rhein-Verlag, Zürich, 1955.

TAKAKUSU, J. *Essentials of Buddhist Philosophy.* University of Hawaii, Honolulu, 1947.

WALEY, A. *Zen Buddhism and Its Relation to Art.* Luzac, London, 1922.

WATTS, A. W. (1) *The Spirit of Zen.* Murray, London, 1936. 2nd ed., 1955.

(2) *Zen Buddhism.* Buddhist Society, London, 1947.

(3) *Zen.* (Same as above, but enlarged.) Delkin, Stanford, 1948.

(4) *The Way of Liberation in Zen Buddhism.* American Academy of Asian Studies, San Francisco, 1955.

(5) "The Problem of Faith and Works in Buddhism," *Review of Religion,* vol. V. 4. New York, May, 1941.

WENTZ, W. Y. E. *Tibetan Yoga and Secret Doctrines.* Oxford, 1935.

WILHELM, R. (1) *The Secret of the Golden Flower.* A translation of the *T'ai I Chin Hua Tsung Chih,* with commentary by C. G. Jung. Kegan Paul, London, 1931.

(2) *The I Ching or Book of Changes.* 2 vols. Tr. Cary Baynes. Pantheon, New York, 1950.

WONG MOU-LAM *The Sutra of Wei Lang (Hui-neng).* Luzac, London, 1944.

CHINESE NOTES

Read horizontally, from left to right

I. 1. THE PHILOSOPHY OF THE TAO

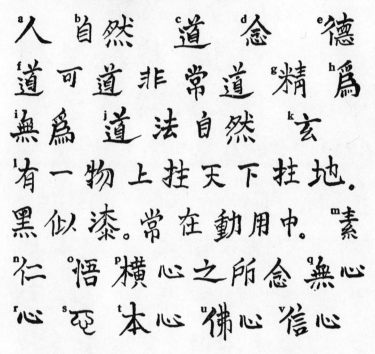

I. 2. THE ORIGINS OF BUDDHISM

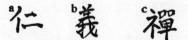

I. 3. MAHAYANA BUDDHISM

^c事 ^d理 ^e理事無礙
^f事事無礙

I. 4. THE RISE AND DEVELOPMENT OF ZEN

^a道指 ^b頓悟 ^c格義 ^d坐禪
^e帝問如何是聖諦第一義、
師曰廓然無聖、帝曰對朕
者誰、師曰不識。 ^f壁觀
^g二祖云、弟子心未安、乞師安
心。磨云、將心來爲汝安。祖
云、覓心了不可得。磨云、爲汝
安心竟。 ^h問答

ⁱ教外別傳、
不立文字、

212

直指人心、
見性成佛。

ʲ至道無難、唯嫌揀擇。
任性合道、逍遙絕惱、
繫念乖真。勿惡六塵、
六塵不惡、還同正覺、
智者無爲、愚人自縛。
將心用心、豈非大錯。
ᵏ來禮師曰、乞與解脫法門、
師曰、誰縛汝、曰無人縛、師
曰、何更求解脫乎。
ˡ身是菩提樹、心如明鏡臺、
時時勤拂拭、莫使惹塵埃。

213

菩提本無樹、心鏡亦非臺。
本來無一物、何處惹塵埃。
來去自由通用無滯即是
般若三昧自在解脫名無
念行。若百物不思當令念
絕即是法縛即名邊見。
住心觀淨是病非禪。長坐
拘身於理何益。
起心著淨却生淨妄。何名
坐禪此法門中無障無礙
外於一切善惡境界、心念
不起名爲坐。
若有人問汝義問有將無對。

問無將有對、問凡以聖對、
問聖以凡對。二道相因生
中道義、汝一問一對。
「君不見絕學無爲道人、
不除妄想不求真、
無明實性即佛性、
幻化空身即法身。
「往問曰、大德坐禪圖什麼、
一曰、圖作佛、師乃取一塼
於彼庵前石上磨。一曰、師
作什麼。師曰、磨作鏡。一曰、
磨塼豈得成鏡耶。師曰、坐
禪豈成佛耶。 「喝

道不屬修若言修得修
成還壞即同聲聞若言不
修即同凡　泉云、平常心是
道。趙州云、還可趣向否。泉云、
擬向即乖。　無　僧　雲水
無事　山僧與麼說意在什
麼處、祇為道流一切馳求
心不能歇、止他古人閒機
境、道流取山僧見處坐斷
報化佛頭十地滿心猶如
客作兒等妙二覺擔枷
鎖漢羅漢辟支猶如廁穢
菩提涅槃如繫驢橛。

佛法無用功處、祇是平常無
事屙屎送尿著 衣喫飯困
來即臥愚人笑 我 智乃知。
你且隨處作主立處皆真境
來回換不得、縱有從來習氣
五無間業自爲解脫大海。
心外無法內亦不可得、求什
麼物你諸方言道有修有證、
莫錯設有修得者皆是生死
業、你言六度萬行齊修我
見皆是造業、求佛求法即是
造地獄業。[bb]五位 [cc]正 [dd]偏
[ee]公案 [ff]疑 情 [gg]汝學坐禪爲

學坐佛。若學坐禪禪非坐臥、
若學坐佛佛非定相於無住
法不應取捨汝若坐佛即是
殺佛若執坐相非達其理。
[hh]生來坐不臥、
死去臥不坐、
元是臭骨頭。

II. 1. "EMPTY AND MARVELOUS"

[a]至道無難、唯嫌揀擇、
但莫憎愛、洞然明白、
毫釐有差 天地懸隔、
欲得現前、莫存順逆、
違順相爭、是爲心病。

受災如受福、受降如受敵。

黃昏雞報曉、半夜日頭明。

問終日著衣喫飯如何免得著衣喫飯、師云著衣喫飯、進云、不會、師云、不曾即著衣喫飯。

寒即圍爐向猛火、
熱即竹林溪畔坐。

雨中看果日、火裏酌清泉。

樹呈風體態、波弄月精神。

經云但以眾法合成此身、起時唯法起、滅時唯法滅、此法起時不言我起、滅時不言我滅、前念後念中念念念不相待念念寂滅。

[1]春色無高下、花枝自短長。

[2]長者長法身、短者短法身。

[3]老僧三十年前未參禪時、見山是山、見水是水。及至後來親見知識、有箇入處、見山不是山、見水不是水。而今得箇體歇處、依然見山秖是山、見水秖是水。

[4]空劫之時無一切名字、佛纔出世來便有名字、所以取相、大道一切實無凡聖、

若有名字皆屬限量。所以江
西老宿云、不是心不是佛不
是物。汝但無事於心無心
於事則虛而靈空而妙。

宗門七縱八橫殺活臨時。僧
便問、如何是殺、師云、冬去春
來僧云、冬去春來時如何、師
云、橫擔拄杖、東西南北、一
任打野榸。

神通並妙用、運水及搬柴。

II. 2. "SITTING QUIETLY, DOING NOTHING"

如刀能割不自割、
如眼能看不自看。

兀然無事坐、春來草自生。

青山自青山、白雲自白雲。

妙用 不可以有心得、

　　　　不可以無心求。

去 不生 若虛空勿涯岸

不離當処常湛然、覓即知君

不可見、取不得捨不得、不可

得中、只麼得、默時說、說時默、

大施門開無擁塞。

一擊忘所知、更不假修治、

動容揚古路。

不信只看八九月、

紛紛黃葉滿山川。

相見呵呵笑、園林落葉多。若是本分人須是有驅耕夫之牛、奪飢人之食底手腳。驀直去　念　任運著衣裳。要行即行、要坐即坐、無一念心希求佛果。你諸方言道有修有證、莫錯、設有修得者皆是生死業、你言六度萬行齊修、我見皆是造業、求佛求法即是造地獄業、求菩薩亦是造業、看經看教亦是造業、佛與祖師是無事人。諸方說有道可修有法可證、何法修何

道、你今用處欠少什麼物、
修補何處。

p爭如著衣喫飲、
此外更無佛祖。

q識得本心本性、
正是宗門大病。

r入林不動草、入水不立波。

s護生須是殺、殺盡始安居。

t一句定乾坤、一劍平天下。

u若人修道道不行、萬般邪境
競頭生。智劍出來無一物。

[a]本証妙修・[b]體 用 [c]法身、
機關、言詮、難透、五位。
[e]孤掌難鳴 [f]有 時 奪 人 不
奪 境、有 時 奪 境 不 奪 人 有
時 人 境 俱 奪、有 時 人 境 俱
不 奪。

[g]移 花 兼 蝶 到、達磨道不知。

[a]易 [b]江月照 松風吹、
　　　　永夜清宵何所爲。
[c]寂 [d]侘 [e]哀 [f]幽玄 [g]風流
[h]風穴和 尚因僧問、語默涉離

微如何通不犯、穴云、

　　長憶江南三月裏、

　　鷓鴣啼處百花香。

i風定花猶落、鳥鳴山更幽。

j破鏡不重照、落花難上枝。

k無有生相刹那無有滅相、
更無生滅可滅是則寂滅
現前當現前時亦無現前
之量乃爲常樂。

INDEX

Proper names of persons are printed in capitals, and, in the case of Chinese Zen masters, the Japanese pronunciation follows the Chinese in parentheses. Titles of works are printed in italics.

227

About the Author

ALAN WATTS, who held both a master's degree in theology and a doctorate of divinity, is best known as an interpreter of Zen Buddhism in particular, and of Indian and Chinese philosophy in general. Standing apart, however, from sectarian membership, he has earned the reputation of being one of the most original and "unrutted" philosophers of the century. He was the author of some twenty books on the philosophy and psychology of religion. He died in 1973.